CAUGHT IN THE CURRENT

ADVANCING STUDIES IN RELIGION

Series editor: Sarah Wilkins-Laflamme

Advancing Studies in Religion catalyzes and provokes original research in the study of religion with a critical edge. The series advances the study of religion in method and theory, textual interpretation, theological studies, and the understanding of lived religious experience. Rooted in the long and diverse traditions of the study of religion in Canada, the series demonstrates awareness of the complex genealogy of religion as a category and as a discipline. ASR welcomes submissions from authors researching religion in varied contexts and with diverse methodologies.

The series is sponsored by the Canadian Corporation for Studies in Religion whose constituent societies include the Canadian Society of Biblical Studies, Canadian Society for the Study of Religion, Canadian Society of Patristic Studies, Canadian Theological Society, Société canadienne de théologie, and Société québécoise pour l'étude de la religion.

Caught in the Current

*British and Canadian Evangelicals
in an Age of Self-Spirituality*

SAM REIMER

McGill-Queen's University Press
Montreal & Kingston • London • Chicago

© McGill-Queen's University Press 2023

ISBN 978-0-2280-1695-3 (cloth)
ISBN 978-0-2280-1696-0 (paper)
ISBN 978-0-2280-1779-0 (ePDF)
ISBN 978-0-2280-1780-6 (ePUB)

Legal deposit second quarter 2023
Bibliothèque nationale du Québec

Printed in Canada on acid-free paper that is 100% ancient forest free (100% post-consumer recycled), processed chlorine free

This book has been published with the help of a grant from the Canadian Federation for the Humanities and Social Sciences, through the Awards to Scholarly Publications Program, using funds provided by the Social Sciences and Humanities Research Council of Canada.

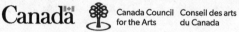

Funded by the Government of Canada   Financé par le gouvernement du Canada   Canada   Canada Council for the Arts   Conseil des arts du Canada

We acknowledge the support of the Canada Council for the Arts.

Nous remercions le Conseil des arts du Canada de son soutien.

Library and Archives Canada Cataloguing in Publication

Title: Caught in the current : British and Canadian Evangelicals in an age of self-spirituality / Sam Reimer.
Names: Reimer, Samuel Harold, author.
Series: Advancing studies in religion ; 14.
Description: Series statement: Advancing studies in religion ; 14 | Includes bibliographical references and index.
Identifiers: Canadiana (print) 20220465495 | Canadiana (ebook) 20220465606 | ISBN 9780228016953 (cloth) | ISBN 9780228016960 (paper) | ISBN 9780228017806 (epub) | ISBN 9780228017790 (ePDF)
Subjects: LCSH: Evangelicalism—Canada. | LCSH: Evangelicalism—Great Britain. | LCSH: Christianity and culture—Canada. | LCSH: Christianity and culture—Great Britain.
Classification: LCC BR1642.C3 R435 2023 | DDC 277.108/3—dc23

This book was typeset by True to Type in 10.5/13 Sabon

*To the pastors, priests, and laity
who generously participated in this study*

Contents

Figure and Tables

FIGURE

TABLES

Preface

In my teens, I loved going to summer camp, particularly one Christian camp near the Pacific Ocean. Each afternoon, campers rushed to the beach to swim and body surf, but could not enter the water until a strong swimmer tested the ocean swimming area for undertow. Then the lifeguards would form a wide semi-circle in the water that the campers were required to stay within. The lifeguards not only watched the swimmers but also kept an eye on the shore to make sure they were not being pulled away from a set location on the beach where the head lifeguard stood watching. On some days, campers and lifeguards would constantly adjust, swimming against the ocean's pull. I remember being pummelled by the powerful waves and resisting the currents to keep within the designated boundaries. But on most swims, I was unaware of the current; I just loved being in the water.

Similarly, evangelicals often find themselves carried along by the powerful current of Western culture. And, as with an undertow, they cannot see it on the surface – it is hidden beneath the pounding waves. The laity/campers try to resist and stay within the boundaries of their faith, while still enjoying all the pleasures that "the world" offers. The clergy/lifeguards keep one eye on their flock and the other on the set location on shore – the "unchangeable" biblical standard. They hope their preaching and teaching keep the laity within the semi-circle of the faith. Yet, all are caught in the current, and many are drifting outside the boundaries of the faith. The pages that follow look at the pull of Western culture, and the ways evangelicals are conforming and not conforming to it.

In this book, I am hoping to bridge two audiences, the scholar of religion and the educated practitioner (both clergy and laity). On the one hand, this book brings new findings to the academic study of evangelicalism in Canada, Britain, and beyond, which I hope will engage scholars. On the other hand, I have tried to avoid getting bogged down in the details of academic debates and theory, so that this book is engaging for non-scholars. Further, I have tried to engage audiences on both sides of the Atlantic. This may mean that each audience will wish I had written more (or less!) on certain topics.

During the writing of this book, the global COVID-19 pandemic shook up all our lives and emptied evangelical churches in both countries. Much is being written (and is yet to be written) about the effects of this pandemic on religion in general and·evangelicalism in particular. The reader may be surprised that the pandemic is hardly mentioned in this book. That is because the data collection was (thankfully) completed in 2018, before the pandemic hit: obviously, such an event was not on the radar of anyone I interviewed. I could speculate on its effects, but a book like this should be based on research, not speculation.

This book tends to focus on evangelicalism as a monolithic whole, and some readers may view it as glossing over important demographic differences, like race, class, gender, denomination, and so on. But much has been written about evangelicalism and race, class, gender, and sexuality by other scholars,[1] and so, rather than revisiting these subjects, I have chosen to focus on external influences rather than internal diversity. While evangelicalism is not monolithic, it is clear that many evangelicals contend with cultural change in similar ways on both sides of the Atlantic.

In a preface, it is typical to acknowledge all those who contributed to a work, and, in my case, this is hardly perfunctory. I am most grateful to have received the Alan Richardson Fellowship at the University of Durham, so that I could complete data collection in England. There were many benefits to being at Durham, not least of which was being able to enjoy beautiful northern England with my wife and son. Those in the scholarly community around Durham – Durham's Department of Theology and Religion and Cranmer Hall/St John's College – were particularly helpful and gracious hosts. Special thanks to Mathew Guest for letting me use his office (and read his books!) while he was on sabbatical. Crandall University also provided financial and research support through the Stephen and Ella Steeves' Sabbatical Research Scholarship, for which I am grateful.

Many scholars and leaders offered helpful advice and information, including Dan Goodwin, Beth Greene, Derek Purnell, Alex Fry, Andrew Nicholson, Andy Byers, David Bebbington, David Goodhew, David Muir, David Voas, Joe Aldred, Ephraim Radner, Grace Davie, Greg Smith, Ian Parkinson, Joel Edwards, Liz Kent, Martin Kreplin, Peter Robertson, Ram Gidoomal, Roger Sutton, Ruth Perrin, Sam Hailes, Justin Brierley, Susie Thorp, William Challis, David Wilkinson, Jessamin Birdsall, Malcolm Martin, Mark Bonnington, Nick Spencer, Peter Brierley, David Edwards, Linda Woodhead, Yemi Adedeji, Rick Hiemstra, and Steve Clifford. Of course, the over 100 clergy and laity who trusted me enough to tell me about their churches and their spiritual lives deserve my special thanks. I am always surprised at how many people are willing to help when a complete stranger requests an interview. These are truly generous and helpful people, and I dedicate this book to them.

I gained much from the insights of John Stackhouse Jr, Keith Grant, Galen Watts, Mathew Guest, and Adam Stewart, who read all or parts of this manuscript and gave helpful comments. Research assistants Cassidy and Kennedy Steeves did both theme analysis and proofreading. Emmett Fawcett, Julianna Hisey, and Samantha Anderson completed the painful task of transcribing interviews with grace. My daughter, Dani Reimer, provided editing and offered helpful comments on some chapters. My wife always provides significant behind-the-scenes support, for which I have been grateful for over thirty years.

Finally, I am thankful to be working again with the capable staff at McGill-Queen's University Press, including editor Kyla Madden. Copyeditor Barbara Tessman went well beyond my expectations, to make this book more readable and engaging. Her extra help getting my citations in order deserves particular recognition.

CAUGHT IN THE CURRENT

Introduction

With the culture around them seeming increasingly hostile and post-Christian,[1] many British and Canadian evangelicals are feeling unsettled and anxious. New Atheists disparage their faith. Moral attitudes toward sex and sexuality are becoming increasingly liberal. Children from evangelical families are taught values in schools that their parents do not agree with. Fewer people are going to church. Evangelicals are surrounded by increasing numbers of non-Christians and those who claim to have no faith at all.

Such unsettledness, of course, is nothing new. On the one hand, evangelicals have had some degree of tension with society for most of their history. They are known for their orthodoxy and orthopraxy,[2] holding fast to conservative positions in spite of growing secularism. They take seriously the biblical command to not "copy the behavior and customs of this world" (Romans 12:2).[3] On the other hand, this tension should not be overstated. Most evangelicals feel comfortable being part of Western culture most of the time, and many have a mixed view of society, seeing both good and bad.[4] Open confrontations between individual evangelicals and non-evangelicals are rare in day-to-day life, and few evangelicals feel limited in what they can do or where they can go. Most evangelicals are fully engaged in society. They do not want to be radically countercultural or out-of-touch with present realities, for they wish their beliefs and lifestyles to be appealing, partly so that non-Christians will be attracted by their faith and ultimately be "saved." However, it is difficult to be relevant and attractive to non-evangelicals while maintaining orthodoxy.

Evangelicals' unsettledness is due not only to cultural change, but also to the fact that Western culture is changing them. Clergy see consumerism, busyness, individualism, and secularism creeping into their congregations. Unorthodox views are common among those in the pews – and it is hard to get people in the pews. Secular entertainment, children's sports, vacations, and travel keep the faithful away. A few clergy whom I interviewed noted that an hour on Sunday does not inoculate parishioners against the unchristian values and viewpoints they absorb from dozens of hours spent on secular media. Regardless of how much they try to keep the "world" out, it worms its way in. As Alan Wolfe (2003, 3) has said about the United States, "In every aspect of the religious life, American faith has met American culture – and American culture has triumphed."

Evangelicals' dis-ease is also about their reputation. Many of the evangelicals in Britain and Canada whom I interviewed do not like how they tend to be perceived by non-evangelicals. Secular media often presents them as intolerant, homophobic, patriarchal, and narrow-minded (Haskell 2009; Wright 2010). "Evangelicals have a PR [public relations] problem," one evangelical academic states bluntly (Yeh 2018, 104). However, the issue is not simply that non-evangelicals unfairly berate them. British and Canadian evangelicals recognize that negative stereotypes are partly deserved because of the behaviour of their fellow evangelicals, especially those in the United States (Hatcher 2017). Many evangelicals in Canada and England try to separate themselves from the stereotype of white American evangelicals, 81 per cent of whom voted for Donald Trump in 2016. (Of course, some white American evangelicals also try to distance themselves from Trump supporters (e.g., Noll, Bebbington, and Marsden 2019; Labberton 2018).) Several clergy and evangelical leaders I interviewed stated that even the label "evangelical" is problematic (see also Stringer 2021; Mouw 2019; Hatcher 2017), and they wonder if they should completely rid themselves of it and its negative connotations.

Evangelicals are aware of their cultural milieu. For them, this world is not their (final) home, and they recognize that they do not always fit into it. They are also self-aware. They know that not everyone likes them, and that this is partly their fault. And they know that Western culture is seeping into their subculture.

This book focuses on the influence of Western culture on evangelicals, mainly in Britain and Canada, although many of my findings apply to other Western countries as well. A book could also be written with the causal arrow going the other way – that is, on how evangelicals influence, and have influenced, Western culture. Evangelicals were and are formational in both Britain and Canada, but that will not be the focus here. Rather, this book is about how evangelical beliefs and practices are adapting to or resisting the cultural changes around them.

Evangelicalism is changing in response to the Western cultural milieu. These changes are not just demographic, although demographic change is an important part of the story. Evangelicals are also changing in their beliefs, practices, and attitudes. Some of these changes, like shifts in some moral attitudes, are obvious to researchers. Others are subtle changes that quantitative surveys – which only scratch the surface of beliefs and morals – cannot pick up. My qualitative interviews reveal the reframing of beliefs to make them more palatable to Western non-evangelicals. Still other changes are organizational and structural. Evangelicals are adjusting the way they "do" church, seeking to get outside the walls of the church building to impact their community. Denominational structures are changing as well. New international networks are growing, sometimes to the detriment of traditional denominations. Many of these changes show a level of conformity to Western culture. Indeed, a careful study of evangelicals reveals that they have accommodated to the society around them (Quebedeaux 1978; Shibley 1998; C. Smith 1998; Guest 2007); in the words of Hexham and Poewe (1997, 43), they "take on local color."

Yet, evangelical history is far more complex than a linear series of accommodations, and a balanced view of evangelical interaction with Western culture includes nonconformity. Evangelicals have long been (and have viewed themselves as) the defenders of Christian orthodoxy and orthopraxy (Hunter 1987). While some Christian traditions have liberalized in response to social trends, evangelicals often resisted accommodation (Penning and Smidt 2002). Even if some influences seep in, evangelicals protect their distinctiveness. They fortify boundaries to resist the "world" – boundaries defined by conservative religious beliefs (Hunter 1987; C. Smith 1998; Reimer 2003). Their orthodoxy is supported by a plethora of institutions, which include evangelical churches, Bible colleges, seminaries and universities, book publishers, music labels, conferences, and many non-profit organizations. The cultural "goods" produced by these institutions, along with evangelicals crossing national borders throughout their history, result in many similarities among evangelicals in Canada, Britain, and beyond.

In my previous comparative study of Canadian and American evangelicals (Reimer 2003), I argued that a pervasive interdenominational and international evangelical subculture exists in Canada and the United States and that it spawns significant similarities between evangelical individuals, churches, denominations, and schools. In fact, active evangelicals on both sides of the border have matching core beliefs, share similar views of in-groups and out-groups, and have similar moral attitudes and similar levels of commitment (Reimer 1996 and 2000). My more recent research confirms that this evangelical subculture spans the Atlantic. I attended many evangelical church services in England, and often felt that, with a change in accent (and often newer buildings), many church services could have easily taken place in North America.

Cultural similarities will be the focus of this book. For most of what follows, I will look at broad cultural changes affecting both the United Kingdom and Canada, and other Western countries as well. Admittedly, using such broad brush-strokes means that one risks oversimplification, including overlooking important regional and national differences. Yet, as I showed in my previous work on US and Canadian evangelicalism (Reimer 2003), similarities outweigh differences, and between-country differences were more important than within-country differences. Here, I risk using an even wider brush by looking at recent cultural changes that exist in many Western countries (and beyond).

It would not surprise my respondents to hear that evangelicals in Britain and Canada show a family resemblance, reporting striking similarities in beliefs, practices, and discourse. How do we explain these similarities? First, there are globalizing subcultural flows *internal* to evangelicalism that span the Atlantic and the forty-ninth parallel (Guest 2017). Evangelical books, music, speakers, blogs, denominations, apostolic networks, and so on cross the Atlantic and the Canadian-American border quite easily in this age of the internet and global travel. Evangelical denominations and churches have a long history of cross-Atlantic linkages (e.g., Carte 2021) and form vast networks of connections, both local and international (Chapman 2004). Second, the broader cultures of Britain and Canada have much in common. Thus, *external* influences are similar. They were both influenced by the Enlightenment and Romanticism; the disestablishmentarianism of the 1960 and 1970s; modernity and postmodernity; increased religious and ethnic diversity due to immigration; capitalism; and global trade.

However, if one looks closely, there are also differences between each country's brand of evangelicalism. Comparing evangelicals cross-nationally reveals a few dissimilarities stemming partly from slight differences in cultural context. To quote eminent sociologist Seymour Martin Lipset, "Nations can be understood only in comparative perspective. And the more similar the units being compared, the more possible it should be to isolate the factors responsible for differences between them" (1990, xiii). Scholars typically locate Canada between the United States and Britain culturally and religiously (e.g., Noll 1992), as the British and American influences on Canadian evangelicalism are substantial (Bebbington 1994a). Differences between evangelicals based on national context stand out when similarities predominate. These dissimilarities tend to reflect differences in the broader cultures of each country. Canada's and Britain's evangelicalism look more similar to each other, whereas US evangelicalism looks more distinct. As a result, US evangelicalism serves as a foil, a point of comparison – and the vast material on American evangelicals generated by scholars and the media facilitates such comparisons. I will have more to say about both similarities and differences and their sources below. At this point, I must attend to some important definitional and methodological issues.

CULTURE AND SUBCULTURE

"Culture" can be understood as the values, norms, material goods, language, and symbols that make up a group's understanding of the world. This is not the place for a lengthy, academic explanation of culture, but a metaphor may help. Culture, suggests sociologist Tim Clydesdale (2007), is like a computer's operating system (os). An os is the software – like Microsoft Windows – that runs your computer; it is the default way of orienting you to the world of your computer. You have come to expect it to work in certain ways, with, say, pulldown menus or icons that you can tap or click. For people with any degree of experience in the world of computers, their os is natural and taken for granted. Just like we do not need to think about how to access or navigate the internet, we do not think about whether we should get dressed or not before we go outside, or whether we should eat with our fork or use our fingers, or what to say when someone says "hello" on the street. Our "os" culture has default settings for all of that. Sometimes our computer's OS receives updates or downloads without us knowing it (and sometimes they are obvious and annoying!). Similarly, we internalize cultural norms and values without even being aware of it. Culture seeps in, influencing our behaviour and thinking, whether we like it or not. Even evangelicals who are wary of "worldly" influences "download" Western cultural norms and values. Normally, we do not think about our culture any more than fish think about the water around them.

However, the norms and values of our culture do become evident when they change or they are breached. For example, moving from an evangelical private high school to a large secular university can be something like switching from a Mac to a PC. Fortunately, there are some similarities between a Mac and PC OS, so not everything is new, but there is enough that is strange (language use, big classes, parties, hooking up, and so on) at a secular university that evangelicals feel like they do not quite fit in. In these circumstances, it is easy to feel uneasy. This is because there exists an evangelical subculture (or a distinctive culture within a bigger national culture) that has some of its own norms, values, language, symbols, and material goods.[5] Evangelicals may wear material goods like WWJD (What Would Jesus Do?) bracelets, follow norms like daily Bible reading and prayer, and use language like "the blood of the lamb" (referring to Jesus' sacrificial death) or "devos" (personal devotions), all of which would be foreign to most non-evangelicals. Evangelicals may love their church, listen to Hillsong music, and read books by Francis Chan. They encounter atheists, pro-choice activists, and Gay Pride marches, and realize that those groups do not share all their values and beliefs. They do not quite feel at home in the "PC OS" world of Western culture.

In addition, subcultures are distinctive because they have symbolic boundaries. Such boundaries help one distinguish those who are "in" the evangelical subculture and those who are "out." They enable evangelicals to identify a fellow evangelical. Do they go to (an evangelical) church? Can they quote Bible passages like John 3:16? Do they use evangelical language or know evangelical worship songs? Do they avoid certain behaviours, like getting drunk or engaging in premarital sex? Do they believe that salvation is possible only through Jesus? My previous research showed that there is general agreement among active evangelicals in Canada and the United States on who is in the evangelical fold and who is outside of it, what groups they feel far from (like atheists and New Agers), and those that they feel close to (like conservative Catholics and pro-lifers). In sum, this international evangelical subculture not only has similar norms and values, but similar boundaries.[6]

Yet, most evangelicals are comfortable in modern Western culture in many ways. They work in secular jobs and may attend public schools, where they make non-evangelical friends; they play video games, own smartphones, use social media, and go to movies and pubs; they dress, eat, sleep, buy houses, and procreate like everyone else. They are not separate from Western culture (like a Luddite who refuses to use computers for any reason) but, rather, are engaged in it (C. Smith 1998).[7] Indeed, someone could live next door to an evangelical and never know it. Some are not very distinctive at all. As a whole, evangelicals embrace (to varying degrees) a lot of the "world," even while they seek to remain distinctive in ways that align with biblical teaching.

Consider a walled city whose inhabitants seek to maintain a distinctive way of life.[8] The problem is that the wall is broken down in places and vulnerable to infiltration by outsiders. If the city's inhabitants fear a "northern" invasion, the north wall is built up and patrolled by sentries. Meanwhile, the southern part of the wall is unguarded and in disrepair, and can easily be breached. Outsiders enter from the south, but the inhabitants are relatively unconcerned about southern influences. An occasional sentry may voice concerns about southern invaders, but few take heed. After all, the southerners bring such delights into the city that few wish to stop them. Over time, leaders in the city may become aware that southern invaders are threatening their distinctive way of life, so they send workers to repair the south wall and sentries to guard it.

Like this metaphorical walled city, the evangelical subculture is aware of certain threatening influences from Western culture – like liberalizing sexual ethics, for example – and clergy, apologists, authors, and other "sentries" are warning of their dangers. While this part of the subculture's boundaries or "wall" is built up and protected, other areas are unguarded, and other societal influences, like consumerism, stream in. As a result, someone's evangelical status is not questioned if they love to shop; but if they condone sex outside of traditional marriage, their loyalties indicate to some that they should move outside the walled city. Over time, evangelical spokespersons may draw attention to another threat – "New Atheism," for example – and attention moves to reinforce another section of the subculture boundary. Authors and clergy warn against New Atheism and pro-

duce arguments to defend the faith. In other cases, some former outsiders – like Christian rock musicians or conservative Catholics – live
close enough to the city that they are no longer viewed as "other" and
are invited to live within the walls of the city.

Thus, evangelicals are influenced by the broader Western culture –
in some areas more than others – but are also distinct, resembling
those in other "walled cities." However, evangelicalism is not simply a
combination of external cultural influences and internal subcultural
influences: it is not just global-national-regional cultural "pieces" and
evangelical subcultural "pieces" mixed together, like a bag of mixed
nuts, where peanuts, almonds, and pecans are clearly distinguishable.
It is more like combining eggs, flour, sugar, and other ingredients to
make a cake. In other words, evangelicals (or any subculture) draw elements from Western culture and from the evangelical subculture (and
other local influences), which combine to make something that is not
completely predictable. By the combination something new is created – something that is greater than the sum of its parts. Evangelicals
adapt Western culture to fit their needs, or they import evangelical
influences from elsewhere and then make them uniquely their own.

Canadian evangelicalism is not just a combination of British and
American versions, even though both countries substantially influenced Canada's evangelicalism. Canadian evangelicalism is shaped by
its own unique history and geography (Bebbington 1997). This is
because people "make" culture, drawing from a dizzying number of
cultural elements (which sociologists call "repertoires" or "schemas")
and combining them over time in unique ways (Brubaker, Loveman,
and Stamatov 2004). Since culture is created as persons interact, each
church has a unique "feel," a slightly different culture than a church of
the same denomination in close proximity (Becker 1999). Denominations, evangelical schools, evangelical philanthropic organizations,
and other institutions, also may differ in important ways, even though
they are clearly all evangelical and hold many things in common.

Let me try one more metaphor, which gets past some of the limitations of the "walled city" comparison. Drawing from Eliasoph and
Lichterman (2003), consider a bebop singer making a Christmas
album that includes Irving Berlin's song "White Christmas," made
famous by Bing Crosby. The bebopper draws from an external (outside
of bebop) musical genre and adapts it in ways that are creative ("no
one sings 'White Christmas' quite like that") but somewhat predictable
("still sounds like bebop"). Similarly, evangelicals will draw elements

from external culture, "baptizing" or "sanctifying" them for use within the evangelical subculture. "Evangelicalism's genius is its plasticity," writes evangelical theologian Chris Armstrong. "Look for trends in popular culture and then look for them in similar-yet-different forms in evangelical churches" (2016, 66). Evangelicals will also draw from within their subculture, based on what they have seen or experienced elsewhere. In doing so, they adapt the elements slightly or significantly for better fit within their context. Some elements are intentionally brought "inside" the subculture from the "outside": media use, musical styles, fundraising techniques, and much more are drawn from Western culture and used by evangelicals for their ends. Other elements seep in undetected. Thus, there is an international coherence within the evangelical subculture, since a globalizing Western culture and a globalizing evangelical subculture share elements that breed similarities. At the same time, there are differences, as these similar elements are combined and adapted in complex ways by local actors.

As a result, conformity (to Western culture) and nonconformity (because of subcultural boundaries) always exist in tension. Evangelical churches tend to be innovative and adaptive, drawing elements from Western culture. After all, they want their churches to be "seeker-sensitive" – that is, they hope their church services attract unsaved persons. The style of the worship music should resonate with those (beboppers) outside the evangelical fold. The language used from the podium should avoid "evangelicalese," and the sermon should impact the spiritual seeker. However, this use of broader cultural forms cannot tamper with the timeless truths of the faith. The central tenets stated in the Bible cannot be compromised. The tension between relevance and resistance is a tricky balance to achieve. One strategy is to downplay the more offensive parts of orthodoxy, especially when seekers or new converts are present. Thorny issues can be raised once new members become more committed.

In spite of the permeability of evangelical boundaries, similarities abound within the evangelical subculture. Sociologists argue that cultures have a "thin" coherence (e.g., Sewell 1999), with similarities existing along side many differences. However, the evangelical subculture is pretty "thick."[9] Its coherence is increased because of what sociologists call "cultural anchors," some of which are more robust than others, like evangelicalism's strong biblicism (Hoffman and Bartkowski 2008; Ogland and Bartkowski 2014). The commitment of evangelicals to biblical authority increases their similarities across nations because it "anchors" their orthodoxy and orthopraxy. These anchors are affective and transposable to diverse settings and have broad influence within the subculture. This notion of "cultural anchors" is helpful when attempting to define evangelicalism.

DEFINING EVANGELICALISM

Defining evangelicalism is not easy, partly because the group is internally diverse (Bebbington 2009; Dayton and Johnston 1991). Evangelicalism is divided within itself. This is particularly evident in the United States, where evangelicals are politically polarized. Indeed, some recent scholarship has indicated that (white) US evangelicalism is defined more as a political movement than a theological one, adding to difficulties of definition.[10] Others wonder if evangelicalism is so shaped by cultural factors that it is not distinct from Western culture or unified enough to form a separate entity (see, e.g., Trueman 2011). Still others wonder if the word "evangelicalism" is so tarnished that is should be replaced (see, e.g., Stringer 2021). In response to these debates, I argue that evangelicalism remains an international and distinct entity or subculture that must be defined primarily with reference to its theology.[11]

However difficult, definitions are important. Evangelicalism can be defined, variously, based on self-identity (those who say they are evangelicals), beliefs (those holding orthodox Christian beliefs), and affiliation (those who affiliate with evangelical churches and/or denominations). All strategies have their weaknesses and result in very different estimates of the number of evangelicals (Hackett and Lindsay 2008). The issue becomes more complicated when dealing with evangelicalism as an international movement. Possibly the best-known definition of evangelicalism uses Bebbington's quadrilateral (1989),[12] which defines evangelicals based on four characteristics that have distinguished them throughout their history. These are "conversionism, the belief that lives need to be changed; activism, the expression of the gospel in effort; biblicism, a particular regard for the Bible; and what may be called crucicentrism, a stress on the sacrifice of Christ on the cross. Together they form a quadrilateral of priorities that is the basis of Evangelicalism" (3).[13] This definition is broad enough to include evangelicals across time and space, and works well with the notion of cultural anchors. The point is that conversionism, activism, biblicism, and crucicentrism are foundational to the evangelical subculture, and speak to norms, values, boundaries, symbols, language, and material goods. For example, evangelicals value the Bible, and it is normative for the dedicated to spend significant time reading and studying it.[14] Biblicism forms subcultural boundaries, and evangelicals normally reject external influences that do not align with biblical teaching. Material goods like translations of the Bible, Bible study books and guides, Bible reading schedules, Bible apps, and Bible commentaries, are common in the evangelical subculture. Strong cultural anchors like biblicism spawn similarities within the evangelical subculture, even across national boundaries.

Counting evangelicals is also difficult, particularly in Britain. Of course, the proportion of evangelicals in each country depends on our definitional strategy. Typically, the percentage of the population that is evangelical is said to be about 10 per cent in Canada (Reimer and Wilkinson 2015) and 25 per cent in the United States (Pew Research Center 2014), but these figures may be too high now due to increasing disaffiliation. A 2019 representative poll of Canadians showed that 6 per cent of the population identified as evangelical (Hiemstra 2020), for example. In Britain, where evangelical Anglicans and non-denominational churches make up a much higher proportion of evangelicals, it is harder to get good data. The Evangelical Alliance estimates two million evangelicals in the United Kingdom (Hatcher 2017), or about 3 per cent of the population, but some argue that the proportion is higher than that (G. Smith 2015).

THE STUDY

In 2018, I completed 124 interviews with evangelicals in England and Canada,[15] either face-to-face or online, sixty-seven with clergy and fifty-seven with active laity in sixty-seven different churches. Why a sample of committed evangelicals, both clergy and laity? My purpose is to examine the ways in which the cultural milieu is reshaping evangelicalism within the churches. Clergy are uniquely situated to observe such change. They provide a validity check to what I am hearing from the laity in their pews. In addition, one would expect to find minimally involved evangelical affiliates to be shaped by the broader cultural milieu, but to show that active laity selected by their clergy (or the clergy themselves!) are absorbing secular cultural trends makes the argument that evangelicalism is changing more convincing.

In England, I completed eighty formal interviews, in northern cities and London (and surrounding areas, to include some rural congregations); in Canada, forty-four formal interviews took place in New Brunswick, Alberta, Manitoba, and southern Ontario (see the appendix for a list of British and Canadian cities where interviews were conducted). Denominationally, evangelical Anglican (roughly twenty-five in each country) and Independent church (twenty-eight in England; eight in Canada) interviews dominated, but Baptist, Salvation Army, Vineyard, Redeemed Christian Church of God (RCCG), and conservative Presbyterian interviews were also completed in both countries (see the appendix for numbers of interviews by country and denomination).[16] All church leaders identified their churches as evangelical and were considered evangelical by reputation (according to regional/denominational leadership). I used similar sampling strategies and matching denominations across the two countries. In addition, I completed some forty informal interviews (conversations over lunch or tea, phone discussions, a few face-to-face discussions formally recorded) with scholars in Britain and Canada, and I attended over twenty Sunday morning services in churches where I also did interviews. I took notes at each service related to the building and neighbourhood, the demographics of the congregants, the music, the liturgy, and the sermon.

Clergy interview questions covered four areas: basic demographics of the congregants, including changes in attendance over time; theological beliefs and ethical positions; cultural connections, including cooperation with other churches and organizations, and transatlantic influences (authors read, conferences attended, network connections in North America or Britain); and finally, cultural influences, particularly the effects of Western culture on evangelical beliefs and practices. Lay interviews included questions on theological and moral beliefs and the influences of Western culture. In addition, I asked questions about practices such as church involvement and devotionalism. Finally, I asked interviewees about their religious background and current non-religious practices, to uncover possible connections to their religiosity. (See the appendix for the content of the clergy and lay questionnaires.) Of course, I did not expect either clergy or laity to be experts on cultural influences, but many gave insightful answers to these questions. My informal and formal interviews with academics who study religion and evangelicalism in Canada and England and with evangelical leaders in both countries also provided helpful information. You will hear their voices in later chapters.

CONTENT AND ORGANIZATION OF THIS BOOK

This book is not solely about my analysis of the interview data, although that is an important part of it. Some of the book consists of my analysis of trends in Western culture and their effect on evangelicals and evangelicalism. Such analysis is influenced by my formal and informal interviews, and also by my review of the academic literature and many years of participation within and observation of the evangelical subculture. My goal is not primarily prescriptive, although I hope some of what is written below will be helpful to evangelical leaders, clergy, and laity. Rather, my focus is mostly descriptive and analytical. I describe macrocultural trends and how societal change is perceived by my interviewees. In addition, I analyse how Western culture is changing evangelical beliefs and practices. Such an examination is necessary because the direction of most change is toward less orthodoxy or orthopraxy, partly because Western societies are increasingly post-Christian. That said, unlike some commentators (e.g., Dickerson 2013), I am not an alarmist who thinks that evangelicalism is disappearing from the West, nor do I think that all the influences of Western culture are secularizing or corrosive to evangelicalism. Some are positive. Moreover, there never was an idyllic state in which evangelicals were pure and uncontaminated by secular influences. While the nineteenth century may have been a time when evangelicalism had considerably more social influence than it currently does,[17] this did not represent a golden age when society was morally good and just.

This book is primarily about how evangelicalism is changing in England and Canada. Its central argument is that we cannot understand recent evangelicalism unless we understand the dominant cultural force that is reshaping it. This external force is what Charles Taylor (1991, 26) calls the "massive subjective turn." This "turn" has led to a sea change, with the rejection of institutional religious authority, and the relocation of authority inside the individual. As a result, most Britons and Canadians no longer feel obligated to attend churches or to hold orthodox, institutionally sanctioned beliefs. While the subjective turn affects all major institutions in society – including those related to politics, the economy, media, and families – it has a particularly powerful effect on religion. The subjective turn spawns self-spirituality, often seen in those who claim to be spiritual but not religious. I refer to this subjective turn as the transition from an external locus of authority to an internal locus of authority. This change has been glacier-like – massive but gradual – and has been largely undetected by evangelicals. Instead, they focus on adjusting to the most visible consequences of this move to internal authority – unorthodoxy and declining orthopraxy. As a result, they misread Western culture and some of its effects on evangelicalism.

My interviews reveal that evangelicals are focused on two main concerns. The first is related to their perception of society's effect on them. They point to the increased secularism and individualism of Western society as the cause of their woes: declining churches, youth leaving the faith, and compromised theology. The second issue is related to society's perception of them. They are working on damage control due to their tarnished public image.

According to the evangelicals I interviewed, their unpopularity stems primarily from two sources: their conservative sexual ethics and exclusive beliefs, and, more recently, their American counterparts. White evangelicals in the United States were instrumental in electing Donald Trump in 2016, and evangelicals in Canada and Britain feel that they have been conflated with their American co-religionists, who draw most of the (negative) media attention. Ironically, this self-image problem reveals that evangelicals are being re-formed from within in response to the same cultural zeitgeist that pervades Western culture. The zeitgeist that undermines institutional authority and church participation – resulting in widespread hand-wringing among my evangelical respondents – is the same cultural force that draws evangelicals' gaze inward, so that they focus on their identity and public image. Both of these responses are evidence of the turn toward internal authority and self-spirituality.

My central argument is that these two main concerns of evangelicals – decreasing orthodoxy/orthopraxy and unpopularity – are surface symptoms of a much more foundational and formational change that many fail to see. Evangelicals misread Western cultural change, partly because they operate with a traditional paradigm of external authority, partly because of a degree of separation that they maintain from Western culture, and partly because of the slow, surreptitious nature of that change. Just as one cannot see an undertow by looking at the water's surface, so they fail to perceive the move to internal authority.

As Christians who try not to conform to worldly standards, evangelicals intend to resist some of Western culture's changing beliefs and values. Yet, since they do not see gradual, foundational changes, they misdiagnose their own fundamental vulnerability. Their greatest concern should not be declining church attendance or liberalizing sexual strictures. These are symptoms. Their primary concern should be that they, too, are vulnerable to sliding from an external to an internal locus of authority. By exploring the "subjective turn," this book is not only about *how* evangelicalism is changing, but also about *why* it is changing.

In chapter 1, I explain the glacial change to an internal locus of authority. I consider it the most important social change (related to religion) in Western culture since the 1950s. This idea is not new, but I hope to articulate it in a way that is helpful for understanding its massive impact on transatlantic evangelicalism – and, for that matter, on Western culture. I then relate this change to secularization. The shift toward internal authority brings about religious change, moving away from institutional religion toward a self-spirituality that focuses on authenticity and self-discovery. Finally, I look at the impact of self-spirituality on evangelicalism. As in most chapters, I include the perspectives of the interviewees. How do they perceive this change? Is there evidence that this change in the locus of authority is internalized by even the most active evangelicals?

Chapter 2 focuses on beliefs, including theological and moral tenets. Unsurprisingly, when evangelicals are asked about the influence of "secular" culture on evangelicalism, the area they most commonly identify is liberalizing sexual ethics. This "top-of-mind" issue is constantly confronting evangelicals, who are concerned with both softening sexual mores within evangelicalism as well as antagonism from without. According to my interviewees, their conservative position on sexual ethics is not a minor blemish on an otherwise spotless reputation. Rather, it defines them in the eyes of the non-evangelical world. As if that were not enough, evangelicals in Canada and Britain feel that they again bear the brunt of the negative press related to evangelicals in United States, whom many observers view not only as homophobic and transphobic but also as anti-immigration and far right. In response, their co-religionists in Britain and Canada work hard to show that this image does not reflect most evangelicals outside the United States. As a result, their responses to ethical questions were qualified: yes, they hold conservative positions on sexual ethics, but they are not like those who (embarrassingly) lack compassion and eirenicism. The same qualified answers were not evident in their theological views, as biblicism, conversionism, and crucicentrism were largely confirmed without hesitation. Most active evangelicals think that their beliefs are stable inner convictions. I explore how having such convictions is antiquated in post-Christendom: beliefs are now much more fluid, as identities remain under construction. I connect this new understanding of beliefs to the internalization of authority and self-spirituality.

Chapter 3 focuses on practices, including both private religious practice (devotionalism) and public practice (ritualism). Given the emphasis on self-discovery and authenticity presented in chapter 1, it is unsurprising that the institutional religiosity practised by evangelicals looks decidedly inauthentic from the outside. In addition, public scandals involving well-known (mostly American) evangelicals – Ted Haggard, Jimmy Swaggart, Todd Bentley, Bill Hybels, Ravi Zacharias, to name a few – add to this perception. But is it correct that evangelicals do not "walk the talk"? In this chapter, I examine data to test this perception. Further, I examine how religious practices are changing. Practice looks different in a culture where ecclesial expectations are trumped by internal authority and self-spirituality. The inward turn changes church attendance, volunteering, and evangelism. I also look at research on Bible reading and biblical literacy, prayer, and what evangelicals tend to pray about. I also examine evangelization practices. In pluralistic societies where tolerance is a virtue, pushy proselytization is not appreciated. Those I interviewed are working hard to change negative perceptions by using non-confrontational methods, if they evangelize at all. Other effects of Western culture on practices are also explored.

Chapter 4 looks at faith transmission, a topic that concerns most evangelical parents and leaders. Many youth no longer attend a church, and many are leaving the evangelical faith, even those raised in devout homes. It is hard to keep youth in church when they have embraced self-spirituality, but, again, evangelical parents rarely see past the surface evidence of changing beliefs and practices. I review some of the literature about transmitting one's faith to the next generation, including the factors that are most important in keeping children committed to the faith.

In chapter 5, I examine the evidence for international differences and similarities within evangelicalism. The focus is on similarities that support the notion of not only a transnational evangelical subculture, but also of similar cultural influences that breed similar changes in belief and practice within evangelicalism. I examine the responses of evangelical leaders in both Canada and England regarding how they have been shaped by evangelical authors, leaders, and institutions from the United States, and how Canadian leaders have been influenced by British writers. Such connections point to a transatlantic, even global, evangelical subculture. In spite of the positive influence of many American evangelical leaders, those I interviewed were also eager to distance themselves from US evangelicals as a whole, especially the Trump-supporting kind. Evangelicalism in Canada and England is different from US evangelicalism politically, indicating differences in evangelical subcultural boundaries (Bean 2014; Hatcher 2017). I conclude the chapter by discussing differences between Canada's and Britain's brands of evangelicalism.

Chapter 6 looks at organizational change, exploring questions such as the following: With declining denominational loyalty and less interest in doctrinal differences between denominations, are the traditional evangelical denominations (like the Baptists, Wesleyans/ Methodists, Pentecostal, and Reformed groups) going to survive? Are they being replaced by non-denominational churches, megachurches, emerging churches, or new apostolic networks? Are evangelical organizations conforming to secular organizational change? Another demographic force bringing organizational-level change is the increasing percentage of immigrant evangelicals, from Asia, Africa, and South America. Decreasing birth rates and poor retention among British and Canadian non-immigrants would mean considerable reduction in evangelical membership, if numbers were not being bolstered by immigrants. Many of these immigrants are not joining white evangelical churches but are starting their own. Yet, some others are joining, and often invigorating, declining white evangelical churches. Such changes bring some surprising results, including increasing rates of church attendance in big cities, like London, England (Goodhew and Cooper 2019). Finally, recognizing that not all institutional forms are equally well suited for the move to self-spirituality, I examine those institutional forms that have a competitive advantage in Western culture.

In the conclusion, I make a few tentative predictions about evangelicalism's future in Canada and Britain.

In all these chapters you will hear the voices of evangelical clergy, laity, and leaders as they seek to navigate their way through an ever-changing cultural milieu. Some are hopeful, others are not, but all want to see their churches and fellow evangelicals thrive. Unfortunately, their picture of modern Western culture is dark and out-of-focus. I hope this book provides increased clarity and light to navigate by; not just for them, but all who seek to understand their uneasy relationship with Western culture.

1

The Modern Zeitgeist: The Changing Locus of Authority and Self-Spirituality

New Age beliefs and attitudes are now so widespread in our society
and its culture as to effectively dominate all areas of life.

Campbell 2004, 40

Inner-life spirituality has permeated a great deal of the culture and its
institutions.

Heelas 2008, 61

A sea change has occurred in Western culture's view of authority. The development has variously been called "expressive individualism" (Bellah et al. 1985), "individualization" (Beck 2010), "subjective-life" (Heelas and Woodhead 2005), and "subjectivisation" (Berger 1967). As noted in the introduction, for philosopher Charles Taylor (1991, 26), it is a "massive subjective turn of modern culture." Heelas and Woodhead (2005, 2), describe it as "a turn away from life lived in terms of external or 'objective' roles, duties and obligations, and a turn towards life lived by reference to one's own subjective experiences." They believe (along with Taylor and many others) that "the subjective turn has become the defining cultural development of modern Western culture" (2005, 5). This change has existed in various iterations over the past one hundred years or so, with roots in the Protestant Reformation, the Enlightenment, and Romanticism; more recently, it became widespread among the baby boomers and was passed on to their children (Roof 1999). This is a cultural internalization, as people understand themselves as autonomous humans with individual rights. The individual person is free to create their own identity, unhampered by the expectations of family, institutions, or society. When applied to religion, it has been called "a god of one's own"

(Beck 2010), a "congregation of one" (Arnett and Jensen 2002), or "religion of the heart" (T.A. Campbell 1991; Watts 2022), and is most commonly found among the "spiritual" but not religious. This sea change toward internality is widespread, shaping the culture and structure of late modernity. It is the modern zeitgeist. In this chapter, I explicate how this change, which I describe as a move from an external to an internal locus of authority, is reshaping religion and spirituality in Western countries and beyond. I look at both the *inner journey*, which is the *means* by which one realizes one's spiritual self, and *finding the authentic self*, the *end* or terminal goal of one's quest. Regarding the former, our spirituality is no longer anchored in a congregation (Wuthnow 1998). Instead, the quest is internal, and each person is responsible for finding their own way toward wholeness. One's journey is toward a new life-goal or telos. One's life purpose is no longer about fulfilling one's (occupational) calling in the world, gaining prestige or wealth, or creating a better future for family or community. The goal of life has also moved inside. This telos, at least as it relates to religion and spirituality, is to *find one's authentic self*. This "teleology of self-realization" (Watts 2018, 1026) or personal quest for inner wholeness culminates in discovering who one is meant to be.

THE INTERNAL LOCUS OF AUTHORITY

One's locus of authority is external if one's behaviour and beliefs are shaped from outside, largely by parental, religious, educational, or political authorities. Among the Silent Generation (those born before 1946), an external locus of authority was common. The hierarchical structure of workplaces during industrialization, the duty to country promoted by the world wars, and high religiosity, among other things, reinforced deference to external, institutional authority. Much of what this generation believed or did was unquestioned or taken for granted. Identity was mainly ascribed at birth, and it was fairly stable. One hundred years ago, Christendom was taken for granted by Canadians and Britons. They lived under a "sacred canopy" (Berger 1967) – a society where deference to Christian norms was assumed. Post-Christendom, the canopy has been replaced by individual umbrellas (Carwana 2021).

Deference to external authority was eroded particularly with the baby boomer generation (Bibby 2006), who were born between 1946 and 1964. The countercultural movement of the 1960s and 1970s, energized by Watergate, the Vietnam War, and rock and roll music, promoted a critical attitude toward traditional authorities. Many rebelled against their parents, refused to climb the corporate ladder, and criticized religious and political leaders. Young people experimented with drugs, sex, and Eastern religions. As external authority weakened, the result was a move toward an internal locus of authority.[1] This authority comes from inside each person – that is, it is up to the individual person to choose their behaviours and beliefs. Indeed, each person has the right to decide who they are; they must discover their own identities. Beliefs, practices, and identities are more fluid and contested, as people rethink their beliefs in light of new attachments and changing priorities. For people living one hundred years ago or more, religious beliefs and practices were prescribed by religious authorities. Religious leaders were honoured, and straying from their teachings was socially deviant and sanctioned accordingly. Children were expected to adopt the religious beliefs and identities of their parents, and they usually did.

I define "authority," as Max Weber does, to mean legitimate power (Weber [1922] 1964).[2] Legitimate power is accepted by the one under authority. For example, if robbers take your money at gunpoint, they have power over you, but it is not authority, because you do not think they have the right to take your money. However, if a cashier takes your money in exchange for a product, this is acceptable and legitimate: based on accepted norms of economic exchange, the cashier has the authority to do so. In the past, religious leaders had authority over the beliefs and behaviours of the laity. Inevitably, some deviated from prescribed expectations; but the point here is that the social expectations were clearly prescribed. Now many affiliates reject the official teachings of their religious groups, and, therefore, beliefs within a church can vary considerably (D'Antonio, Dillon, and Gautier 2013; Reimer 2011b). Although there is no central institutional authority within evangelicalism, many raised as evangelicals feel free to depart from the beliefs and practices of their parents, pastors, or denominations (Bielo 2011; Brophy 2016; Martí and Ganiel 2014). We have known that inward authority is typical of the "spiritual but not religious" (Ammerman 2014; Beaman and Beyer 2013), but what is less well known, or expected, is that it is also widespread in institutional religion, including evangelicalism (Watts 2022).[3]

In reality, external and internal loci of authority exist along a continuum, rather than in separate categories. The categories are not "either or," but "more or less." As the person embraces internal authority, they view external authority as increasingly suspect. This trend is evident among evangelicals. On the one hand, it would be true that evangelicals are, on average, more religiously devout than mainline Protestants or Catholics, and that the more devout tend to have higher levels of external authority. For some evangelicals, the Bible is the external authority to which they submit. They seek out "Bible-centred" churches, where pastors preach the true "Word of God." Of course, the Bible must be interpreted and applied, something that is often done by pastors, Christian authors/speakers, and other leaders. So it would not be true that pastors and leaders in evangelicalism have low authority, as long as their lay followers are convinced that they accurately teach the Bible. On the other hand, the zeitgeist of our modern age infiltrates the evangelical subculture as well, pushing evangelicals toward internal authority, as I will demonstrate below.

The transition toward internal authority has been particularly hard on institutional authority. Leaders in politics, medicine, science, law, education, and especially religion, can no longer assume deferential submission. As Heelas and Woodhead (2005) note, all areas of modern society show signs of increased subjectivity and inward authority – child-centred education, customer-centred stores and restaurants, patient-centred healthcare, and an emphasis on personal development at work.[4] Woodhead (2016) states that "most British people place great value on the freedom of the individual and are decidedly liberal when it comes to matters of personal morality – they believe that it is up to individuals to decide for themselves how they live their own lives" (251). This liberal position is "the opposite of 'paternalism,' understood as the view that one should defer to higher authority, whether of parents, God, scriptures, managers or whomever/whatever" (255). When individuals are their own authority, they are quite comfortable accepting and rejecting the views of experts and leaders based on their preferences, experiences, or personal whim. They take pieces that they like and leave the rest (Nichols 2017).

Consider a buffet, with dozens of items to choose from. There are succulent meats, rich desserts, fresh fruit, and exotic foods from around the world. Institutional religion, for the typical Western consumer, is something like the raw vegetables at the buffet (Clydesdale 2007). Vegetables, like religion, may be good for you, but, with limited time and stomach capacity, it would be silly to eat too many vegetables when there are so many more tantalizing options. Besides, your mother is not there to remind you to eat what is good for you. The sensible conclusion is to eat whatever you desire. Similarly, if religious leaders no longer have authority over you, and there are many more enjoyable ways to use your Sunday morning than going to church, one would be wise to consume religion sparingly. After all, it is up to you. You are your own authority.

It is easy to assume that the move to an internal locus of authority means that social or cultural influences have less effect, as people think for themselves instead of simply acquiescing to external authority. Yet, this assumption may not be true. The move from external to internal authority does not necessarily equal a move from deference to discernment (Bibby 2006). A quick trip to a mall or school may reveal a group of teens, dressed similarly, with similar hairstyles, all texting on their iPhones. Clearly social conformity and peer pressure is still active. My argument is not that people today are more discerning and therefore resist getting on a bandwagon. Instead, *society itself* endorses the internal locus of authority. Thus, moderns are *conforming* when they embrace an internal authority. As Woodhead (2017) states, freedom to decide for yourself is the default position. Guest et al. (2013), in their study of Christianity in UK universities, wonder if the growing subjectivism among students is really due to greater autonomy from social influences, or if the groups and institutions that influence them are simply more eclectic. Indeed, societal influences still wield significant power to define beliefs, values, and identities. The visual presentations of media and the strategic logic of the market shape moderns, even evangelicals (Guest 2022). One wonders if persons are really more free or autonomous, or if they simply are under the influence of new powers.[5]

The inward turn is not about society's power to influence behaviour and beliefs, but about legitimacy. Who or what has the legitimate right to decide what I should believe, do, or be? Under an internal locus of authority, the answer is me. The expectation is that I should define myself. I am told to be "true to myself," not to be "what others tell me to be."

Labelling this turn inward as a move toward an internal locus of authority is clearer, in my view, than other terms used, including the tendency to label Millennials (born between 1981 and 1996) (Dimock 2019) as "individualistic" or "narcissistic." The word "individualism" has multiple meanings, so it is increasingly unclear what exactly is meant by the term.[6] Additionally, to say that narcissism,

Table 1.1
Characteristics of external or internal loci of authority

External loci of authority	Internal loci of authority
Institutional authority – from parents, priests, experts, etc.	Individual authority – personal experience and what resonates with one's heart
Deference to institutions and leaders	Suspicion of institutions and leaders
Beliefs, behaviours, aspirations are prescribed	Beliefs, behaviours, aspirations are discovered and chosen
Identity is ascribed and stable	Identity is created and flexible

commonly understood to refer to self-adoration, accurately describes baby boomers (the "me" generation) and later generations is inaccurate (Watts 2018). Cultural historian Christopher Lasch, the author of *The Culture of Narcissism* (1979) and *The Minimal Self* (1984), clarified his use of the term: "narcissism signifies a loss of selfhood, not its self-assertion" (1984, 57). He suggests that many people are self-absorbed, not because they adore themselves, but because they are trying to find or create themselves.

To recap, Western culture is in the process of moving from external loci of authority toward internal loci of authority. This change has been glacial – gradual, quiet, under-the-radar – but extensive in impact. Most do not grasp its implications. Its effects include undermined institutional authority and increased tolerance for and affirmation of diversity in belief, practice, and identity. The modern zeitgeist avers that, regardless of class, race, gender, sexuality, or inherited religion, people should be free to make their own choices, at least as long as they are not seen as limiting other people's freedom to define themselves. Table 1.1 summarizes the characteristics of those with external loci of authority and those with internal loci of authority, although it is important to emphasize that these characteristics fall along a continuum, and few are likely to be pure externalists or internalists. Most people are located somewhere in between, and all the characteristics may not be equally evident.

Whence internal authority? Many forces have encouraged the move toward an internal locus of authority, and I will list only some here. First, levels of education have increased. Higher education has a critical edge, calling into question taken-for-granted norms and values. It also exposes the young person to a wide swath of ideas and viewpoints. Students are encouraged to think for themselves and develop their own views. Second, Western societies are experiencing increased immigration, increasing the heterogeneity of the population and world views within it (Bibby, Thiessen, and Bailey 2019). Third, the internet provides instant access to a plethora of ideas through blogs, social media, podcasts, and so on. As spiritual influencers move online, religious and cultural authorities are levelled and diversified (Flory and Miller 2008). These social changes, among others, point to an underlying reason for the inward turn: societal influences have become increasingly *multi-vocal*,[7] particularly for evangelicals. The messages or social influences received by a person are diverse, disparate, even contradictory. The values and beliefs heard at school or in the media vary from what is heard at home or at church. Moreover, the messages within any given social sphere (like education or politics or religion) can be disparate. Gone are the days (more typical of decades prior to the 1960s) when the messages coming from home, school, television and radio, church, and other institutional authorities were generally consistent and mutually reinforcing. Gone, too, are the days when beliefs, values, aspirations, and even identities were negotiated within a rather homogeneous community, where key influencers reinforced shared norms and beliefs. Options for what a person could believe or become were limited. Now, options are increasingly open.

The Venn diagrams in figure 1.1 illustrate this gradual change in the multi-vocality of social influences. The diagram on the left shows spheres of influence with greater overlap, representative of more traditional and more homogeneous societies. Clearly, as the non-overlapping parts of the circles indicate, some messages within each sphere are unique, often not reinforced in other spheres. But there is a significant core where all the circles overlap. This represents those messages from all sources that are similar and mutually reinforcing. This core provides a foundation on which an individual can build their beliefs, behaviours, and identity, often consistent with social prescription. In a more heterogeneous society, as shown in the Venn diagram on the right, influences from the major spheres are more multi-vocal and less mutually reinforcing. Social cues are more diverse, often with little overlap. Thus, the expectations of external authority are unclear, leaving the individual without clarity on beliefs, behaviours, and identity. The result, then, is that individuals must be the authors of their own beliefs, behaviours, and iden-

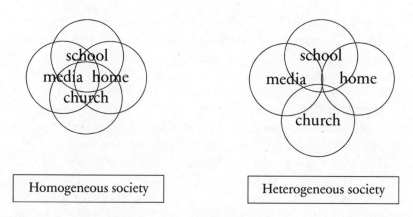

Homogeneous society	Heterogeneous society

Figure 1.1   The multi-vocality of societal influences

tity. The perceived need to create oneself is, I suggest, a natural adaption to a heterogeneous society's increased multi-vocality. Finally, even though the circles in the diagram on the right overlap less than those on the left, they do still overlap, indicating that certain messages are consistent across multiple institutional spheres. As I will argue below, part of this overlap reflects a cultural "script" about religion and spirituality that is reinforced within Western culture and its institutions.

The transition from internal to external loci of authority, then, is not driven by an increased narcissism or rebelliousness of individuals. It is not primarily a change at the individual level. Rather, people are adapting to a macrosocial reality. If society does not clearly prescribe beliefs, practices, and identities, then persons are left to come up with their own, pasting together what they can glean from what is available around them. Of course, there is no such thing as a society that does not prescribe or ascribe. Prescriptive influences that implicitly or explicitly communicate expectations and obligations always exist. The point is the prescriptions are not uni-vocal. What a person hears from home can conflict with messages they get at school, in church, or in the media. These conflicting messages require a filtering process, one that is more up to the individual than it used to be.

This argument is not new. Eminent sociologist Peter Berger and his co-authors made a similar argument in *The Homeless Mind* (1974). Pluralism, aided by mass communications and technology, creates many diverse sets of values that contradict each other, whereas traditional societies were more homogeneous and coherent. So modernization means that we lack social cohesion and cannot easily maintain a single symbolic universe. This weakens the authority of institutions and leads to (micro-level) anomie and frustration (Watts 2022). Each person must create their own sense of identity. The result is turning inward, a "subjectivization." But this situation is precarious, because humans need community, social institutions, and traditions to situate the self. As these fall away, the result is a "homeless mind."[8]

People experience varying degrees of multi-vocality, depending on their primary and secondary socialization (Berger and Luckmann 1965). Religious parents, in particular, seek to engage their children in settings that reinforce the beliefs, values, and practices they are trying to inculcate at home. They take their children to church activities, enrol them in religious schools, limit access to certain media, encourage them to make "good" friends while avoiding others, refuse to take them to parties, and so forth. In this way, spheres of influence are bounded and can be more mutually reinforcing (Smith 2003b). However, diverse ideas and influences are readily available, so it is hard to keep disparate voices out completely. In a globalized world, isolating children enough to monitor and control incoming messages is increasingly difficult (Waters 1995). The ubiquity and accessibility of the internet and other media, along with increased diversity in our towns and cities, means that the "sacred canopy" is full of holes, and the external culture seeps in. In *The Heretical Imperative* (1979), Berger observed that "modernity pluralizes both institutions and plausibility structures" (11), resulting in diverse influences. As a result, he states, humans are forced to choose their own beliefs, values, and lifestyles subjectively. In the words of Galen Watts (2019,) *"disenchantment of the outer world has always meant a simultaneous enchantment of the inner world"* (1032; emphasis in original).

INTERNAL AUTHORITY AND RELIGIOUS CHANGE

The relationship between the changing locus of authority and religious change is complicated, but certain trends are correlated. The decline of institutional religion in Western countries, often referred to as "secularization," is one such correlate. This trend is well documented across the West. Church attendance has fallen in Canada (Bibby 2017; Clarke and Macdonald 2017; Thiessen 2015), Australia (R. Powell 2013; Bouma 2008), European countries (Voas and Doebler 2011; S. Bruce

2011), and elsewhere (Inglehart 2021). Also on the decline has been trust in religious leaders (Bibby 2017) and the increase in religious "nones" – those who no longer affiliate with any religion (Thiessen and Wilkins-Laflamme 2020). Declines in trust, affiliation, and participation all point to decreased influence. However, the best measure of the ebbing authority of religious institutions is not declining affiliation or belief in God, although they are related. The clearest evidence is perhaps the willingness of people to ignore the official teaching of the religious hierarchy on matters of doctrine and practice (Chaves 2011).

Thus, Mark Chaves (1994, 749) has suggested that secularization is best understood "not as declining religion, but as the declining scope of religious authority." In his view, secularization means that religious institutions can no longer control the access to certain supernatural goods. People may still affiliate with religion and believe in God but no longer feel obligated to abide by prescribed religious beliefs and practices. This is consistent with a societal move toward an internal locus of authority, which happens when religious (and other) external authorities lose their legitimacy. They no longer are the ultimate authority for what a person does or believes. For Carole Cusack (2011), the secularization process is "intimately connected" with

> the individual as the agent of choice, the centre of human decision-making. In earlier times institutional Christianity had wielded considerable power in the enforcement of morals and the disciplining of public culture, but modern Western individuals favour affective experience over authoritative tradition and construct their identities through the acquisition of consumer items, body-based practices including working out at the gym and sexual experiences, and a multitude of other meaning-making activities derived from art, literature, film and television. Decisions are made on the grounds of tastes and inclinations, rather that family ties or community values. (410–11)

Although secularization and internal authority are tightly coupled, one should not assume that the modern Westerner follows a linear path toward secularization. No single continuum adequately describes a person's self-spirituality. Rather, identity formation in the religious realm is fluid and contested, following multiple trajectories that do not match well with traditional categories of Christian commitment or lack of commitment (Beyer, Craig, and Cummins 2019). Young people do not uniformly dislike institutional religion, nor are they all apathetic about it. Some are more ambivalent, sometimes loving it and sometimes hating it. Many struggle to integrate their religious upbringings into the identity they are constructing (Shipley 2019; Halafoff and Gobey 2019).

Charles Taylor (2007) is not particularly interested in the secularization debate. For him, the key issue is not religious decline, but how religious plausibility structures became contestable. Religion has become increasingly "fragilized," and, in a "secular age," all beliefs (including agnosticism/atheism) are questioned. As Taylor puts it, "we are now living in a spiritual supernova, a kind of galloping pluralism on the spiritual plane" (300). The supernova – an explosion of options for finding meaning, significance, and fullness – is the new reality. Coupled with this change is the "great disembedding" (152), where people no longer see themselves as embedded in society, but now understand society as a collection of individuals. This disembedding and multiplication of options provide fertile ground for self-spirituality.

Another correlate to internal authority is growing religious diversity. The decreasing percentage of Christians in most Western countries and the increased diversity of religious groups (both Christian and non-Christian) create more between-group variation. There is also increased within-group variation. Theological diversity within denominations and traditions is increasing, as evidenced by divisions over same-sex marriage among Anglicans worldwide or among United Methodists in the United States. Meanwhile, the number of non-denominational churches and networks is growing. State churches have lost their monopoly as sects and "free" churches flourish. Even Christian religious voices are diverse. With the Christian religion becoming increasingly multi-vocal, the inward turn is not surprising.

Finally, the massive turn inward is also correlated with certain types of religiosity. Modern individuals tend to take a consumerist approach to religious institutions: the church is there to serve them when they want it; they are not there to serve the church. As in the buffet example above, or a trip to the mall, consumers pick and choose the religious options they want. Their use of religious institutions is pragmatic: to the degree that they are useful in individuals' quest to find their true self, they will engage them. Christian churches are useful when rites of passage (e.g., christenings, marriages, burials) are desired, at times of corporate grief, or at Christmas, Easter, or other high feast days. Davie (2015) uses the term "vicarious religion" to describe the expectation that an active religious minority will perform religious services for the inactive majority when desired, and argues that this perspective it typical of religion in Britain. It should not be surprising, then, that "regular" church attendance tends to be one or two times a month, not more than once a week (Bibby 2017), even among evangelicals.

SELF-SPIRITUALITY

Influenced by the glacial shift toward internal authority, religion also moved internally.[9] Heelas' (1996) term "self-spirituality" is useful because it indicates both the individual nature of the spiritual quest and its goal, the true self. For Heelas, "self-spirituality is characterized, most fundamentally by the belief that the sacred resides within rather than without the self; in short, it sacralizes the self" (cited in Watts, 2018, 346).

However, simply because religion has taken the inward turn toward self-spiritualty does not mean it is devoid of any institutional supports. The view that such spirituality is free-floating, existing only in individual minds, is mistaken. Self-spirituality is not idiosyncratic, random, or unique to each individual. Rather, the sacred has relocated, finding other institutional homes that provide the "plausibility structures" (Berger 1967) to maintain it. Self-spirituality's institutional homes include what Heelas and Woodhead (2005) call the "holistic milieu" (including yoga studios, mediation groups, twelve-step programs, clinics that provide aromatherapy and alternative medicine, and so on, promoted by websites, advertising, books, blogs, and social media). Indeed, one can easily see the discourse of self-spirituality in the arts, healthcare, education, and particularly in popular culture and media (Watts 2022). Self-spirituality's institutional embeddedness provides it with coherence and structure, as I discuss below. Thus, spirituality does not signal a loss of the sacred (as some accounts of secularization suggest) but rather a decline in institutional religious authority.

So, what are the common characteristics of self-spirituality? Is there coherence around both the final *goal* and the *means* to reach that goal? I look first at the "means" of self-spirituality and its attributes.

The spiritual person generally eschews institutional religious authority and embraces private spirituality. For the self-spiritual, spiritual needs cannot be fulfilled in a physical place, like a church building; such fulfilment requires a personal *quest* (Wuthnow 1998). The self-spiritual quest is characterized by various features. First, it is a private journey for which the individual is responsible. The journey usually requires spiritual practices – yoga, meditation, mindfulness, tai chi, homeopathy, reiki, and so on – that counter dis-ease in one's subjective well-being and moves one toward wholeness. At best, institutional religion may be useful in this journey for a time, to the extent that the place of worship enhances the person's private journey toward wholeness. Once the religious group is no longer helpful, the seeker moves on, but the quest continues.

Second, for those on a self-spiritual quest, all major religions are basically the same at their core – a belief called "perennialism" (Heelas 1996). Beneath the layers of historically created divisions, the same metaphysical truth is foundational to all religions. Hiemstra, Dueck, and Blackaby (2018) found what they call the "Universal Gnostic Religious Ethic" common among emerging adults in Canada. These young Canadians felt that all religions shared the same core ethic, which was to help one become a good person and create social harmony. In this way of thinking, the enlightened realize religions' common core, and those who are not enlightened often create division, elevating their religion and rejecting others. Naturally, then, any religion is fine, as long as one does not hold exclusive beliefs. "Bricolage" (Heelas 1996), the practice of drawing from a variety of religions to create a spirituality of one's own, is typical.

Third, this quest involves an inner epistemology (Heelas 1996; Watts 2022). The way a person knows something is based largely on personal experience. Morality (what is right and wrong) and spirituality (how we know anything about God or the divine) is based on what is sensed internally. Truth is what resonates with the inner self or the heart. The rational mind, then, is not the ultimate source of authority in subjective areas like morals and spirituality. Rather, the heart allows access to what is "right for me." Truth is reached when a person senses love, wholeness, unity, peace, or joy – those feelings that come from the heart. Intuition, the "inner voice," guides our choices (Heelas 2008). The internal is the source of guidance for everyday decisions and choices. Indeed, one should not let society determine one's beliefs, for society divides us from others, undermines a healthy and authentic self, and generally puts demands and expectations on us that compete with what our inner voice is telling us. Listening to the cacophony of external voices trying to tell us what to think and who we are can add to one's dis-ease.

Fourth, a spiritual quest requires freedom from external restraints that can impede spiritual seekers as they travel their own path. Under external authority, freedom is understood to be the ability to make a choice between right or wrong, since right and wrong are defined by God, religious authorities, or societal norms. This understanding has been replaced by a broader privileging of individual freedom: one must be able to enjoy the personal liberty required for self-expression and self-direction. Thus, personal liberty and individual rights are sacralized (Heelas 2008; Watts 2022). Impediments, whether real or perceived, on the road toward self-realization are negative, even evil. If societal norms or external authorities are keeping a person from being all they can be, they are impediments that the person must learn to overcome. If someone is less than affirming of another's chosen path (assuming that path does not harm others), then their influence is negative and bad. We should all empathize with the struggle to get past impediments and negativity to discover our beliefs and identity, so it is unkind in the extreme to be critical of another's sense of self. One's identity and views in private areas of morality and spirituality are to be "liked" on social media. Since people should have an internal locus of authority, and since they should decide for themselves what they think and who they are, how could anyone not affirm their identities and views? As an individual on a spiritual journey, I may encounter people who disagree with me, but they are obviously wrong – my heart tells me so.

Fifth, self-spirituality involves a relocation and reattribution of God (that is, the God of orthodox Christianity and other world religions), or what might be called the sacred or divine. The sacred is now *immanent* (Taylor 2007), relocated from the transcendent to the inside (Heelas 2008; Placher 1996). God or the sacred is close and present. He (or she or it) pervades the natural world around us and our own bodies. Spiritual but not religious persons reject dualisms – God versus human, body verses mind, and so on – and thus tend toward monism (Chandler 2008). There is a unitary nature to self-spirituality, in that it recognizes a life force that flows through all things (Heelas 2008). This relates to the internal locus of authority because the sacred is now inside and must be discovered and accessed through an internal quest. The person, then, is imbued with inner sacredness, and when they learn to discern their inner voice, they access the divine within. Further, the attributes of God or the sacred are *good and positive*. Those influences that are not good and affirming to the self – fear of the divine or feelings of guilt and judgment – are not from God.

Negative feelings and self-doubt stem from the world around us. The sacred within fills us with wholeness, love, awe, beauty, and goodness. In this way, then, the immanent sacred, which is present in us, becomes undiscernible from our own inner sense, our true selves. The authentic self becomes sacred.

If the "means" by which we accomplish the spiritual is a private quest, then the "end" or telos is *finding the authentic self*. If the way we "know" what is right for us is internal, then the goal is also internal. The goal is to find that inner part that is authentically "me," the real self. There are really two selves: "a 'mundane', 'conventional', 'unnatural' or 'socialized' self, demonized as the 'false' or 'unreal' product of society and its institutions," contrasted "with a 'higher', 'deeper', 'true', 'natural', 'authentic' and 'spiritual' self" (Houtman and Aupers 2010, 6). The authentic self is hidden behind (or beyond) the mundane self, and must be discovered. Charles Taylor (1989) called this belief "expressivism," where the "ultimate purpose of life is to fulfill one's own nature" (347). One is told to "be true to yourself" or to "be who you are," however that is understood. The true self is hard to define, because it is different for each person, as each person is an original. Again quoting Charles Taylor, this time from *The Ethics of Authenticity* (1991, 29), "Being true to myself means being true to my own originality ... something only I can articulate and discover." Self-spirituality has a unitary, monistic nature but also emphasizes individual uniqueness (Heelas 2008). Everyone is equal, and the same sacredness lives in all of us, but everyone is also unique. What is clear is that once one finds one's authentic self, one finds wholeness and flourishes. While the precise end cannot be identified, there is a script or shared understanding of this telos. It is part of the zeitgeist in late modernity (Houtman and Aupers 2010; Watts 2022).

One aspect of this shared understanding of the late modern spiritual telos is that the authentic self is *good*. While historical Christianity sees the person as both good (made in the image of God) and bad (all are sinners), modern self-spirituality sees the self, at least the true self, as only good. It is good in the sense of it being innately virtuous. Love and acceptance are natural for the authentic self. It is in harmony with the world around it (monism) and full of compassion and kindness. The self is also good in the sense that it provides feelings of wholeness and well-being. Smith states that the central goal of life for the American youth he studied was "to be happy and to feel good about oneself" (C. Smith with Denton 2005, 163). Since the heart, not the head, has primacy in this inward journey, travellers can know that they are acting in accordance with the true self if they feel good (Houtman and Aupers 2010; Watts 2020). Being true to yourself just feels right.

A second aspect is that the authentic self is *divine* or *sacred*, and thus has divine characteristics. If God is immanent, then the true self is part of the sacred or the divine. When someone taps into their real self, they are tapping into the divine – the God within (Houtman and Aupers 2010). Like God, the authentic self is *pre-existent*. The inner self existed before culture or society began to distort it. It is innate and natural. It is also sacred in the sense that it has great *potential and power*. It is endowed with supernatural capacity. Not only does the inner voice guide us, but, once we become who we were intended to be, our innate potential is released. This great potential allows a person to have victory over suffering and weakness (Watts 2018).

While the authentic self is full of goodness and power, the path to finding oneself is fraught with obstacles and hardship. Since internal authority is required to find the self, conformity to external authorities obstructs the search. Fears, insecurities, unkindness, and not reaching one's potential indicate that the person is not being true to themselves. If someone is not acting virtuously, it is because they are not acting in accordance with their authentic self. Immoral behaviour and vice are caused by a distorted self, one that has been misshapen by society. The distorted self means the true self has not been realized, whether because the person has not embraced the inward journey or is not free to achieve or discover their self. While the orthodox Christian view is that vice is caused by inborn sin and requires the salvific work of God through Christ, self-spirituality would understand sin as sickness, and therefore the self as in need of healing (not redeeming). And this healing must be achieved on one's own. Since the journey to wholeness is an inward journey, travellers are responsible for their own healing, even if they make use of guides along the way (Watts 2020). Those who blame others for their problems are shirking their responsibility to find their authentic selves.[10]

SELF-SPIRITUALITY AND EVANGELICALISM

The zeitgeist of our time, with its internal authority and journey toward inner wholeness, is so widespread within Western culture that few are unaffected by it, even if they are unaware of its subtle influence. Western culture is not neutral. What Heelas (2008, 62) calls "subjective wellbeing culture" has a strong pull toward internality and away from institutional religion. If I might expand on the earlier analogy of swimming in the ocean, swimmers enjoying the water and waves are often unaware of the power of the undertow – unaware, that is, until they look up and find themselves far from shore. Caught in the current, even strong swimmers tire of resisting it. Swimming against the current requires an exceptional swimmer; many do not even try, and those who do may not succeed.

Since evangelicals are engaged in the culture around them, they find themselves floating along with everyone else, even if they may be dragging their feet in the water to slow themselves down. The more sectarian take refuge in the backwater or a secluded cove where there is very little current because it is protected from the main flow. Yet this strategy is only partially successful, because it is increasingly difficult, in our connected and globalized world, to isolate oneself. Efforts to stop the rush of water may keep out some influences but can never completely stop others. The zeitgeist of our time is reshaping evangelicals, including in ways that they do not perceive. Yet it is not just evangelicals who are ignorant of this under-the-surface gradual change. Most non-evangelicals are as well. The perceptive and historically informed may see it more clearly, but most see only the surface effects. Just as most of an iceberg is submerged under the water, so most only see a few consequences of the move to internal authority.

We can be sure, based on my interviews, that evangelical leaders want people in the pews to avoid being pulled along by the current of our modern zeitgeist, at least in areas that the leaders are aware of. They want them to pray, read their Bibles, and participate in church regularly. They want their flock to submit to the transcendent God and be guided by biblical directives instead of their own inner sense. In short, pastors hope congregants can avoid going with the flow. From what I heard, clergy try to teach them to resist the world's seductions, but clergy are themselves not immune to the pull of the current.

Many symptoms of the move to inward authority were not lost on the active evangelicals I interviewed. I asked clergy and lay interviewees about the influences of society or culture on the Christian faith. Most commonly, they pointed to the ways media, particularly the internet, were exposing evangelicals to views that ran counter to their religious practices – church attendance, Bible reading, and prayer – and their conservative sexual ethics. Individualism, busyness, and consumerism were also frequently mentioned causes of eroding orthodoxy and orthopraxy. The clergy were, unsurprisingly, particularly articulate about these cultural effects.

Most clergy were aware of some symptoms of the modern zeitgeist, including a therapeutic approach to faith, the centrality of individual experience, loss of institutional authority, and especially increasing liberalism and relativism. One Church of England priest near London came very close to saying "internal locus of authority," but his response focused mostly on the perception that religion was to be therapeutic. He suggested that many Britons see Christianity as "self-medication":

And I believe ... it's not all about me. You know, if I make myself and my experience the locus of, or if I use my experience as the test of everything ... and I judge everything on that basis, does it enhance my life? Do I feel better about myself? Do I have more energy and enthusiasm and, you know, what's my serotonin level? Christianity is kind of self-medication. And I think that therapeutic models [are] quite strong in a lot of people.

The theme of "individualism" was raised by several interviewees, focusing on the importance of one's own experience and feelings. Some evangelicals see society as all about individual rights, with a focus on the self. One well-read leader called this tendency "expressive individualism" (after sociologist Robert Bellah), while others noted that such individuality undermined biblical and ecclesial authority. One western Canadian Anglican priest saw its effects on church attendance and devotionalism: "I think individualism and this idea of authority as being your feelings, I think that has really hit church attendance. I think Bible reading ... people [are] so used to being entertained that I don't think they have a lot of patience for trying to fight through difficult-to-understand literature."

A conservative Presbyterian pastor in the Maritimes pointed to declining authority among clergy, stating that "if you're a clergyman in Canada, up until fairly recently, I think, there's a certain cultural acceptability or credibility ... But I get different reactions from younger people than older people." He continued:

In fact, if somebody finds out [I'm an] evangelical minister (this is a bit of an exaggeration) – I say this to people in the [American] South where there still is a lot of deference for the clergy – if I tell somebody that I'm an evangelical pastor, it's almost like telling them I'm in the Klan. They say, "Oh, you don't seem that bigoted. You seem so kind and nice." And my wife runs into this too. People find out at work that she's married to a pastor, and people are like, "But you seem so normal. You don't seem at all like what my stereotype of an evangelical is."

The above quotes suggest that, while, in general, evangelical clergy were aware of a few effects of the inward turn – declining religious authority, the rise of therapeutic spirituality, a negative public image – they apparently did not understand their source.

Most respondents emphasized the negative effect of Western culture on evangelicalism, but a few thought that its effect was sometimes positive. An independent (male) pastor in Newcastle, England, noted that "sometimes social pressure is good when it's things like feminism or helping oppressed women." An independent pastor in the Maritimes said that "there's so much that is really good" about Canadian culture, but that sometimes our desire "not to offend and be accepting of diversity (which are good things) clashes with the importance of evangelism and (exclusive) truth."

The clergy were concerned about the effects of the cultural milieu on evangelical faith, as were many of the laity, as we will see in future chapters. More important for the argument here is evidence from the lay interviews of self-spirituality and the move to an internal locus of authority. While I did not ask lay respondents directly about the effects of Western culture on their faith, I did ask directly about beliefs and practices. Because these lay interviews deliberately targeted the most involved parishioners, identified by my asking clergy interviewees to recommend active members of their churches, most of the evidence for the influence of the modern zeitgeist is in areas of belief, not practice, since all were actively practising their faith within a church.

At least three-quarters of the lay interviewees showed signs of inward authority and self-spirualty, and these were most common among younger evangelicals.[11] Most laity showed evidence of internal authority by disagreeing personally with the official positions of the church or denomination. Many qualified or softened their positions to appear less dogmatic. Several stated that what people believe is "up to them." Note the response from a thirty-something eastern Canadian who attends a Vineyard church, was previously in full-time ministry, and continues to serve actively in her church in worship and youth ministry. The question was about her view of same-sex marriage, to

which she said she was "neutral" and was clearly "torn" between her
desire to accept it and her understanding of theology. She indicated
that she thought it was up to the individual, a response associated with
the "inner voice" of self-spirituality and internal authority:

> I'm a real fan of a personal relationship with God, and if someone
> says to me they feel right with God and that they, 100 per cent
> theologically, believe that this is okay and that they've had a con-
> versation with God and God agrees ... I can't call that out because
> I'm a fan of having a personal relationship with God, and I have
> to say, "Well, that's your personal relationship with God and I'm
> going to love you as my brother and sister in Christ," and let God
> be the judge of working that out with Him. So, yeah, it's [same-
> sex marriage] a hard one.

Many others, both young and old, demonstrated an internal locus
of authority by indicating that positions on moral issues were up to
the individual. Micah, a young Asian man from an evangelical Anglican church in Toronto is a good example:

> Sam: How about co-habitation, premarital sexual relationships,
>   people who live together before they are married or are sexually
>   active, how do you feel about that?
> Micah: I don't really care one way or another.
> S: So it's up to them?
> Micah: Yeah, up to them.
> S: For Christians – it's fine for them to cohabit or live together
>   before they get married in your view?
> Micah: I haven't exactly formulated my opinion on that, but in
>   general I would say it's up to them.
> S: Okay, and how about same sex relationships, like gay
>   marriage ... ?
> Micah: Yeah, right, right, again role of the individual to decide,
>   not government ...

A highly educated man who attends a Vineyard church in England,
when asked about premarital sex, said:

> It is better if there was a stable marriage between a couple ..., in the
> interest of that, a trial-run isn't such a bad idea. I understand that

that's heresy and it's outside of the views of the church. I am technically wrong in that view. But I don't think it's such a bad thing. However, I understand there are people who will adopt a higher moral standard than me who would decide that they want to be celibate, whatever, until after they are married and I would respect and support that, if that is their choice and how they are inspired.

His response indicates that he recognizes that he is going against the position of the church in which he is actively involved when he expresses that, for individuals, premarital sex is "their choice" – a position associated with internal authority. On same-sex marriage, he noted that his niece is a lesbian, and he said that, "while gay marriage seems alien to me personally, if it works for other people, I don't see that it is doing intrinsic harm. I do like the idea of equality in society and I hate to see people marginalized. If that seems to be the way people are made, who am I to argue with creation?" Note the emphasis on equality, typical of self-spirituality, which is used to defend a view that is contrary to his church's position.

Jem, a young woman who attends a Vineyard church in England and is very active in her faith, indicated that cohabitation or premarital sex was not acceptable for her personally, but went on to say:

Jem: I think it's one of those things that has to come out of a personal choice rather than being shamed or forced into it. If people look at it for themselves and have chosen that personally for themselves, that's a good thing. If they've been forced into it, it's as bad as doing it, really.
S: Forced into not doing ...?
Jem: Yeah.
S: So, forced to not do it, like parents saying, "You absolutely can't do this." Is that what you're thinking?
Jem: Yeah ... I think it has to come out of a place of personal conviction.
S: So, for you, why do you think it's not okay?
Jem: I just think that ... the best place for sex is in marriage and the reasons in the Bible and because of all the emotional stuff attached to it because to have that closeness to someone and not even have a permanent decision around it isn't good for you as a person either.

Jem clearly indicates that reference to internal authority ("personal conviction") is the right way to make relational or sexual decisions, whereas giving in to external authority (the edicts of parents or society) was the wrong way.

It is not only the young who demonstrate an internal locus of authority. A sixty-something woman attending a Redeemed Christian Church of God (RCCG) in Canada said, "my position is a little different from the church" and that she is fine with same-sex marriage as long as "people love each other and they are deeply committed ... Love is from God, and so I can't judge about that or berate anybody. The Holy Spirit is in the makeover business, not me."[12] In this case, the respondent defended a disagreement with official church doctrine by quoting a biblical statement, that "love is from God" (I John 4:7), indicating that her personal interpretation had priority over that of her church. Knowingly holding a stance that does not align with her church's position indicates that her authority is (at least partially) internal. In this case, her stance stemmed from her personal experience. Her adult children were both unmarried but living with their romantic partners, and one had a child with someone who was not her current partner. She connected this experience to a change in her views and said, "Yes, I am [more open in my sexual mores]. Love is the thing, not the piece of paper [a marriage certificate]." Similarly, an eighty-year-old Baptist woman from England stated that "I don't believe that church authority is the final say."

It is important to recall that all the lay persons interviewed were selected by their pastors (based on certain demographic criteria), are regular (usually weekly or more) attenders, and usually are actively serving in their evangelical churches. To be fair, some evangelical interviewees, young and old, were staunchly orthodox in their theological and ethical positions, and thus show less movement toward internal authority. Yet the research evidence shows that the cultural zeitgeist is common among the most dedicated. So we can assume that it is much more common among less committed evangelicals, which is consistent with other research (Castle 2019).

While these interviews indicate that an internal locus of authority is in tension with the traditional biblical or ecclesial authority of evangelicalism, we should not assume that evangelical authority is unidimensional. As Molly Worthen (2014) has made clear, evangelicals struggle to balance multiple authorities, including biblical authority, reason, experience, and scientific evidence.[13] While authority for evangelicals will continue to be contested, I am arguing that there are many evangelicals who, due to the influence of the inward turn, are questioning old authorities. They make up their own mind on what beliefs to hold and practices to engage in, and, even if they personally accept an orthodox position, many do not expect others to share their convictions. Individual people, even if they are evangelical Christians, need to decide for themselves what beliefs and practices they will embrace. This validation of individual authority, I submit, is the primary battle of evangelical leaders today, but they are mostly unaware of it and are thus trying to treat symptoms rather than the fundamental issue. As an external authority, a church leader can clearly describe God's standards and commands, but doing so would not translate into changed lives, because of internal loci of authority operative in the pews (and possibly behind the podium). "Sure," the lay person will respond, "religious leaders are expected to say things like that" or "that is their view, but I see things differently." Authoritative statements bounce off, or do not even compute, because they assume external authority. For those with an internal locus of authority, it is normal to disagree with or be apathetic toward what the church or Bible teaches, because one has to decide for oneself. Few feel the need for a well-formulated world view or a coherent set of beliefs because their identity and views are fluid. They are still on a journey.

Is there quantitative evidence that some evangelicals are embracing self-spirituality and inner authority? The answer is yes. In table 1.2, I use Canadian data from 2019 to show that many evangelicals accept beliefs typical of the modern zeitgeist: these include perennialism (the belief that all religions are the same at their core), relativism (there is no absolute right or wrong), and privatization (beliefs are personal and should not be dictated by institutional religion).[14] The table includes the percentages of all Canadians and Canadian evangelicals who agree (strongly or moderately) with statements associated with these beliefs. The table divides evangelicals into two groups, the first by affiliation to an evangelical denomination, and the second by "alignment" – that is, based on regular church attendance and agreement with evangelical beliefs. While evangelicals are less likely than most Canadians to agree with the statements, approximately one-fifth to one-quarter of evangelicals agree with the statements related to perennialism and relativism, and closer to half agree with the statement related to privatization.

Obviously, none of the statements in table 1.2 are compatible with evangelical orthodoxy, and the majority of evangelicals still reject

Table 1.2
Canadian evangelicals' agreement with perennialism, relativism, and privatization

% who agree (strongly or moderately)	All Canadians (N=5,011)	Evangelical affiliation (N=328)	Evangelically aligned (N=507)
"All world religions are basically the same if you can get behind their rules, rituals and beliefs."	58.4%	21.2%	21.3%
"I believe there is no absolute right or wrong, it depends on the situation."	58.0%	23.0%	25.2%
"When it comes to making decisions, my personal beliefs are more important than what is taught by any religion."	77.0%	49.4%	43.9%

Source: 2019 Maru Blue/EFC Church and Faith Trends survey in possession of author.

them. Yet, these beliefs seem to be making inroads, especially among less-active evangelicals. If young evangelicals go to church and continue to do so after they leave home, it is likely that they have acquired an external locus of authority, at least to some degree. They may understand the "lordship of Christ." They may agree that there is an external divine authority and that they are not divine. In embracing such beliefs, they do not conform to the modern zeitgeist – in some areas at least. Such acceptance of external religious authority requires swimming against the dominant cultural current.

On the surface, it seems like evangelicals should easily recognize that the views and values of self-spirituality are unorthodox. For Heelas (2008), the Christian God is incompatible with self-spirituality:

Logically, it is impossible to reconcile an inner "god" which facilitates self-actualization, the expression of the uniqueness or originality of the person, with the transcendent, theistic God ... which emphasizes adherence "to" and places limits on autonomous self-development and expression ... The "god" within and the God without cannot serve at one and the same time as absolute and different sources of significance and authority ... Neither ... can one reconcile a spirituality which is generally taken to flow through all that lives, where we "are all god/s," and which is thus egalitarian, with spiritualities bound up with an emanating from a hierarchically located Godhead on High.

Yet, his observations in Britain led him to conclude that "in practice, a great many of those participating in ... activities operating on the 'edges' of theistic Christianity are more or less at one and the same time drawing on the two sources of authority and significance. The God within and the God without" (58). I argue that this is the case not just among those "on the edges"; active evangelicals in the pews also draw authority from the "God within and the God without."

Like Heelas, other scholars doubt that the efforts of pastors and priests to guide the laity to safe backwaters (or train them to be exceptional swimmers) will be successful. Instead, many discern elements of self-spirituality within the evangelical subculture. Sociologist James Davison Hunter says that conservative Protestants have "accommodated to the anti-institutional, therapeutic, and cultural preferences of the baby boomers" (cited in Coleman 2000, 24; see also Hunter 1982). David Martin (2002, 15) points to a "discernable consonance" between charismatic Christians and the neoliberal zeitgeist of this age. Galen Watts (2022) argues that the evangelical C3 church he studied in Toronto embodies many of the aspects of the broader ethos of spirituality that shapes Western culture.[15] He found these characteristics to be particularly evident among charismatic evangelicals, the emerging church (Bielo 2011), and those influenced by the prosperity gospel (Bowler 2013).

Watts' evidence suggests that the "means" of the inward journey is present among evangelicals in at least three ways. First, personal experience is central at the C3 church. Experiences are evoked through emotive worship. Congregants are encouraged to sense the Holy Spirit and feel God's presence. The transparency of church leaders about their lives, including their prodigal ways and their struggles, convinces attenders that they are authentic. Testimonies of changed lives give attendees hope that they too can experience internal healing. Second, individual freedom is embraced. Church leaders introduce people to Jesus but are not to prescribe what they should believe about dogma or morality. Even if the church has clear positions on sexual ethics and theology, leaders rarely take a stand from the pulpit on thorny issues, allowing lay persons to find their own way through the guidance of the Spirit, which may not be distinguishable from one's "inner voice" (Guest 2007). Third, God is clearly presented as benevolent and immanent. God in the form of the Holy Spirit is inside each individual, a God of love and kindness is portrayed, and little is heard of God's wrath or judgment (Watts 2020, 2022).

Watts (2020) also found evidence of the telos of self-spirituality, which is to realize one's authentic self, in the C3 church. First, the church understands the self to be good. The "real you," the person God intended, is virtuous and imbued with great gifts. It is supernaturally empowered. The problems faced in life are external, including demonic powers and pressures from the world, which keep persons from reaching their potential. Second, God is present to help people overcome their weaknesses and insecurities and to help them on their journey toward healing. If the true self is aligned with what God wants the person to be, then God, naturally, will help them on their journey toward authenticity. The Holy Spirit is the inner guide on this quest (Watts 2020).

CONCLUSION

The research clearly indicates that evangelicals are not immune to the ethos of Western culture, even though they try to keep it at arm's length. The chapters that follow look at this tension between conformity and nonconformity in more detail. Here, I can state precisely what evangelicals misdiagnose. First, they remain unaware of the unifying doctrine or zeitgeist that underlies the seemingly chaotic secular and spiritual fragments they observe. Just as surface waters can hide a powerful undertow, evangelicals fail to see that a "doctrine of self-spirituality constitutes the common denominator of the wide range of beliefs, rituals, and practices found in the contemporary spiritual milieu" (Houtman and Aupers 2010, 6). Speaking to this common denominator, Woodhead (2016, 256) observes that, "contrary to the view that there is pervasive moral fragmentation, [British surveys] show that there is actually a massive moral consensus about the importance of individual freedom of choice" for about 90 per cent of Britons. To evangelicals and non-evangelicals alike, self-spirituality appears diverse, idiosyncratic, and antinomian on the surface, and they seem to be largely unaware of the unified ethos that drives it. This should not be a surprise, as many academic observers also fail to see the foundational coherence of self-spirituality (Houtman and Aupers 2010). Second, evangelical clergy and leaders tend to see changing beliefs and practices, not the source of these changes. As a result, they misdiagnose a deeper, internal change, and instead try to address only its symptoms. Partly because external authority is still their *modus operandi*, and partly because they insolate themselves from aspects of cultural change, they misdiagnose the prevailing milieu.

2

Orthodoxy:
Believing Right

Jessica is the kind of congregant any evangelical pastor would love to have in their church.[1] She and her husband attend their church about "seven out of eight Sundays." She leads a group for parents of toddlers that meets weekly, is involved in two other ministry teams (both also weekly responsibilities), and co-leads a small group with her husband. She reads her Bible daily, prays daily with her husband, and journals during her devotional times. They tithe over 10 per cent of their pre-tax income, and give on top of that to charitable causes. Although no one can doubt her commitment to her faith or her church, her beliefs show the influence of the modern zeitgeist – self-spirituality and internal authority.

Jessica was a delight to interview, thoughtful and articulate. She had just managed to put her three year old down for a nap when our video interview began. She was intrigued by the research project and contacted me immediately when her pastor asked her if she would participate in my study. I had interviewed her pastor, Brock, two days before. He was also articulate, an informed observer of society. Their church, in northern England, has about 300 weekly attendees and is part of the global New Frontiers network. I asked her why she and her husband chose that church. She said that they did research online when they arrived in the area four years ago, and she was looking for a church that was led by a leadership team, not just a solo head pastor. They did not "church-shop" but went directly to that church and have stayed.

Jessica grew up as a preacher's kid – her father was a Church of Scotland minister. When asked whether she had had a conversion experience, she states that she did when she was about thirteen years old. For her, and many other evangelical interviewees, her conversion was not a one-time event when she said the "sinner's prayer" but a gradual process of "growing into a relationship with Jesus." She attributes her faith development to an influential youth leader, who taught her that if "I was a Christian, that Jesus would impact all the different areas of my life." She went on a Youth with a Mission (YWAM) trip, which "was really formative for me because I was suddenly immersed in this culture of people that expected to hear from God, expected to hear prophetically ... So, all that was happening around the time I was thirteen, fourteen, fifteen [and] really shifted it for me." These experiences strengthened the charismatic side of her faith, leading her to attend an independent charismatic church in Scotland in her late teens. Her view of the Bible was typical of other evangelicals I interviewed – inspired but not word-for-word literal. She said the Bible is "inspired by the Holy Spirit" but that some passages were not to be taken literally and instead should be understood as poetic or figurative.

Based on her answers, Jessica had clearly thought about controversial ethical issues. On abortion, Jessica said she believed that life begins at conception. She recalled that she and her husband struggled to conceive but would not consider in-vitro fertilization (IVF) because some fetuses are destroyed in the process. Their own daughter came as a surprise. Yet her views on abortion had changed over time. "I feel like God's primary sadness about abortion is that we have a world that necessitates it. I think God is probably a lot more angry that families and communities are so broken that women feel abortion is required or so often their only choice." She recognizes her position of privilege that allows her to raise a child, and she would not consider abortion herself, but her ethical decisions might not work for everyone: "If someone told me that they had had an abortion or were considering an abortion, I certainly wouldn't tell them that I think God thinks abortion is wrong because I feel like that issue is so complex."

Without being asked, she moved right into opining on sexual orientation, another area where her views had changed:

When I was twelve or thirteen, I would have said, "God hasn't designed us to be gay; God's designed us to be straight and God feels sad about people who choose to be gay" ... I don't believe that anymore. I think our sexuality, like everything else about us, is subject to the Fall,[2] and we're broken people living in a broken world, and I feel like none of us has a sexuality that reflects God's intended purpose for all of us.

She made it clear that she believed that same-sex attraction is no more "broken" than heterosexual attraction. Regarding gender, she calls herself "gender cynical" and says that much of what we consider to be male or female is "messy," created by society and the church through its history. In her view, there is "something female in God and there is something male in God," and God created male and female because "the entirety of God's gender cannot be expressed in [a single] human form." She recognized that her position on gender (and sexual orientation) was not perfectly clear: "I'm not trying to not land an opinion. I feel like I'm being very wishy-washy," she said. She continued, "if someone wanted to start a conversation with me about that [same-sex attraction] ... I feel that the heart of God is so much more saddened ... by the demonization of people who do not have this extremely narrow sexual expression [advanced by the church]."

When I asked about her view on women in leadership in the church and elsewhere, Jessica exhaled very audibly. She asked if I wanted her church's view. "Not necessarily," I responded, and reminded her that I was looking for her views. (According to her pastor, Brock, the New Frontiers churches are "very strongly complementarian" and committed to "biblical manhood," and thus do not allow women in church leadership. He has, however, softened his position over time on this issue.) Jessica believes that Jesus was a "radical" egalitarian and that "women should be released and empowered in leadership in ways that are equal to men." But, she stated, there is something different about the marriage relationship, which, while completely free from oppression or pride, "looks like headship and submission." No doubt she had in mind the passage in the Bible (Ephesians 5: 22) where the apostle Paul instructs wives to submit to their husbands.

Whatever one makes of Jessica's beliefs, it is beyond doubt that, first, her beliefs have changed over time, and in a more accommodating and less dogmatic direction. Some beliefs, like her views on gender, are still not completely settled. She specifically pointed out her changing views on abortion and sexual orientation (without prompting). She stated, "Had you asked me when I was a kid about same-sex attraction, abortion, IVF ... any of the juicy ones, I would have had the very black-and-white, Christian, judgmental view of all of them." By contrast, she made no similar statement about change in her views of the Bible or conversion. Second, the changes in her beliefs demonstrate a genuine effort to balance biblical authority with her egalitarian and accepting posture toward ethical issues. Like many of my respondents, Jessica did not suggest that she had carte blanche to discard her conservative beliefs, nor had external (biblical and church) authority disappeared from her ethical beliefs. Nonetheless, there seems to be a tension between biblical authority and cultural pressures toward more open ethical views. Finally, it is equally clear that her beliefs are not based on complete deference to church authority – neither to her Church of Scotland upbringing nor the official position of her current church. Rather, her beliefs and ethical positions were developed based on relationships (e.g., with her youth leader) and experiences (her YWAM trip), along with her own thinking. For most respondents, it was clear that formulating beliefs was a process, and that it was up the person to settle on their own beliefs as they traversed their own spiritual path.

This chapter examines the beliefs of evangelicals on doctrinal and ethical issues. These include the "hot" issues of abortion, gender roles, and same-sex marriage. In the eyes of many, conservative stances on these issues distinguish evangelicals from non-evangelicals and make the former increasingly unpopular. My respondents understood this. They consistently seemed to reframe and qualify their views on these controversial issues to avoid sounding like fundamentalists.

In this chapter, I examine how my interviewees' beliefs reflect the influence of Western culture's inward turn. I explore this turn to an internal locus of authority in several ways. First, I examine research that provides evidence of changes in beliefs. I explore religious (and non-religious) beliefs and whether they are primarily based in adherence to propositions made by external, institutional authorities or are increasingly fluid, relational, and identity based. Second, I discuss *how* beliefs change, examining the roots of this change in shifting relational networks and cultural norms. Finally, I examine what the evangelical leaders and laity say they believe, first in theological beliefs (about the Bible, conversion, and so on) and then in areas of ethics (abortion, same-sex relations, on so on), to determine whether the data point to a growing internal locus of authority and tendency toward self-spirituality among some evangelicals.

BELIEFS — RELATIONAL OR PROPOSITIONAL?

Contrary to popular belief (pun intended) – at least among evangelical Christians – what people mean when they say they "believe" something is not what Christians have historically meant when they use the term "believe." The 1828 version of *Webster's Dictionary* defined belief as "a persuasion of the truth, or an assent of mind to the truth of a declaration." For Webster in the early nineteenth century, belief was also clearly linked to religion, as the definition portrayed belief as "a firm persuasion of the truths of religion" or as "religion; the body of tenets held by the professors of faith."[3] In the New Testament, the Greek word *pisteuo*, normally translated as "belief" in English, is also translated to "commit to," "trust in," or "have faith in." Christian creeds, like the Apostles' Creed or the Nicene Creeds, start with the affirmation that the person praying believes in (one) God. These creedal beliefs are affirmed regularly. We can conclude that beliefs were understood to be fairly stable, inner convictions, which involved assent to doctrinal propositions. They are also assumed to be based on external authority, as persons "trust in" or "have faith in" a God who does not change.[4]

Some scholars define religion as fundamentally belief-based, as religion came to be thought of as a "set of propositions to which believers gave assent" (Asad 1993, 40–1). This propositional, assent-based view of belief – and its centrality to religion – is still prevalent among evangelical Christians. However, the notion that religion is primarily about belief has been challenged as Protestant-centric by scholars, and some argue that definitions of religion should centre on ritual and practice, not belief (e.g., C. Smith 2017). Regardless of how one defines religion, it is easy for (Protestant) evangelicals to be biased toward propositional, doctrinal beliefs as central to their faith. However, I suggest that belief is increasingly about *adherence to* (significant others) and less about *assent to* (doctrinal propositions). This is because the beliefs that "feel right" to the person are shaped by their warm relationships with the family and friends in whose company they "feel right."

In her book *Believing in Belonging* (2011), Abby Day argues that beliefs should be relocated in the social, particularly in relationships. She found that people generally refer to "belief" "as a type of faith in deeply held, non-verifiable values or truth propositions that reflect their identities and sense of belonging to social relationships" (Day 2013, 278; see also Day and Lynch 2013). For most of the Britons that Day interviewed, their beliefs were grounded in relationships with their friends and family, which she designated as "anthropocentric" belief, while a minority pointed to God or some transcendent authority, which she designated as "theocentric" belief. The anthropocentric majority might say that they believe in "their mates," "their family," and significant others, and that, by doing so, they are signalling their adherence to a group.

For Day, not only do beliefs indicate belonging, but they also mark *boundaries* of belonging. Beliefs function to locate a person within a group they identify with, and to distinguish "us" from "others." For example, Day found that, when her anthropocentric respondents identified as "Christian," it was not because they held theocentric beliefs or attended a church; it was because they were identifying themselves with white Britons of Christian heritage ("us"), to the exclusion of immigrants ("others"). They may also hold to some aspects of Christian morality, which serve as a marker of British cultural superiority. Thus, beliefs have a "performative" function. Day (2013, 289) states that "performative belief refers to beliefs that are brought into being through rituals or social acts and are then repeated to reinforce their salience and function."[5] Such beliefs are created and reinforced in our social interactions. Day maintains, then, that we must attend to the function of beliefs – what beliefs do – not just the content of beliefs.

Further, Day focuses on the *sources* of belief. She shows how beliefs are not created *ex nihilo* but are powerfully influenced by people's close and warm relationships. She rejects arguments of increased individualism, if by that one means that young people are creating beliefs on their own, free from relational influence: "I found that young people's beliefs tend to be co-produced, through participating with family and friends in creating and maintaining beliefs" (Day 2011, 90). Young people *believe in others* – the warm relationships in which they are situated. According to Day, this is believing in belonging. Beliefs are influenced by legitimate authorities, like friends and parents, but such believers no longer view religious authorities (and other institutional authorities) as legitimate.

To suggest that close relationships shape beliefs may sound like a contradiction in relation to notions of internal authority and self-spirituality, where the person is to create their own beliefs. However, as I tried to make clear in the previous chapter, the internal locus of authority does not mean that persons are not influenced by significant others. Personal identities and beliefs are powerfully shaped by relationships. While beliefs are to be freely chosen and should reinforce and align with one's authentic self (Day and Lynch 2013), the inner or authentic self is shaped by the modern zeitgeist, and by friends and family. Beliefs are legitimate if we *perceive* them to be "our own," derived from our inner self.

Lastly, beliefs are not solely, and possibly not primarily, cognitive. They are usually not derived from intellectual examination of the evidence. Some religious scholars have argued that religion and religious beliefs are primarily about providing purpose and meaning to life. Religion is about making meaning out of the chaos: it provides theodicies for liminal experiences and helps us decide what is good or bad, true and false (e.g., Berger 1967). Day thinks that people get along just fine without needing religion to make their lives meaningful. For her, beliefs have more to do with belonging.[6] Thus, anthropocentrics articulate beliefs "primarily in reference to their human relationships," while theocentrics "cite God and their relationship to him as central to their lives" (2011, 157). Both anthropocentric and theocentric beliefs are relational. Both orientations strengthen *adherence to* others or to God. As Durkheim (1915) argued, religious beliefs have a community-binding function. If beliefs are increasingly relational and less cognitive, then it should not surprise us that people hold intellectually incompatible beliefs without cognitive dissonance. One could also belong to a church, and even frequently attend it, with little concern that one disagrees with the church's official doctrine.

If Day is right, then we can assume that the beliefs of committed evangelicals are partially about belonging and relationships. Evangelicals, like Jessica, emphasize a relationship with God as foundational to their faith. They believe because they belong – both to a group of believers and to God. This means that beliefs are not only "in the mind," but also have emotional and physical (embodied) components. For example, the following exchange between myself and Claire, a British Methodist minister, shows how relationship shapes beliefs about sexual identities. In response to a series of questions about the evangelical Methodist Church's position on sexual ethics, she noted that a "not out" young gay man, an active and influential lay leader in the church, was entering into a same-sex relationship. As a result, she suspected his sexual orientation and relationship would soon become public:

> Claire: So I think it's going to be a huge problem. I think there
> will be people who very much say, "Why shouldn't he be in a
> [same-sex] relationship?" And that comes less from a theological

conviction, I think, and more from a personal relationship ...
[Others] say, "Well, the Bible says gay marriage is not a possibility," [but] because they know this individual I think they will
now face significant conflict ... Some more say, "I don't know
what to think about this."

S: I guess your concern is that will split the church apart?

Claire: It could do. I would like to hope we're united by more
than that, but ...

S: [What about your church's views on] premarital sex or
cohabitation?

Claire: Interestingly, I think that the general line ... would be, it's
frowned upon. So I think the general expectation is [that] it's
not compatible with Christian practices.

S: So they would be less open to that than same-sex marriage, possibly, hard to say?

Claire: It is, it is very hard to say, I am just trying to think of various examples. Because there is no one in that congregation who
is living with a partner.

S: I see.

Claire: I'm just trying to think of people who might have ... are
living with partners and how that sits, but I think people would
be fairly clear on Christians don't live together before they are
married; they don't have sex together before they are married.

Belief for evangelicals is not just relational, but a mix of the relational and cognitive aspects. Yet even "assent-to" doctrinal beliefs have
a relational function. Based on her research in an evangelical Anglican church, Anna Strhan (2013b) argues that propositional, creedal
beliefs function to bind believers together. Belief is not to be understood as only individualized, cognitive assent but is "habituated
through embodied techniques of listening, reading and speaking"
(17). Evangelicals strengthen their beliefs, their religious identities,
and their bonds with co-religionists as they hear the Bible preached,
as they read the Bible devotionally, and as they talk about their beliefs
with other evangelicals. Her point is that beliefs are more than cognitive: they are embodied – requiring physical action, emotion, and
relationship. People hold to beliefs partly because their behaviour
reinforces the belief. Since beliefs speak to their identity and relational attachments, people are emotionally attached to them. Beliefs
are not simply cognitive categories available for intellectual critique.

They reveal "me." Beliefs say something about who I am. Critiquing my beliefs may be seen as criticism of me.

A few conclusions about evangelical belief stem from Day's and Strhan's analyses. First, when evangelicals say they believe something, it is also performative. By performative, I am not suggesting that pronouncements of belief are somehow disingenuous or attention seeking, but that beliefs serve the function of signalling allegiance and belonging to a group. It is a way to show and reinforce one's identity. Of course, beliefs are also propositional to evangelicals. They *assent to* beliefs cited in the creeds, but they are also signalling *adherence to* something or someone. Second, if beliefs are partly about relationships and identity, then we should expect them to be relatively unstable. As social groups change, so might belief. If identities are slow to develop and are in flux, then we should expect beliefs to be in flux as well (see, e.g., Perrin 2016). In chapter 4, I will have more to say about the long and difficult process of creating the self or one's identity. For now, it is enough to recognize that if beliefs say something about "me," and if that "me" is still under construction, then my beliefs will be under construction as well. Third, as persons espouse an internal locus of authority, beliefs are expected to be internally produced. What "I believe" is authentic if it is freely chosen and it resonates in my heart. Naturally, what resonates (feels right or makes me happy) with me is shaped by my significant, warm relationships (which also feel right and make me happy). However, my beliefs are fragile if some, or most, of my significant others do not hold them (Taylor 2007). Thus, it is difficult for the evangelical minority to maintain their beliefs. On top of that, some evangelical beliefs are unpopular, even offensive, because they critique others' identities. As Strhan (2013a) has argued, it is awkward to talk about one's religious beliefs with others if they do not share those views. This is made worse if one's views are exclusive, thereby suggesting that another's private beliefs are wrong. To insinuate that someone holds wrong beliefs breaks tacit social expectations of polite conversation in Britain and Canada, where open acceptance of different beliefs is normative. As a result, evangelical beliefs are susceptible to softening, particularly in those areas where social pressure is strongest.[7]

Finally, and most importantly for this discussion, I am suggesting that what beliefs *are* is misunderstood by evangelicals. Disagreements about what evangelicals and non-evangelicals believe are not just over the content of belief. Beliefs are becoming less about stable inner convictions involving cognitive assent to propositions and more about statements of belonging and identity, which are more pliable, emotive, and embodied. I am suggesting that the change in what beliefs *are* parallels the slow, glacial change toward an internal locus of authority in society. There is a logical affinity between internal authority (and the inward journey toward the authentic self) and beliefs as "markers of identity" and "expression of socially significant relationships" (Day and Lynch 2013, 199). If the inward turn dictates that persons must "find" themselves and their beliefs, following their heart, then beliefs will reflect that identity-creating quest, with "who we are" being shaped by our relations with significant others along the way. Alternatively, if external authority dictates beliefs, then they are more stable because they require assent to religious traditions or "unchanging" biblical authority. Evangelicals, still embracing (to various degrees) external authority, may wonder how Westerners can attend churches where they do not believe what the preacher says. They express incredulity that persons can say they pray and yet do not believe in God or a higher power (see Reimer 2003). For some, it is because what they mean when they say "I believe so-and-so" is not about a timeless truth that fits nicely into a "systematic theology" or an intellectually coherent worldview. They often are signalling something they value, as shaped by experience, relationships, and identity.

Consider the difference between saying "I believe in God" and saying "I believe in you." The first is assent to a creedal doctrine, which speaks to the person's religious convictions. Generally, it is a stable belief based on external, religious authority that has been internalized ("I believe it in my heart") by the individual. Although it is personal, it is more objective than subjective, in the sense that it is understood to be true for others as well – the belief is widely shared, held in common with all Christian "believers." In comparison, "I believe in you" refers to a vote of confidence, an affirmation of someone. It is a statement that reflects a relational bond with the person and serves to strengthen it. It is not assumed to be a widely shared objective truth, but is true "for me" in the context of a specific relationship. I suggest that beliefs are becoming more like the latter, as persons embrace internal authority. Even when someone with internal authority says "I believe in God," it is meant in a more relational, subjective way, like "I believe in you." My interviews bear this out: respondents do not assume that their religious beliefs are "true" for everyone. Evangelical ethical positions, even if based on biblical fiat, are guidelines for me, and maybe for other evangelicals, but they do not apply to everyone in society. Beliefs are increasingly based on one's personal "relationship with God" or the "inner guidance of the Holy Spirit," not on a religious tradition's interpretation of the Bible.

BELIEFS AND THE INWARD TURN

What do religious beliefs look like for those who have embraced an internal locus of authority? Research shows that the new "enlightened" religious position is perennialism. As Houtman and Aupers (2010, 7) state,

> According to perennialism, all religious traditions refer to one and the same esoteric truth, i.e., the presence of a sacred kernel in the deeper layers of the self through which one can "connect with all that exists." This perennialism firmly rejects the idea that such a thing as a tradition superior to all others exists. It is instead held that, by their very nature, religious traditions have lost sight of this common source because of their dogmatic clutching to sacred texts, elaborating and systematizing religious doctrines, establishing priesthoods, etcetera – by engaging in the side issue of traditionalizing, routinizing and institutionalizing "pure" spirituality.

Perennialism is a natural conclusion if beliefs are relational, and one's significant others come from diverse religious backgrounds.[8] Perennialism works well when everyone is to create their own beliefs, as it allows the community-binding function of beliefs to be operative among groups that were previously thought to hold incompatible religious views (like a Muslim and a Christian, for example). If this belief is part of the modern zeitgeist, then exclusive religious beliefs, including evangelism, make for awkward conversations with (non-evangelical) friends. Such beliefs are viewed as xenophobic and bigoted. Inclusive beliefs are more functional, especially if relationships are mediated through social media.

Even though users generally avoid discussing religion on social media (Freitas 2017), values and beliefs are shaped by the online experience. The average young person checks social media about twenty times a day (Freitas 2017), and users averaged 144 minutes per day on social media in 2019.[9] Kane (2013) has argued that social media provide a venue where identities can be developed and beliefs can be "tested" in a virtual environment that gives a sense of personal freedom and control (and, thus, the perception that "my beliefs originated with me"). Facebook, for example, allows users to "like" another's post, and "likes" can be quantified to gauge how popular one's visual presentation (through a profile picture or "selfie") or one's views (e.g., supporting Black Lives Matter or Pride Month on social media) are. The more "shares," affirmative "comments," or "likes" one gets, the more likely the communicated viewpoint is to become a personal value. On Facebook and Twitter, affirmation ("likes") is the only option; there are no "dislikes." This may feed a tendency toward the affirmation of all identities and most (inclusive) ideas. As chapter 1 has shown, even the god/sacred of self-spirituality is only good and affirming to the self.

Hiemstra, based on his research of youth in Canada, has argued that the golden rule is no longer "do unto others what you would have them do unto you" (Matthew 7:12). Rather, a Canadian youth summarized her understanding of the biblical Ten Commandments with a new golden rule, which was widespread among young interviewees: *"Don't do anything that is going to make someone feel bad about themselves"* (Hiemstra et al. 2017, 6; emphasis in original). For Hiemstra and his colleagues, "judgement ... that might make someone feel bad about themselves is not consistent with being a good person" because it undermines social harmony. In multicultural society, "one way to reconcile difference is to say that the differences are only apparent" (2017, 6). If the dominant flow of Western culture is toward perennialism and the new golden rule of affirmation, then there would be significant pressure to avoid non-affirming beliefs, particularly those ethical positions that do not "like" other person's identities. Change in belief will result.

INTOLERANT EVANGELICALS?

Evangelicals are normally not perennialists or all affirming. Even if internal authority is making inroads into the subculture, most evangelicals are closer than the average non-evangelical to the external authority end of the continuum. They still assent to biblically based doctrinal beliefs and assume that beliefs that are not consistent with the Bible are wrong. Some observers theorize that such exclusive beliefs breed evangelical intolerance toward outgroups (Wilcox and Jelen 1990; Reimer 2021).

Exclusive beliefs are not the only possible cause of evangelical intolerance, however. Recently, some researchers have argued that

evangelicalism in the United States is not just a theological movement but also a cultural one that has embraced a unique form of
Christian nationalism (Whitehead and Perry 2020). This nationalism envisions a time when America was white, Christian, and male-
led, and breeds intolerance toward non-white and non-Christian
minorities (Davis and Perry 2021). Some evangelicals desire to
return to this "golden age" and "make America great again." In *Jesus
and John Wayne* (2020), Kristin Du Mez argues that overwhelming
support for Donald Trump's presidency among white evangelicals is
not an aberration, but a culmination of a long-held ideology of
"rugged, aggressive militant White masculinity" that binds evangelicals together into a "coherent whole" (4). They believe that Trump
has the John Wayne–like toughness and swagger to bring America
back to its Christian roots. But, in those roots, she sees intolerance
toward immigrants, minorities, and non-Christians, and opposition
to gay rights. Others (Rah 2009; Martí 2020; Butler 2021) show how
white evangelicals have marginalized non-whites and the poor,
evincing a racism and classism rooted in white nationalism, along
with a desire to protect free-market capitalism. Whitehead and Perry
(2020) show that it is Christian nationalism – not evangelicalism
per se, even though a high proportion of white evangelicals embrace
Christian nationalism – that is the key predictor of xenophobia and
Trump support.

Yet, Britain and Canada are not the United States, and Christian
nationalism seems comparatively weak among evangelicals in those
countries (Hatcher 2017; Malloy 2019). Furthermore, most Britons
and Canadians see diversity as good for their country (Hargreaves et
al. 2020; Reimer 2021). So, are evangelicals outside the United States
being unfairly painted with the same brush as American evangelicals?

Does research show that evangelicals are intolerant, whether inside
or outside the United States? Sometimes the answer is yes, but it
depends on how tolerance is measured. There is a lot of research in the
United States on political tolerance – defined as the willingness to grant
civil liberties to disliked groups (Stouffer 1955; Boch 2020). For example, the US General Social Survey lists various unpopular groups (e.g.,
racists, gays, communists, Muslim extremists, and so on) and asks
respondents if they would grant civil liberties to each group (e.g., allowing a member of these groups to make a public speech, hold a
rally/demonstration, and so on). Based on this method (called the
"fixed-groups" method), evangelicals, and others who are religiously
conservative and committed, come out as more intolerant than most

Americans (Nunn, Crockett, and Williams 1978; Eisenstein 2006 and 2008; Schwadel and Garneau 2019). However, research generally shows that US evangelicals are not more intolerant than non-evangelicals if an alternative method of measuring tolerance is used. In this alternate method, respondents are asked to select, from a long list of unpopular groups, the group they like the least (called the "least-liked" method, based on the work of Sullivan, Piereson, and Marcus 1982). Then respondents are asked if they would grant civil liberties (e.g., the right to make a public speech, hold a rally/demonstration, and so on) to the least-like group they selected. Research in Canada using the "least-liked" method also shows that evangelicals are not more intolerant than other groups (Reimer 2021). It seems that the relationship between conservative and committed religiosity and intolerance is actually an artefact of the oft-used "fixed-groups" method (Busch 1998; Eisenstein 2008).

Social tolerance – as distinguished from political tolerance – can be defined as "people's willingness to accept disliked others in their everyday life" (F. Lee 2013, 713), including having them as neighbours. Whether or not evangelicals come out as more socially intolerant depends on the groups studied. Not surprisingly, evangelicals feel less warm than non-evangelicals toward LGBTQ+ people in both Canada and the United States, but, in Canada, evangelicals feel at least as warmly as the general population toward racial/ethnic and religious minorities (Reimer 2011a). We can conclude that there is not much evidence to suggest that evangelicals (at least those outside the United States) are more xenophobic, racist, or intolerant of people of different religions. But what about homo- and transphobia? Recent research shows that evangelicals are still less accepting of LGBTQ+ orientations and same-sex marriage than is the general population. However, even here, there is evidence of softening views, especially among the young in the United States (Bean and Martinez 2014; Farrell 2011; Castle 2019) and in Canada (Reimer 2011a).

BELIEF CHANGE

Jessica's interview suggests that evangelical beliefs are changing. The above discussion suggests *why* they are changing. If the evangelical understanding of beliefs overemphasizes cognitive assent to propositions and beliefs are more relational and identity-focused, then belief change should start with changing relational networks. Belonging will do more than apologetics to change beliefs. Does the research support this? Pål Repstad (2008) and about twenty other researchers studied multiple conservative Christian organizations in the Agder region of Norway over three years. Their goal was to understand religious change since the 1960s. Like Hunter (1987) in the United States, they found an overall trend toward liberalization. Their findings include the following:

1. Liberalizing beliefs would "first manifest themselves as changes in everyday practice, without explicit and public theological reflections accompanying them" (2008, 20). For example, the researchers found that evangelicals became less isolationist over time, participating in sports, going to movies, and so on, which broadened their list of acceptable activities and their relational circles.

2. With expanded networks, evangelicals found non-evangelicals to be likeable, good people. These encounters could lead to theological change. For example, the researchers found that pastors and leaders would reconsider their understanding of certain biblical texts that no longer fit their relational experiences.

3. Silence on a controversial subject is a means of change. Repstad and is co-researchers found that a lengthy public controversy on the nature of hell led to topic fatigue, and, after a few years, the subject was rarely mentioned in public discourse. Preachers stop talking about it to avoid conflict, and parishioners came to hold diverse views on the subject. The views of clergy also changed. Follow-up interviews with evangelical leaders found that they would say hell is "separation from God" and would say nothing about suffering, fire, and brimstone. They said they didn't want to scare people into salvation.

4. Change can initially be justified as a change in form, not content. "The message we preach is the same, we just package it differently," an evangelical innovator might say. Repstad wonders if it is possible to change the form without changing the content, at least in the way it is processed and received.

5. Changes can be defended as necessary to reach a higher good. For example, changes in worship style are justified as a means to keep young people engaged, or the Christian emphasis on "loving others" and not "judging others" justifies acceptance of same-sex attraction.

6. Ethics change before dogma does. Conservative Christians are more likely to change their views on ethical and social issues

like premarital sex before they change their views of the divinity of Christ, for example.

Repstad relates these liberalizing beliefs to a larger shift in culture.
Sociologists, he notes, point out that religious persons are "becoming
less committed to dogma and more oriented towards experience and
expressiveness" (2008, 27) and that "the scope of sin has been shrinking and the scope of legitimate and God-willed human self-realization
has increased" (23). Thus, Repstad's findings in Norway seem indicative
of what I call the move toward internal authority and self-spirituality in
Western culture.

Repstad's longitudinal data suggest both the *direction* (toward more
open and accommodating positions) and *areas* (in contested ethical
beliefs) of change. My interview data are cross-sectional – a "snapshot"
of one point in time – and do not allow me to measure change over
time. However, the content of the interviews themselves provides evidence of change. First, interviewees such as Jessica often stated that
their views have softened, indicating change over the life course. Second, younger respondents tend to be less orthodox than older ones,
indicating intergenerational change.

Although there were a few exceptions, nearly all interviewees' beliefs
moved in a more accommodating, eirenic, civil direction. This is not
the same as saying evangelical beliefs are liberalizing en masse. Indeed,
some research indicates that responses to survey questions on the
divinity of Jesus, on abortion, or other doctrinal and moral issues show
little-to-no change among evangelicals in recent decades (Reimer
2003; Penning and Smidt 2002). What I contend here is that the language evangelicals use to talk about their beliefs is changing, because
how beliefs are understood in society (what beliefs *are*) is changing.
The actual *content* of belief may not change, but the way the belief is
presented is gentler; it is more accepting of diverse beliefs. This change
in what beliefs *are* is more important and more subtle than content
change, and is often missed by "broad but not deep" survey results.
Beliefs are becoming less creedal, less propositional, less generalizable.
They are more qualified, more personal, and less dogmatic.

THEOLOGICAL BELIEFS

In societies that embrace diversity, like Britain and Canada, evangelicals perceive that they are expected to relegate their religious views to

the private sphere. Even more, exclusive beliefs should be rejected. For some, such beliefs are reminiscent of hegemonic power, of colonization and oppression of religious minorities. They indicate a blind adherence to external authority. Exclusive beliefs suggest an objective correctness of my views as opposed to yours. This is not compatible with the subjective nature of religious belief held by those with internal authority. As a conservative religious group that holds to exclusive propositional beliefs, it is not a surprise that evangelicals are concerned about their presentation.

Can evangelicals soften their unpopular beliefs without necessarily conforming to worldly standards? The answer is yes: evangelicals can and do smooth the rough edges off their beliefs without compromising their positions. This can be seen in several ways. First, the interviews showed that exclusive theological beliefs – those that exclude non-evangelical beliefs or, worse, exclude non-believers from salvation – are most likely to be softened. Lay evangelicals and clergy work hard to present exclusive theological beliefs in a gentle way. Two examples are the belief that Jesus is the only way for salvation and the belief that hell (as a real place of physical suffering in the afterlife) is the ultimate destination for all those who have not received salvation through Jesus Christ. While nearly all interviewees agreed that Jesus is the only way to get to heaven, they answered questions about this belief in a way that is as unoffensive as possible.

In the lay and clergy interviews, I asked about views on the Bible, salvation, and women in leadership. These questions were initially asked in a general way, so as not to be leading: the open question "What is your view of the Bible?" would be followed up with "Would you use words like 'inspired,' 'authoritative,' 'infallible,' 'inerrant' to describe it?", as needed. In the clergy interviews, I would ask for their church's position on a theological issue (often stated on the church or denomination/network website), but a significant minority of clergy would respond that the theological views in the church were diverse. This is particularly true in mainline denominations – like Anglicanism – which research has shown to be much more internally diverse theologically than evangelical denominations (Francis et al. 2006; Reimer 2011b). In this case, I would ask for the personal views of the clergy being interviewed. For the lay interviews, I emphasized that I was interested in the respondent's personal views, not those of their church. The following sections discuss responses to two questions that are central to evangelical orthodoxy: Biblicism (a high view of the Bible) and crucicentrism (the centrality of Christ's salvific work on the cross for salvation). In addition, an area that is not a central tenet of evangelicalism – women in leadership – is also discussed.

The Bible Is Inspired, but Not Literal

If evangelicals are sliding toward internal authority, then their central external authority – the Bible – should allow some room for personal interpretation. Most evangelicals emphasize the priesthood of all believers, so deference to historical ecclesial interpretations of scripture is not required. Evangelicals can interpret the Bible on their own, and this awareness and practice is widespread. As I have shown and will show, lay evangelicals (and sometimes even clergy) often deviate from the official views of their denomination or network. Yet most verbalized orthodox positions. Nearly all respondents – clergy and lay – agreed that the Bible was inspired, and the majority indicated that it was authoritative (even if they did not use those words). A minority thought it was inerrant, but *no one* thought the Bible was word-for-word literal. Even the most conservative pastor I interviewed, a Presbyterian in England, self-described as "more conservative theologically than Oak Hill" (a conservative evangelical college in London), did not always take the Bible literally. He did confirm that the Bible was inerrant and infallible, but, when I asked if he would say it is "word-for-word literal," he responded: "Yeah, we believe the Bible to be the word of God, but also that you'd have to interpret that in certain ways. God does not have to write out [that] he has no body parts."[10] Research has shown that even biblical literalists actually interpret the Bible in non-literal ways (Bartkowski 1996; Malley 2004), and that claiming to be a biblical literalist has much to do with signalling one's conservative religious identity (Crapanzano 2000). Even back in 1996 in Canada, evangelicals were much more likely to agree that the Bible was inspired (88 per cent) than literal (59 per cent) (Hiemstra 2020a).

In my interviews, responses often emphasized that the Bible should not be taken literally. Consider the views of Chris, a young man I interviewed at the University of Manchester and who attended an independent evangelical church in the city:

S: Describe to me your view of the Bible.
Chris: Okay. I think it's the inspired word of God. I think it is also a text that was written at a specific time for a specific purpose

and you shouldn't be separating that away from the Bible,
what's written there. It can't just be taken as – I guess, [I'm]
not a fundamental[ist].

Chris goes on to note that he rejects the idea that the creation story
in Genesis literally took seven twenty-four-hour days, as this would
misinterpret the intention of the text. Most respondents emphasized
the "human component" of interpreting the Bible, indicating that
human subjectivity and historical context play a role in the way the
Bible has been, and still is, interpreted.[11]

Other lay respondents described the Bible in relation to what it did
for them personally, not to what it is. Talia, a middle-aged woman
attending an evangelical Anglican church in London, stated that the
Bible is the word of God and guides her in all areas of life:

Talia: I still think it's a relevant book and it's a way of learning
　　about God and being closer to God as well, reading His word.
　　…
I think it gives guidance and comfort and wisdom and, you know,
　　inspiration as well.
S: … Would you refer to the Bible as the inspired word of God?
Talia: Yes, I would. I think the Bible inspires you to do things and
　　whatever you've got to do, so don't be afraid to do anything
　　because God's with you all the time.

"What it does for me" explanations of the Bible were more common
among the young, Anglicans, and those without theological education. Talia's explanation, which indicates that she did not understand
the word "inspired" in a theological sense, is also more typical of
respondents with a stronger internal locus of authority.

While there are signs in the interviews of less propositional views
of the Bible among the laity, the majority of interviewees still used the
Bible as their central authority in practice. One Church of England
priest near London affirmed that his church leadership view the Bible
as inspired and authoritative (though not inerrant), but that "people
know we're Anglican … [so] its rare that we talk about any of those
sort of key markers [like inspired or inerrant]." Chris's pastor, David,
pointed to the centrality of the Bible for the church:

So for example, we've moved away from a complementarian position and would embrace women in leadership … but we did that

on the basis of a thorough searching of the scriptures and seeking to be faithful to that, interpret them faithfully, not from a point of view of we just fancy changing. So I would say scriptures are as important to us as ever; we place a really high value on the preaching, teaching of scripture. We've just begun to grapple a little bit more with the way we interpret and apply.

Salvation through Jesus Only – With an Addendum

Nearly all respondents confirmed that salvation is through Jesus alone, keeping with evangelical orthodoxy. Canadian Anglican lay interviewees were more liberal than their evangelical Anglican counterparts in England. Some affirmed "salvation through Jesus alone" but, after I probed, stated that non-Christians (like a devout Hindu) may also be saved vicariously through Jesus. They added that it was up to God – not them – to judge who merits salvation. Here we see an affirmation of an orthodox belief (salvation through Jesus alone) with a non-exclusive addendum. More common overall were responses like Jackson's, a twenty-something youth leader in a Canadian Anglican church:

> I believe ... salvation through what Christ has done for us with his life, and death and resurrection ... We haven't lived according to his law, or we haven't always loved him or our neighbour. And, because ... God isn't just loving and merciful he's also just and righteous, ... there's a sort of consequence to ... our choices and to our actions, and God offers us forgiveness; he offers us reconciliation through what he provides in Christ. So I would say that is the salvation message and how we receive that is just through faith. It's just a gift to be received, not something to be earned. It's not something we have to sort of strive after; it's something we have to accept by faith.

Many lay persons emphasized, like Jessica in the example at the beginning of the chapter, that salvation is a process, a growing relationship with God, not a one-time "say the sinner's prayer" or "Damascus Road" event.[12]

Although I did not ask questions about hell, two clergy mentioned that belief in a "literal hell" was debated in their church. When I asked an independent pastor in Manchester if his church held to the belief that "salvation was through Christ alone," he affirmed that belief, but added that "the existence of Hell, or of eternal punishment, we've debated as a staff team. We've not come to any fixed view and we've not stayed to anything other than the standard evangelical viewpoint."

To this point, there is some evidence of slippage in orthodoxy in areas of exclusive beliefs, as one would expect if beliefs are increasingly relational and relationships are increasingly diverse. Much stronger evidence of softening, however, shows up in areas of gender and sexuality. As Repstad's research (2008) shows, accommodation is more likely to happen in ethics than in doctrine.

Qualified Complementarianism

Some US researchers have argued that an ideological commitment to male headship, and the anti-feminism inherent in such a stance, is an important part of American evangelical identity (e.g., Stasson 2014; Du Mez 2020). Yet such commitments were not evident in my sample. While some conservatives spoke of male headship, most evangelicals (and nearly all young evangelicals) I talked to were egalitarian – espousing the view that women can hold all leadership positions in the church, equal to men. Some of the network churches (and the Salvation Army) have leadership couples, where both the husband and wife are co-pastors/co-leaders and are thus egalitarian. As one pastor emphatically stated, his wife is "not a *pastor's* wife, but a *pastor* wife." Other networks, like New Frontiers and Acts 29 churches, are complementarian (Aune 2006). In this view, women hold positions that are "complementary" to men, and certain positions of leadership in the church are limited to men only. For some complementarian churches, women should not be part of the leadership team; some say women should not teach (or preach to) men; others accept women in all roles (including ordination and preaching), except for lead pastor. Complementarianism can also include male headship in the home, where the wife "submits" to the husband's leadership. In most cases, complementarians experienced some inner tension with respect to their views. For example, a young Anglican priest, Andrew, in a rural parish near London, told me that this was a hard issue for him. While he identified as complementarian, he was "happy for women to preach in a church as long as there's a male vicar taking the headship role." However, he observed that other evangelical Anglican parishes nearby were led by women, and he found himself "in terms of a practical level, just thanking God for their ministry. It's an ongoing battle

for me. There's a tension there." Consider, as well, the response of Candice, a young university student attending an Anglican church in
Manchester:

> S: So, how about women in leadership. What's your position on
> that?
> Candice: Yeah. I'm for it. One of my previous churches, New Fron-
> tiers, is quite anti-women in leadership, which for me wasn't
> really an issue at the time because I wasn't at a stage in my life
> where that was the issue ... I know no church is perfect but, yes,
> I'm for women in leadership (hesitates) ... I think this but I
> don't know if I actually believe this. But I think there's a mas-
> sive advantage to a man and woman being in leadership togeth-
> er. Not that – if there was a single lady as a leader of a church, I
> wouldn't mind that because ... if it was the Church of England,
> let's say, I know there would be other people around her but if
> it was an independent church that was just completely indepen-
> dent and there was just this woman with no one around her
> supporting her, then I would maybe be a bit concerned about
> "Who are you getting your input from?" ... I'm not saying single
> people can't lead because they can, but you need to have people
> around you who are regularly challenging you and keeping you
> accountable.
> S: ... So, would you feel also uncomfortable with an independent
> church with a single man leading?
> Candice: Yes, probably less so, which is a bit sexist. I would proba-
> bly stay away from independent churches altogether, like com-
> pletely independent, but I think probably less so. That could
> just be society and my upbringing or like social construction ...
> I don't know why; that's a little bit sexist. And it could just be
> because of what I'm used to. I think some experiences of ladies
> that have been in leadership and been single haven't been good
> whereas there's been a few men that have been okay. So, I think
> that's it.

Candice is self-reflective, which is probably related to her university
training in a psychology-related field. She recognized a tension
between what she was used to and her egalitarian views.

Without prompting, most clergy and lay complementarians qualified their response by noting that they were more egalitarian in prac-

tice. It was rare that respondents would say "We are complementari-an," and stop there. Most answers were considerably longer, as they wrestled with presenting their beliefs (a performative function). The response of Stephen, a pastor in a New Frontiers church in England, was typical. In our discussion of the way his church compared to other New Frontiers churches, he noted that one difference was in his church's "soft complementarian":

> S: Whereas other [New Frontiers] churches would be a harder complementarian?
>
> Stephen: Yeah, massively, yeah. Some churches certainly wouldn't have a woman preach ... We don't have any problem with that at all. In fact, one of our elders' wives ... could well be the best preacher in our church. There's women who take prominent positions in the church in terms of leadership of things, so ... I think on the basis of relationship and friendship with the guys in our network, I think we sort of soft-peddle some of that. If we were just to cut loose [from New Frontiers] and go it alone, we might make some bigger changes. I don't know. Kind of talking off the top of my head a little bit here. So, yeah, I think we're probably a slightly less hard-core evangelical version of New Frontiers. I think. And, yeah. That's a good question.
>
> S: ... So, would the church accept a woman elder ...?
>
> Stephen: Probably not at this point. I think some [in the church] might. I think many probably wouldn't have a strong position either way and would just go with it. A small handful really would object a lot. I won't say any names. There would be ... if we did go in that direction, then I think it would largely be accepted, yeah. I think.

Thus, Stephen, like some other pastors, made it clear that New Frontiers official doctrine had "soft" application in his church.

The fact that official positions of evangelical churches are not always strictly adhered to in practice is not new. Research shows that loose coupling between official protocol and practice is common in both secular (Powell and DiMaggio 1991) and religious (Demerath et al. 1998) organizations. In the area of male headship in marriages, previous research has shown that evangelical couples who verbally assent to male headship are often egalitarian in practice (e.g., Gallagher 2003). For instance, Aune's (2006, 653) study of a New Frontiers congregation in Britain shows the presence of a "postfeminist" tension between traditional complementarianism and "pragmatic egalitarianism." About one-third of the congregation showed egalitarian attitudes. She relates this to the changing roles of evangelical women. For many single women or women in the workforce, male headship is less appealing than it might be for those in domestic, married-with-children roles (see also Aune 2004 and 2008; Marler 2008). The same seems to be the case with my respondents. Verbal adherence to complementarianism may have little practical application to day-to-day life in families and churches. Like biblical literalism, however, complementarianism locates a church within the fold of conservative evangelicalism, and thus serves a performative function.

ETHICS AND INCLUSION

Evangelicals are known for their conservative positions on "sanctity of life" issues like abortion, euthanasia/assisted dying, and sometimes the death penalty.[13] They hold to the view that humans are made in God's image and, thus, that life is sacred. Only God, the giver of life, decides when life begins or ends. Evangelicals are also defenders of traditional marriage and sexuality. They fear that sex outside of marriage, and the changing definition of marriage, undermines the traditional family and thus erodes the very foundation of society (Carwana 2021). They insist that the Bible teaches that sex should be limited to marriage, and that marriage is between one man and one woman. Umbrella organizations like the Evangelical Fellowship of Canada, the Evangelical Alliance in the United Kingdom, and the National Association of Evangelicals in the United States all have statements on the sanctity of life and traditional marriage.[14] Of course, these are not the only ethical issues evangelicals are concerned about. These umbrella organizations and many evangelical denominations and interdenominational organizations have statements against racism, sexual abuse, environmental protection ("creation care"), protection for the poor and marginalized, international development, human rights, and other issues. In general, evangelicals have expanded their areas of concern and activism (Steensland and Goff 2014).

Like complementarians, evangelicals of all stripes in Canada and England qualified their conservative ethical positions toward greater inclusivity. The most common way this was done for clergy was distinguishing between theological position and pastoral practice. When

I asked one independent church leader where his church fit within the range of evangelical churches in the area, he said that they were "soft in tone but conservative in conviction." Michelle, the leader of a small independent church in a poor section of London, stated that they are anti-abortion and believe marriage is between a man and woman, but was eager to qualify her response:

> S: So, you'd be conservative on same-sex marriage and you would be pro-life generally?
> Michelle: But in quite a pastoral sort of ... do you know what I mean?
> S: I know exactly what you mean.
> Michelle: And the whole thing about gay, transgender thing, it's very different pastorally to theologically. So, that's where I think we've really struggled with gay people who have been part of the church. We tend to find they walk with us for a season but when they realize we're not changing our theology, they tend to move to a church that is promoting the gay agenda or whatever. We might have people journey with us several years before they come to that point.

Among both laity and clergy, another strategy was to distinguish between Christian standards and societal standards by recognizing that not everyone in society is Christian, and so Christian ethical standards do not apply to all people. Some responses referred to the group level – where standards applied to all evangelicals but not non-evangelicals – while others indicated individual-level standards. It was common for respondents to qualify their responses by statements like "for me" or "it's up to them," indicating that ethical and moral decisions were up to the individual. Another common way to handle these controversial issues is silence, as we will see below. To avoid offence, they just don't talk about them publicly. In the following sections, I discuss responses to questions about views of abortion, premarital sex or cohabitation, and same-sex marriage.

Abortion Is Still Wrong ... in Some Cases

Evangelical views on abortion are more nuanced than the "pro-life" label suggests.[15] While nearly all evangelicals I spoke to leaned in the pro-life direction and defended traditional views of the sanctity of life (normally beginning at conception), most were also open to abortions in some cases. For example, in cases where pregnancy results from rape or the health of the mother is threatened, many of the evangelicals I interviewed would accept abortion. While a few were blunt ("abortion is murder"), many more qualified their responses. Softened, eirenic responses were the norm. Although I did not ask about activism, several pastors stated that their churches would not join pro-life marches or protests outside abortion clinics, and only one clergy interviewee said she had participated in a pro-life march (which was a personal decision, not a church event). On the whole, evangelicals in England and Canada prefer a non-aggressive, relational approach on the issue.

Nonetheless, there was a range of responses, even within churches. Within the same independent church, one lay respondent stated that he considers abortion to be equivalent to "sacrifice to Molech,"[16] while another attendee stated that she was not "totally anti-abortion" and was still making up her mind on the issue. She said she "had to look into it ... to read more about it." She leaned toward allowing abortion in the first trimester, as she was not convinced that life began at conception. Others distinguish between societal and Christian standards, like Richard, a young Canadian Anglican:

S: How about abortion, what's your view on that?
Richard: You just go right for it; this is awesome (smiling).
S: Yeah, we're in the nitty gritty now (laugh).
Richard: Yeah ... I'd say that I have a kind of complex view of it ...
  In the legal sense, my personal beliefs are that ... it should not
  be illegal ... but I can also recognize the tension that is inherent
  in it, and that ... there is life in the unborn and that, that is a
  tension that is real. And so I can kind of come to a stance of
  like, I can both not support it, but don't want it to be illegal,
  and want access to be available ... I'm sort of in the middle of
  recognizing both sides, and recognizing the tensions and want-
  ing ... as a Christian taking a response: What are the behaviours
  that I can model, what are the actions I can take that make it so
  that isn't the single option?

Some pastors (especially in England) said they did not talk about abortion from the pulpit, and others stated that their church did not have a position on it. Alan, lead pastor at an independent church in

Manchester that ministers to the marginalized, said that abortion was

> [a] very sensitive subject ... We are never gonna be one to judge
> that in the sense of being judgmental. Knowing the statistics of
> any given group of people, chances are 40 per cent of the women
> in the room may have had such a procedure. So, it's not gonna
> help us to make them feel bad. So, we would encourage people to
> consider alternatives. We would be supportive of pro-life initia-
> tives that present a different alternative, particularly stuff around
> adoption.

Like Alan (or Jessica, who was quoted at the start of this chapter),
some respondents saw abortion as a systemic problem, not an individual moral one, and sought to alleviate the societal problems that
contribute to abortion. These included providing support and love
for pregnant single women, encouraging adoption and adopting foster children, and supporting families.

Others – in England, if not in Canada – seemed somewhat surprised by the question. One pastor stated that abortion was not a big
issue anymore in England like it was in the United States. Rebecca, a
major in a Salvation Army church (Salvation Army calls churches
"corps") in London, thought the question sounded "American."

> S: What would be your view on abortion?
> Rebecca: Oh, wow ... I don't know. That's a really interesting ques-
>   tion. Have you interviewed many Brits about this? This is very
>   sort of American, isn't it?
> S: Well, yes, I think I'm on my fiftieth [British] interview.
> Rebecca: Oh, wow ... gosh. This is the thing: I think in the States,
>   I would say that issues such as abortion are very black and
>   white whereas we ... especially maybe this is because we're inner
>   city and we're multi-cultural, I don't know. There is loads of
>   grey. We can't just say, "We're against abortion."
> S: I think that would be ... yeah, remember, I'm Canadian; I'm not
>   American.
> Rebecca: Oh, thank God for that.

Evidently, at least for some evangelicals in England, abortion is not of
such political and symbolic importance as it is in the United States.
Rebecca's response also smacks of anti-American bias and stereotyp-

ing, which was not uncommon among respondents, as we shall see in subsequent chapters.

Premarital Sex/Cohabitation:
Wrong for Me

Most evangelical clergy and laity affirmed the position that, in their view, sex should take place only within marriage, which they considered as being between one man and one woman. Yet, some softened their position by saying that what mattered was a "covenant" or "committed" relationship between a man and a woman, not the actual marriage ceremony. Some younger respondents stated that all sexual relationships were "up to the person," but such responses were a small minority. More common were two other broadening strategies: separating between Christian and non-Christian ethics, and advocating that these issues be handled privately and personally rather than by public declaration. Julie, a young woman active in a Vineyard church in Canada, said:

> I am very passionately committed to chastity, and I might be the only one! Um, yeah, I think a shared life should start with a life-long commitment and I see that as happening in marriage. Um, it seems like a more and more unique position even in the church. A lot of my friends cohabit. Um, certainly I don't expect people who don't follow Jesus to have any value around chastity or … um, like chastity being the belief that sex belongs inside marriage only … I don't expect people who aren't trying to follow Jesus to hold to that, but I expect people who are following Jesus should. And it troubles me that we don't do a better job of equipping – maybe not just young people, but particularly young people to commit to that.

As noted above, evangelicalism is internally diverse, so, not surprisingly, not all interviewees agreed with Julie's division between evangelical and non-evangelical ethical standards. After she stated her conservative views on abortion, women in leadership (complementarianism), and premarital sex, I asked Kara, a young female university student who attends a conservative and reformed (formerly Anglican) church in England, if her views applied to everyone or just Christians. Her response: "Good question. I think we're all held to God's standard so I would say it is wrong for everybody. But then I know people do it [premarital sex]. So I'm not going to tell them, but I would tell a Christian brother or sister who I thought was making a mistake. I have done that in the past." She was the only lay interviewee who clearly stated that God-given standards on sexual ethics were the same for everyone.

For pastors, sexual issues were not black and white in practice. Peter, a British Hillsong pastor, had this response to premarital sex:

> We're against it but grace has to be there. [I'm] dealing with a [cohabiting] couple at the moment ... They've got two kids together. He's professed to be a Christian, she's just made a decision [to become a Christian], so how do we help them through that process without wrecking the kids' lives by doing a strong, "Yep, you can't live together." How do you then deal with that? How do the kids deal with that? There's a weight of the stuff that's happening that we have to help people deal with as well. Not just, "Well, that's wrong," and not taking into consideration that we can actually wreck their lives as much as the sin [of cohabitation] can.

Similarly, when I asked Martin, an Elim Pentecostal pastor in England, his position on premarital sex, he stated, "I'm too old for it. Sorry (smiles) ... Our stance is that we will always work and would want to work with couples to bring them to a faithful commitment in marriage." For both Peter and Martin, the goal was to help people reach the evangelical standard without disrupting familial ties in the process.

Same-Sex Relationships:
A Qualified Conservative View

Softening strategies dominated responses to the issue of same-sex relationships. It may seem surprising that respondents were often more conservative on abortion and premarital sex than on same-sex marriage. Again, the same strategies apply: distinguishing between societal standards and standards for Christians, and emphasizing the gracious handling of these issues with people in spite of a conservative theological position. More than any other belief, evangelicals are clear that conservative positions in the area of same-sex relationships are unpopular. One highly educated pastor of a large independent church in England saw generational change in sexual ethics. He acknowledged that most of his congregation is conservative on sexual issues, but that there also is some diversity:

I think there's a whole generation of younger people growing up in an education system which has pushed this as a kind of justice issue, kind of civil rights issue for same sex–attracted people and so on. And I think that may be changing generationally, but I still think ... many of these kids are also coming from a framework where there is a tolerance towards what goes on in society and a tolerance towards diversity and, indeed, sometimes an embracing of that diversity. But [we have] an expectation that serious disciples of Jesus live and act in a different way; and that happens right across the board in a number of different issues.

If society sees same-sex marriage as a human rights issue, and evangelicals embrace both universal human rights and the authority of the Bible, they are faced with competing values. We should expect to find accommodating positions in such areas. A retired medical doctor from a conservative Anglican church in England gave the following response. It not only shows how his view changed over time due to relational experiences, but is also an example of the long, qualified answers that were typical when I asked about same-sex relationships.

I've been on a journey on that over the years. When I first became a Christian ... I took a traditional view on same-sex attraction and practice, but, as I have practised over the years as a GP, I've known a lot of gay and lesbian patients and probably the majority of those that I've known have actually been in long-term relationships. They've been the equivalent of a marriage; they've been in very faithful relationships. I've been impressed by what I've seen of those people. With changes in science and understanding of sexual attraction and the fact that that does seem to be something which isn't reversible and which people recognize from very early on, sometimes extremely early on in their lives ... and, frequently, eventually accept after kicking and screaming against it for a long while ... My experience of same-sex couples doesn't fit with what [St] Paul's talking about rebellion and the things he saw in [the New Testament book of] Romans. I think he's describing something different from that ... So, I've been on a journey. I've sort of moved from accepting that this might not be ideal, that this is

how people were, that they shouldn't actually act on that. I think
in more recent times, ... well, people should at least look at their
own conscience, but if they felt that it was right, they didn't feel as
if the scriptures were right to say they shouldn't be having a same-
sex relationship, that I'd actually be supportive of that ... It would
make it a lot easier for the [Anglican] Church if they wholeheart-
edly accepted same-sex marriage in that they would then be able
to have a simple teaching about the ideal was sex only within
marriage. I think it would remove some potential conflicts there
in teaching at the moment. So, as I said, I've sort of moved significantly on that. I would actually now support same-sex marriage.
It's not the norm, it's probably not the ideal, but I believe that
that's the way that some people inherently are and ... they're not
behaving against what is normal for them. It's not a rebellion; it's
an acceptance of the way that they are made.

Note that this British senior concluded that same sex–attracted Christians should "look at their own conscience" and not scripture to
decide whether they would get married. His response both rejected
institutional (Anglican) authority, along with a rethinking of biblical
passages, and supported internal authority.

Others thought the church has overemphasized sexual impropriety
as a "greater" sin. Here is part of my conversation with Cassie, a young
Baptist woman in England:

S: Right, tell me about your view about premarital sex or cohabitation.
Cassie: So I think, like I think again it's not, it's not God's will. I
   think I won't ever chastise people who aren't Christians for
   doing those things, but I think if someone is a Christian and
   partaking in those activities that you should be able to challenge them on it. But through relationships, not just kind of
   straight down the line, just challenging anyone, or not loving
   them because of it. Because I think we all sin, but some sins are
   I think looked on worse than others and I think more damage
   is done by that.
S: Right, so some sins are more hidden or they're more acceptable
   even among Christians ...
Cassie: Yeah exactly, and I think the church often has, like, has a
   massive go at some issues and not others when, yeah.

S: So, same-sex marriage, what's your view on that, Cassie?

Cassie: Is it within the church or outside of?

S: Yeah, you can give me both if you have a different view on each side.

Cassie: Yeah, so I have friends in same-sex relationships. And I think because they don't know God I would never call them out on it. And I think, like, those relationships are good for them. Yeah, and they're really happy there. But as a Christian I do think that that is not God's plan for relationships, that it's not just, like, God doesn't love you because of this, or you need to really think about this before you're involved in the church. I think God's very down the line on what He says about it. But I think that, again some sins are looked at worse than others and I think that's one example; where it's kind of the biggest deal, and it's actually not. Like, I think the Bible says that all sin is a big deal and I think we call out those ones because we want to put blame on other people, and look down on them. But if there is someone who I had leadership over [in the church], I would be questioning them on it. But not, saying "oh, you can't come to the church, you can't take communion," that sort of thing, cause I think that's really damaging.

Among the clergy, several mentioned that they do not talk about same-sex relationships. In some cases, it seems that they are tired of it being the key issue that defines them as (conservative) Christians. One independent pastor in Manchester asked me not to publicize his pastoral discussion with a gay man, because he is tired of it being "*the* issue." An Anglican priest near London was part of an evangelical pastor's group that read together and discussed Todd Wilson's book, *Mere Sexuality: Rediscovering a Christian View of Sexuality*, which he enthusiastically endorsed.

We [the pastors] realized we were all on a conservative page on that issue, but what was important about it was that we were all saying that we've not talked about it ... How do we impart that to congregations in a way which is helpful to them? We've all avoided talking about it. I remember that when I was in training at Wycliffe Hall and I remember Alister McGrath saying, "There are two types of evangelicals: mission-first or defend the truth," and I remember I thought, "Well, I'm mission-first, no doubt about

that." So, I think that's coloured how I express belief in the
church. I'm much more focused on [the] mission of sharing Jesus
than trying to nail down people's beliefs on things.

This pastor indicates that doctrinal precision is not his primary focus
– rather, he is more focused on "sharing Jesus." No doubt, some other
evangelicals in England are more "defend the truth" in orientation,
but it is also likely that there is greater focus on truth defending in the
United States than in Canada or England. Comparatively, the United
States has had a stronger historical impulse toward sectarianism and
fundamentalism, where religious groups splintered off of parent
denominations that were perceived to be moving in a liberal direction (Bebbington and Jones 2013; Reimer 2003; Noll 1997).

To summarize my findings on evangelical ethics and beliefs, there is a
pastoral, "love people first" approach among clergy, along with a softening of conservative positions among the laity. Evidence points to
both intra-generational change in an accommodating direction, and
inter-generational change: many have softened their views over their
lifetimes, and younger respondents were less propositional, more relational, and more likely to distinguish between Christian and non-
Christian standards.
    At least some evangelicals are operating under an outdated under-
standing of belief. As Westerners move toward the internal authority
side of the continuum, beliefs will be more about *adherence to* (relational) and less about *assent to* (doctrinal). As relational networks
become increasingly diverse in heterogeneous Western societies, the
desire to belong encourages inclusive beliefs and internal authority.
However, the pressure toward inclusivity and softening comes not
only from non-evangelicals, but from evangelical Britons and Canadians themselves. Many in my sample were tired of having American
evangelical stereotypes – evangelicalism writ large – applied to them.
British and Canadian evangelicals seek to distance themselves from
dogmatic and harsh co-religionists who often make the news in the
United States. They do this by presenting their beliefs in a qualified,
eirenic way. Softening strategies include silence, separating evangelical and non-evangelical behavioural expectations, and creating space
between belief and practice.
    Yet, these softening strategies do not necessarily mean compromis-
ing their orthodoxy, at least in how they presented it. They can still

say, "Yes, I believe Jesus is the only way to heaven" and yet also assert that "non-Christians can also be saved." Or they can affirm that "Yes, same-sex marriage is evidence of a sinful world and not what God intended" and yet also state that they welcome LGBTQ+ persons in their church and do not judge them. In this way, their beliefs are exclusive, but their practice is more inclusive.

CONCLUSION

It was February in northern England, and my wife, son, and I walked through the slushy snow to attend an independent charismatic (New Frontiers) church with about 250 others. As the site pastor joined the worship band on stage after a lengthy and enthusiastic worship (singing) time (led by a young woman in this complementarian church), a few members got up to offer a "word of knowledge" or "prophetic word" to the congregation.[17]

When it came time for the sermon, Philip, a pastor in his thirties well-known to the congregation, stood up to speak from the book of Romans, chapter 1. Knowing the passage, I was immediately intrigued by how it would be handled. Romans chapter 1 includes Saint Paul's condemnation of same-sex relations. It states that, because humankind had not honoured God, they were given "over in the sinful desires of their hearts to sexual impurity," which includes men and women abandoning "natural" heterosexual relationships (Romans 1: 24–7, NIV) for same-sex ones. Philip's tone was careful and gentle. He recognized that some in the congregation were same sex–attracted, and he emphasized that sexuality was "not the most important deal," even though the "church" (referring to Christian churches in general) sometimes treats it as such. He apologized to those with same-sex attractions that the church had made this into "the biggest sin." He stated that the Bible teaches that same-sex sexual relations are wrong, although same-sex attraction was not. Philip recognized that he did not have all the answers, but he recommended that, when someone turned to Christ, they (the church and same sex–attracted person) would journey together to "figure it out." He emphasized that same sex–attracted persons were deeply loved by God. This was only part of the sermon. Philip spoke for forty minutes, which included admonitions to "not be ashamed of the gospel" (Romans 1:16). In my interview with him about a month later, Philip recognized that there were different opinions on same-sex relations in the church, and suggested that the internet "massively" shapes the sexual attitudes and gender identity of people in Western culture. The two lay interviewees from Philip's church both confirmed that sex outside heterosexual marriage was wrong in their view, but emphasized the need for compassion in the church for people who were attracted to the same sex.

In many evangelical congregations in Canada and the United Kingdom (and the United States), you will find women who have had abortions in the pews, along with cohabiting and same-sex couples. Such people are willing to attend a church that does not affirm their choices or relationships, even if many others would not do so. Their level of comfort may be due partly to softening strategies. None of the clergy I interviewed and none of the evangelical churches I visited presented their beliefs, especially their ethical and exclusive beliefs, in a dogmatic, condemning way. If someone were to attend an evangelical church expecting tirades against sexual promiscuity or graphic descriptions of the agony of hell, they would not find them in any of the churches I was in. To be sure, fiery preaching still exists, but it is uncommon in Canada and England, and did not appear in my sample. Further, orthodox beliefs and ethical standards still exist, even if they are softened in presentation and the lines are blurred in practice. My research shows that evangelical churches in these two countries normally present a gentle, qualified orthodoxy.[18] Several pastors told me that they rarely, if ever, preach against abortion, premarital sex, or same-sex relations in their church. Some said they never talk about it. One evangelical Anglican rector in Sheffield admitted that they spoke about premarital sex every two to three years ("I think any less and I'm failing the people"), and same-sex relations about once every three years. "Every time I preach on it, however graciously, somebody gets upset." He elaborated:

> We always work really hard to do it very graciously ... we always have a question time, we ... quite often brought in a guest speaker who is same-sex attracted to ... teach on that, cause I think it has authenticity. But it's always a difficult area, because we have folks in our church family who are lesbian and gay ... They accept where we're at, some gladly, some I guess would prefer if we changed our mind, but we haven't. We just try and I hope it's a gracious orthodoxy.

3

Orthopraxy:
Living Right

In the wake of Donald Trump's 2016 election to the US presidency, the news quickly became public that he had won partly because 81 per cent of white evangelicals had voted for him. In June 2020, roughly the same percentage said they would vote for him again.[1] During his presidential term, Trump's alleged affair with Stormy Daniels (and other sexual improprieties) came to light, as did the $130,000 "hush money" paid by his lawyer, Michael Cohen, to Daniels.[2]

At the same time, as the #MeToo movement was gaining momentum, four evangelical leaders were accused of and/or admitted to sexual impropriety. They included megachurch pastors Bill Hybels and Andy Savage, and Southern Baptist Convention president Frank Page. More recently, in 2021, allegations of sexual misconduct by well-known evangelical apologist Ravi Zacharias were confirmed. And these are just the latest in a long line of evangelical leaders who have been mired in scandal. In 2006, megachurch pastor and National Association of Evangelicals president Ted Haggard was accused of paying a male prostitute for sex, and the 1980s witnessed the highly publicized scandals of televangelists Jim Bakker and Jimmy Swaggart. All of these examples are from the United States; but, lest British and Canadian evangelicals feel smug, such scandals are not limited to Americans. British evangelist bishop Michael Reid and Canadian evangelist Todd Bentley's extramarital affairs were publicized in 2008; most recently, Canadian megachurch pastor Bruxy Cavey was similarly disgraced. And these are just some examples. They contribute to what seems like an easy connection to make: if the vast majority of white evangelical Trump supporters can overlook his improprieties, perhaps they do not take sexual misconduct seriously. As Peter Wehner, senior fellow at the Ethics and Public Policy Center, stated, "A lot of people are going to think it's [evangelicalism] laced with hypocrisy" (Bailey 2018).

The previous chapter demonstrated that, in spite of loosening sexual strictures in Western culture, most evangelicals hold to conservative sexual ethics, even if they do so quietly. Maybe their conservatism is mostly talk. They claim to be defenders of traditional marriage and families, and yet research indicates divorce is common among evangelicals,[3] as is intimate partner violence (Wang et al. 2009; Nason-Clark et al. 2013; Westenberg 2017).[4] Maybe evangelicals do not walk their talk.

There are plenty of examples of evangelicals behaving in unpopular or immoral ways. The question is, how widespread is such behaviour? As Haskell (2009, 212) put it, "Sometimes, it is a few bad apples tainting the rest; in other times the affliction is endemic." In general, however, the evangelicals probably take more heat than they deserve (Haskell 2009). While rates of abuse and divorce are as high among evangelicals as non-evangelicals in the United States,[5] these rates are higher among those evangelicals who rarely attend, who also tend to have lower levels of education, and who marry at a younger age. Studies indicate that church attendance has a positive impact on families and spousal relationships (Wilcox and Williamson 2007; Wilcox 2004; Wright 2010).

Canadian data suggest similar findings. Although differences are small, Canadians who hold to evangelical beliefs are less likely than the general population to get divorced.[6] As in the United States, those Canadians who are religiously committed are considerably more likely than the general population to be married, and less likely to be divorced, separated, or living common law. Furthermore, survey evidence indicates that Canadians show greater congruence between "talk" (claimed beliefs or moral values) and behaviour (self-reports about what they do) than Americans, and evangelicals have slightly higher levels of congruence than non-evangelicals (Reimer 2003).

So the reason the impropriety of evangelical leaders is publicized may not be solely related to their hypocrisy, although that is undoubtedly a factor. It may also be that prominent evangelicals are evaluated by non-evangelicals using criteria that they do not share. The (secular) press seems eager to point out that evangelicals are not living up to their own standards. Why is that?

The issue, I suggest, is deeper than evangelical incongruity between belief and practice. The issue is that evangelicals' epistemology – their way of arriving at their beliefs and practices – is suspect for many in

Western culture. To many outsiders, evangelicals appear to be "drinking the Kool-Aid," blindly following external authority. Within a society dominated by an internal locus of authority, if evangelicals simply accept church-sanctioned beliefs and ethical standards, they are not living according to their true self, which is the end goal of the spiritual quest. Of course, if an individual evangelicals can convince themselves that their beliefs are freely chosen and going to church helps them on their own path toward wholeness, then that is fine, but it might be hard to convince others that traditional, institutional beliefs and practices are really freely chosen. It seems that Western culture has adopted a new evaluation tool, and evangelicals continue to use an old one.

Evangelicals think they are being evaluated on *hypocrisy* – that is, whether their actions match their words, or whether their lifestyle is the same on Sunday as it is on Saturday (or Monday). That is partially correct. But, for those judging evangelicals the deeper issue is *unauthenticity*.

AUTHENTICITY, THE NEW BUZZWORD

Under Christendom, it used to be that orthopraxy was living according to institutional religious behavioural requirements. These included obeying the Ten Commandments, attending church, confessing one's sin, praying, and reading the Bible. Orthopraxy also involved doing the right things outside the church (like evangelism, social justice activism, or acts of kindness) and not doing the wrong things (like abusing alcohol, cursing, or engaging in sexual impropriety) (Bebbington 1989; Hunter 1987). However, as Western culture drifts toward an internal locus of authority and self-spirituality, orthopraxy is passé. Right living is no longer institutionally defined. Evangelicals who still operate with institutionally defined notions of orthopraxy are out of step with Western culture. Instead, right living is about *authenticity* – the new buzzword, and a new yardstick.

But what is "authenticity"? Analysing online responses from Millennials, Jean McDonnell (2017) determined that the word has five interconnected meanings among younger Westerners. "At the heart of this particular meta-concept," she states, "is the 'Hero's Journey' narrative – a narrative marked by challenge and transformation." The challenge is to "conquer your fears and dare to be you," resulting in "the hero's end-of-journey transformation," where the hero reaches their authentic self. McDonnell uses the image of a swan, gliding peacefully on still waters as a picture of finding the authentic self. Swans do not start off pretty (as the famous story *The Ugly Duckling* indicates), but, by overcoming challenges through daring action and hard work, the individual is able to emerge as a beautiful, authentic person, at peace with themselves. Follow your heart and soar with the swans. Leave the ducks behind, because they are trying to reshape you into their mould. Authenticity means that you are true to yourself, transparent (you have nothing to hide), and "pure" or untarnished by worldly influences. Authenticity includes strength of character, determination, and an inclusivity, where one seeks the good of all, not just the self (McDonnell 2017). Authenticity, then, is a centrally important quality because it is the *telos* of the journey. Authenticity is consistency between who you present yourself to be (especially on social media) and who you are in real life. It is also vulnerability, where you are not afraid to reveal your struggles and inner selves. Religious people who act like they have all the answers or have their lives all together are fake. Authenticity is found in those who are guided by their heart, who have experienced the messiness of life and learned from it. If you are fake or hypocritical, Millennials feel they can sense it in their hearts. Hypocrisy, then, is one aspect of authenticity, but only if hypocrisy is understood to be not living by your own standards, but rather by some externally imposed religious standard.

Those who blindly accept institutional (religious) beliefs and behavioural expectations are not authentic, by definition. Hiemstra, Dueck, and Blackaby (2018) argue that, for young adults, externally imposed expectations are juxtaposed with that which originates from within the person, and only the latter is viewed as authentic (see also C. Smith et al. 2011; Arnett 2015). Millennials and youth tend to distance themselves from external, institutional authority. If they do embrace institutional forms of religiosity, they do so because it is valuable for their private spiritual journey. That is to say, such forms must resonate with their perceived identity and enhance their sense of inner wholeness. And they chose the path. It cannot be dictated to them or inherited.[7]

Evidently, authenticity is what Millennials want in their churches. It is the key to their hearts; it is also key to whether they stay in church or leave (Hiemstra, Dueck, and Blackaby 2018; Penner et al. 2012). Research tells us that Millennials want pastors, leaders, and friends who are honest and open about their own struggles (Watts 2020). They also want community and relationship; people who will spend time with them and affirm them; people who take their input seriously and recognize their talents; to see older Christians living what they say they believe; and an authentic worship experience.

In her book *Singing the Congregation*, Ingalls (2018) speaks of authentic worship singing. Increasingly, evangelical churches have twenty- to forty-minute worship sets, involving contemporary worship songs performed on stage by a rock-style band. Worship singing is emotive and expressive, often with hands raised and eyes closed. Such practices are called (and marketed by the worship music industry as) "worship experiences," because they are intended to overwhelm the participant with feelings of divine immanence. They are authentic if they are God-focused and highly personal – that is, if the individual worships without concern of what people around them are doing. They are also authentic if the worship band is worshiping as well, and not focused on their performance. Worship also creates community and identity by drawing together those who share a collective experience and memory. The emphasis on experience and relational intimacy in singing is hard to miss, and it dovetails well with inner-directed self-spirituality.

While authenticity in the church is particularly important to evangelicals, partly because the modern zeitgeist indicates that institutional religion is not authentic, one can also detect the concern for authenticity in private practice, like prayer. Anthropologist Tanya Luhrmann (2012) suggests that, for the growing number of charismatic-leaning evangelicals, prayer is about developing a personal and intimate relationship with God. As people spend time in prayer, they learn to hear God talk to them. With practice and perseverance, the resulting intimacy with God has all sorts of therapeutic benefits, including a sense of unconditional love. Luhrmann suggests that prayer is no longer a discipline of silence that detaches from mind and emotion, as practised by the ancient desert fathers and mothers. Instead, it is emotive, imaginative, and cathartic; it is the means to feel close, and remain close, to God.

Consider my conversation about societal influences on youth in the church with Brock, pastor of a New Frontiers church in northern England:

S: What have you found has been important for faith transmission to the next generation?
Brock: Authenticity. I think that's probably been true all along. I don't think there's been a big change in that. If you as a parent, or as an older person, are living out faith in a way that can clearly be seen and doing that authentically so you're not ...

what you are on a Sunday morning is what you are on any
other day, in your bedroom ... that's what's gonna speak.

I will say more about faith transmission in the next chapter, but, for
now, note Brock's emphasis on the example of authentic Christians
for the faith of youth. In churches, authentic people are more important than cutting-edge programs or worship. As the famous pastor-
blogger Carey Nieuwhof states, "An authentic B+ worship experience
beats a hollow church experience with A+ programming."[8] In sum,
the new standard for right living is authenticity, not adherence to
institutionally prescribed norms.

ORTHOPRAXY AND THE INWARD TURN

If movement toward an internal locus of authority and self-spirituality is infiltrating evangelical churches, then we must ask how it would
affect practices. For one thing, institutional expectations for "good
behaviour" would be replaced by personal ones. There should be evidence that evangelicals are doing what works for them, not internaliz-
ing standards imposed by religious authorities. For example, we would
expect to see church participation, and even the selection of a church
to attend, increasingly based on personal desires. Second, there would
be softened expectations and even redefining of what certain practices
are, particularly among those practices that are unpopular in Western
culture. For example, evangelism – especially pushy evangelism – is
unpopular if everyone is to find their own path. Third, we would hear
justifications for why the person does not do what evangelicals are
supposed to do under institutionally defined standards. Their language should suggest that such behaviour does not work for them personally. Fourth, we would expect evangelicals to reject hierarchical,
doctrinaire, traditional forms of evangelicalism, and embrace more
accepting, individualized, and "authentic" forms. This is evident in the
emerging church movement, discussed in chapter 5. Finally, there
would be differences between younger and older evangelicals if the
inward turn gains momentum with time, and if the younger are more
engaged than the older in Western (secular) culture.

Before we look at evidence in my interviews for evangelical behavioural changes, it should be noted that I did not observe actual behaviour: interviewees provided reports of behaviour, and such reports
are susceptible to bias. However, the goal is not a precise quantifica-

tion of religious behaviour, but to understand how evangelicals think and talk about their behaviour. That is, the goal is to analyze the discourse of evangelicals to uncover the (often unconscious) underlying understandings and cultural frameworks that guide their behaviour. Do interviewee responses indicate operating assumptions/frameworks that point to movement toward an internal locus of authority? In this and similar types of interviews, the discourse of interviewees reveals underlying "cultural models" (C. Smith, Ritz, and Rotolo 2020) that are (often unconsciously) operative, guiding their beliefs and behaviours. As social theorist Jeffrey Alexander (2003, 3) puts it, the goal is to "bring the social unconscious up for view." Quantitative decline in orthopraxy is not the only evidence of change; we need to look also to the qualitative change in language. So I encourage readers to attune to the differences in tone and language used by younger and older respondents. As will become apparent, younger respondents more often use "language of the heart" (Watts 2022). They are guided more by internal ("heart") feelings and perceptions than external prescriptions or ("head") logic. Their tone is affective, subjective, experiential, non-judgmental – evidence that the modern zeitgeist is having an effect. This language of the heart was evident in responses in the previous chapter, but it is even clearer in those presented below.

Recall that my sample is not made up of "average" evangelicals. They are persons selected by their pastors/priests, and are thus among the most institutionally active and have above-average dedication to their faith. We would expect clearer evidence of internal authority and language of the heart from less institutionally engaged evangelicals than from these respondents. The lay interviewees were asked open-ended questions about devotional practices (like Bible reading and prayer); how they chose the church they attend, and how often they attend it; evangelism; political involvement; volunteering and giving. The practices presented in this chapter are ordered from "the inside out," starting with private devotional practices, then practices in the church (attendance), and finally public practices outside the church (evangelism, political behaviour, and voluntarism).

IRREGULAR, SPORADIC DEVOTIONALISM

As "people of the book" who take responsibility for their own spiritual growth, evangelicals emphasize personal Bible reading and prayer. However, Bible reading is on the decline, both in Western soci-

ety more generally and, to a lesser extent, among evangelicals. Hiemstra (2020a) found that, among the Canadian population as a whole,
weekly or more frequent Bible reading went from 20 per cent in 1993
to 10 per cent in 2019. Sixty-nine percent of Canadians in 2019 said
they never read the Bible, a shocking change from 1993, when only 19
per cent said they never read the Bible. For Canadian evangelicals,
weekly Bible reading held steady over the period at about 61 per cent,
but daily Bible reading dropped from 38 per cent to 28 per cent. In
the general population in the United States, daily Bible reading has
dropped from 14 per cent in 2019 to 9 per cent in 2020, and Bible
reading is also declining in Britain and Australia, even among active
churchgoers.[9] It should not surprise that Bible reading is down in a
culture that is less likely to accept external authority. If authority
comes from inside, then the authority of the Bible will be weakened,
and Bible reading becomes less important, just as the institutions that
prescribe (daily) Bible reading have less authority.

Pastor Brock noted that one of the trends he sees in his church
is "biblical illiteracy," which he connects to a societal-level decline
in reading:

> They don't read. We haven't gone from books to e-book. We've
> gone from book to Facebook. If you watch people relaxing any
> where, at the airport or at home, in between meetings, they're
> flicking through Facebook-type things but they're not reading,
> whereas people used to spend that time reading a book or reading
> newspapers. Reading has just fallen off the cliff.

Or consider Scott, rector at an evangelical Anglican church in Western Canada:

> I think individualism and this idea of authority as being your feel
> ings, I think that has really hit church attendance. I think Bible
> reading ... they're so used to being entertained that I don't think
> they have a lot of patience for trying to fight through difficult-to-
> understand literature. And so I think a lot of people just give up
> on reading the Bible because ... it's not immediately understand
> able, and it doesn't tickle you immediately. It's hard stuff in there,
> and people would just rather not wrestle with it. I think prayer,
> people ... still participate in that, but I think maybe it's less dili
> gent, and less disciplined ... Yeah, like almost by definition a prayer
> done out of obedience, as a disciple of Christ, is almost wrong.

Prayer is the most common spiritual practice. Pew Research Center (2014) found that, in the United States, 55 per cent of the population as a whole and 79 per cent of (white) evangelicals claim to pray at least daily. By comparison, in Britain, about one-third of evangelicals say they find a "substantial period of time" to pray daily.[10] In Canada, 17 per cent of Canadians and 55 per cent of evangelicals pray privately on a daily basis.[11] Regarding what people pray for, research suggests that prayers for friends and family, along with prayers related to personal problems, are the most common.[12]

Regardless of age, evangelical devotional practices (often referred to by respondents as "having a quiet time") were similar. They include Bible reading and prayer, and many read Christian books and listen to worship music. A very few also mentioned spiritual disciplines such as meditation, praying the Scriptures (*lectio divina*), and fasting.[13] While the *content* (what evangelicals do in their quiet time) was similar among different age groups, the *scheduling* (when and how long they do it) of devotional practices varied considerably by age. The lay interviews indicate that daily Bible reading is uncommon among younger respondents, partly because devotionalism is less routine and more sporadic. Younger respondents spoke of having their devotions when travelling or "when I have time." Older evangelicals spoke of a daily devotional period, one that occurred at the same time each day, and usually for a relatively long duration. At one extreme, the extent of one young Canadian Anglican's devotionalism was praying for a "few minutes" a day, before meals and occasionally at other times. At the other extreme, sixty-five-year-old Edith, another Canadian Anglican, has an impressive devotional life:

> First thing in the morning anywhere between 5:00 and 5:30 I just start the day with prayer while I'm still in my bed. I have my usual routine at the start of the day, and by about 6:30 ... I usually read the Canadian Bible Society reading for the day ... and I always close with the Lord's Prayer ... [Then] before I have to go out I usually journal ... while I'm having my breakfast and just jot down things that God's brought into my mind or do some more reading depending on the day and how much work I have to do. And then at night before I go to bed, I always read a passage of scripture and I often reread the same passage [for] several nights, to think about and ponder it. I have a devotional reading that I do especially during Lent ... And, throughout the day I really try to follow to the pattern of Brother Lawrence, always throughout the

day being aware of the presence of the Lord and continuing in prayer, just praying as I breathe you know, like a pilgrim in *The Way of the Pilgrim*, you know, and I put myself to bed with every night is the Jesus Prayer.[14]

Edith goes on to talk about the many spiritual books she reads, including books by Philip Yancey, N.T. Wright, and her favourite, Richard Foster, mentioning specifically his book *Prayer: Finding the Heart's True Home*.[15] Edith's response differs from that of Jennifer, a twenty-five-year-old intern at an independent church in England, who also has a very active devotional life:

> [My devotions are] a combination of reading the scripture ... I try to do that as regularly as possible; I don't have [devotions] neces-sarily strict absolutely every day, but definitely probably five out of seven. [I] pray, read Christian books, [and] try and get into the practice of having something on the go that supplements my devotional life – listening to worship music. I'm aware of the ways in which I connect with God during the day that aren't necessari-ly sitting down, having a quiet time, so whether that's just having a quick prayer when I walk somewhere, when I'm between meet-ings, something like that. [It's] something that helps me feel con-nected to God, but not also being wracked with guilt, like "I did-n't do fifteen minutes [when I] sat down on my bed with my Bible today." Just little things like yes, I am connecting with God and this is good, and this is good for my soul and my spirituality. Yeah, without the kind of legalism of being like this must look like this every single day.

Typical of younger evangelicals, Jennifer's response rejects a "legalis-tic" or guilt-ridden approach to devotions, and is much more aspira-tional in tone. Also, her practices are more unscheduled than Edith's. I submit that the inward turn is evidenced by differences in language and not just practice: compared to their older counterparts, younger evangelicals were often more affective in tone (for example, they "feel connected," and do what's "good for my soul"). Yet, age differences were not limited to tone and language. Younger respondents indicat-ed irregular devotionalism. This is consistent with the findings of a study of evangelicals in Britain. Younger evangelicals were more likely to agree (29 per cent compared to 18 per cent overall) that they do not pray at a consistent time but when the "chance or need arises."[16]

Is this lack of devotional regularity among younger evangelicals a sign of the internal locus of authority, or just a result of more hectic or irregular schedules? I suspect that both factors matter and work together. Regarding the latter, younger cohorts are more likely to have irregular employment, including working part-time, being "on-call," or doing shift work. Millennials have young children who disrupt their plans, and university students have class schedules that vary from one day to the next. However, the research suggests that the issue is about more than time. Younger generations of full-time workers increasingly desire and ask for flexible hours and locations. (This was true even before COVID-19 disrupted work schedules and many were forced to work from home.) They want to work when and where it suits them, so that they can enjoy "good quality of life" and "work-life balance" (Miller and Yar 2019).[17] Research also shows that sleep and eating patterns are irregular among young adults, with negative effects on physical and mental health.[18] Some point to technology as a cause. Life increasingly centers on smart phones, which are not tied to place or time. Social media and online entertainment encroach on sleep, as emerging adults wake up and fall asleep to the blue light of their screens (Snyder and Chang 2019). This schedule irregularity is correlated with increased stress and anxiety, which can further disrupt routines (Schneider and Harknett 2019). Research has also shown how our digitally saturated lives are undermining evangelical spirituality (see, e.g., Song 2021). I am suggesting that schedules among younger cohorts tend to be individualized and irregular, and thus it is no surprise that their religious practices are less regular. And irregular schedules do not affect only devotionalism. Regular church attendance is also out of sync with irregular schedules and schedules that "work for me." Schedules and mental health issues undermine regularity. The result is practices that are increasingly sporadic – unscheduled and of shorter duration.

CHOOSING A CHURCH

If institutional authority is declining, we would expect to see low denominational loyalty and a "church-shopping" approach to choosing a church. That is exactly what I found among my sample of institutionally engaged evangelicals. Elsewhere, clergy have reported noticing a trend toward "circulating saints" (Bibby and Brinkerhoff 1973), where church growth is due largely to Christians coming from other churches, not from conversions. Some (mostly anecdotal) evidence suggests that this circulation or church switching has increased over the course of the COVID-19 pandemic (Kelley 2022).[19] The pandemic forced churches to close, and time away from church provided some laity with the opportunity to switch churches discreetly. Further, divisions over how churches handled masking and vaccination requirements likely promoted switching.[20] Yet even before the pandemic, my interviewees indicated that circulation was common. Pastor Jamie, whose church is part of the conservative Fellowship of Independent Evangelical Churches (FIEC) in Britain, had this response to our discussion about why his church was growing in numbers:

> We long to grow by conversions, and we've seen some, but I feel like it's a trickle, and even what we've seen, in the midst of subsequent discipleship there has been, you know, a high fallout rate. And there's another trend which I've noticed particularly in the last year. It's church transfers ... I wonder if at a site you become attractive to Christians who want something new, and you can't do much about it, but really don't want to grow that way. And one or two smaller churches have suffered because people are leaving them. But I can't forcibly send them back, in some cases I've said I think you should go back there and stay but, you know, it hasn't been a major growth thing, but it certainly seems to be a trend.

This problem of circulation and lack of loyalty to church and denomination is echoed by clergy who saw a consumeristic approach to church.

As with devotionalism, the tone and language used by younger evangelicals was consistently different than that of the older generation. Younger respondents normally talked about church shopping with little regard for denomination. They said that the church they settled on "resonated with my spirituality," or "was genuine," or they "liked the vibe." Their vague language suggests that it is hard to describe a "gut" feeling. In the following extract, a young Anglican mother, Leah, struggled to articulate why they choose to attend the parish of Andrew (a young priest we met in chapter 2) when they moved into the area:

> S: So, you said you checked out a few churches in the area. What attracted you to the church you're at now?

Leah: Well, we just walked in and (pause) – that's a really good question. We had been to quite a few churches and we just walked in and we just ... the sermon was ... I felt like we only had a couple of requirements. We wanted somewhere that was Bible believing and preached the Bible and did it well and lived it out kind of thing ... That was our only criteria [sic]. We just walked in and Andrew was giving this really great talk and there were a couple of other kids there ... [My son] was just running around the church and everyone was fine with it. It was super relaxed, but the sermon was really good. We just really loved the atmosphere there.

S: ... Were you looking just within the Church of England or were you looking more broadly?

Leah: We looked really broadly. We looked at – do you know Hillsong? There's a Hillsong [church] in [a nearby town] so we went there, and we went to a Baptist church in [another town]. We went to another Methodist church and all of them were fine, but ...

S: ... Since you checked out some churches in the area, what makes [Andrew's] church unique?

Leah: I think me and my husband got really excited about it. We just feel like there's a lot of people there that ... I don't know how to describe it ... it's because it's small. When we turned up there, there were maybe ten and twelve people in our congregation ... So, it felt really exciting when we got there; it just felt like the people there were really passionate about bringing other people from [the community] into church and loving them and telling them the gospel, which is just really exciting. That's something we really want to do as well.

We can see the emphasis on authenticity (or integrity) in the response of Cassie (the young English Baptist we met in chapter 2):

S: So what attracted you to [your church]?

Cassie: We were looking for a new church anyway. [I] had some issues with my old church, I didn't really get on with it. And so we'd been touring around Sheffield kind of looking at a couple of different churches for a couple of weeks ... Yeah, we just felt like it was the right place, like it wasn't perfect, but it was right.

S: Yeah, hard to find a perfect church I guess. What did you like about it, Cassie?

Cassie: So I liked the integrity of the leaders ... yeah, that's probably the most important thing, I think, integrity ... You could
   just see in their lives that they were practising what they were
   preaching as well. And they were really pushing toward ... living
   more godly lives and spending more time with God.
S: Yeah, so can you tell me why you left your previous church? I'm
   just interested in that too.
Cassie: Yeah, so I'd only been there for a year ... I just felt like that
   church was all about numbers ... And I think it was more on
   quantity than quality.

Finally, the following response from Julie, the young Canadian who
attends a Vineyard church, gives a sense of the "journey" process of
finding a church and of having "a sense" that the Vineyard was the
right church:

So, I grew up in Lutheran churches and then went to university. I
just sort of found the first Lutheran church and stuck there for
the whole time cause that's what Lutherans do. And ... there was a
period where I wasn't feeling very happy with my church and that
helped me shape, kind of, what I think a healthy church should
look like. So, when I moved to [a different city], I actually was
excited about church shopping, like kind of for the first time I
was gonna check some different churches out and thought it
would be a neat way to get to know the city. But [I] made the mistake, perhaps, of going to the Vineyard first and that ended my
church shopping. So, I appreciated the sense of flexibility in the
service, there was space to respond as people felt the Spirit lead ...
There's a love of good music in our church and, like, a real heart
for worship. I particularly appreciated all the folks that I saw sort
of wandering off the street, there's a very active compassion ministry at [the] Vineyard and that I appreciated. Actually, one other
thing that I noticed on my first Sunday was that in ... the bulletin,
they were listing that the tithe amount that they received was on
budget. And I was like, "wow a church that tithes?! No way!" ... It
was just one of the things in the mix ... that drew me there. And I
just had a sense for me personally, that, like, that God was present
there and at work. Like I had a really emotional experience for the
first several weeks that I went there.

Such affective responses were common. When respondents were able to state specifically what they liked about the church they attend, the most common answer was relational – for example, there was a "sense of community" or it was "welcoming." The second most common was related to "good biblical teaching," followed by lively worship music. Regarding how they became connected to the church, previous relationships were key, and often involved an invitation from a friend or a relative.

REGULAR ATTENDANCE:
THREE OUT OF FOUR SUNDAYS

In Western countries, church attendance is declining (Brenner 2011). It's worth noting, too, that weekly church attendance figures reported in most polls are inflated, because people report church attendance based more on identity ("I am a regular churchgoer") than on actual practice ("I was actually in church in the past seven days") (Brenner 2011; Chaves 2011). In Canada, weekly attendance has dropped from 67 per cent in 1946 to around 10 per cent today (Eagle 2011; Reimer 2017; Hiemstra 2020b; Cornelissen 2021). In the United Kingdom, weekly church attendance has declined from 10 per cent in 1980 to 5 per cent in 2020 (Brierley 2020). In the United States, weekly attendance is around 20 per cent, but is dropping, mostly because younger generations attend less often than older ones (Voas and Chaves 2016). We do not yet know where church attendance will settle after the pandemic, but all indications suggest that COVID-19 has accelerated the decline. Younger and less frequent attenders are least likely to return.[21]

Some respondents reported attending church more than once a week, and almost all of these were older people. They would attend both a morning and evening service on Sunday, or morning or evening prayers on a weekday, or a midweek prayer meeting. Among younger respondents, few would attend more than once a week (unless they were working in the church), and they considered three out of four Sundays to be regular attendance.

The clergy felt the effects of this decline. Several complained that "regular" church attendance was down to one to two times a month. Patrick, rector of an evangelical Anglican church in Toronto, stated:

I think the evangelical church is one of the last to be hit by the declining church attendance as a result of just Sunday not being seen as sacred anymore and parents making decisions for their kids that their sport activity or musical activity is more important than church activity. So, regular attendance is now once every three weeks when it was once every week. We're noticing that trend as families age, they're making decisions for other activities other than church. They'd still be committed and "regularly" attend, but they're now missing more Sundays than ever. I think prayer is probably still fairly present as a practice, but Bible reading is really low.

The idea of family activities getting in the way of church commitment was mentioned by other clergy. Concern about "the idolatry of the family" was raised by three clergy in interviews in England and has also been raised by the US evangelical flagship magazine *Christianity Today* (Shellnutt 2018). The concern is that family routines – like driving children to sports or clubs or a child's naptime – will keep them away from church services and activities. As one pastor of an independent church in northern England stated: "Family first – that's one of the big things you get over here, which, please don't misunderstand me: I love my family. But the kind of, that sort of almost slightly idolatrous take on family life that family life trumps everything else including the family of God."

I followed my question about church attendance with a question about whether or not people would sometimes miss church for vacation, illness, travel, and so on. What I found was also not surprising. All respondents admitted that they actually did not attend every week. In fact, in the end, no one stated categorically that they attend every week, even if they initially indicated that they did so. For example, sixty-seven-year-old Jacob, who attends an independent church in Manchester, answered my question about church attendance emphatically:

Jacob: When we're in town, we're at church.
S: Okay, so you're away ...
Jacob: Both of our mothers live about 250 miles away in Scotland, so six weeks we're visiting them, and we go off and do other things. But, if we're in Manchester on a Sunday, we're at church. There's no question about, "Oh, we can't be bothered this week." It would be as much as we possibly can.

In the end, Jacob concluded that they attended about three out of four Sundays. Similarly, Muriel, a recent retiree who also attends Jacob's church, told me:

> We go weekly. If we're away, then depending where we are and if we're visiting friends, we will go to church with them. If we're on holiday, we're a bit more flexible about that. It doesn't have to be … but when we're in Manchester, then yes, we're at church every week. They're my community and the people I love and want to be with.

Muriel settled on four out of five Sundays. Randall, a seventy-year-old who attends a Salvation Army corps in eastern Canada, said that he attends "whenever the doors are open … unless I work, you know, or I'm away or whatever."

POLITICS

Of late, a lot of media and academic attention has focused on (white) evangelicals and politics in the United States. Since the election of Donald Trump in 2016, the strong link between white evangelicals and conservative politics has been in the spotlight (e.g., Fitzgerald 2017; Whitehead and Perry 2020; Du Mez 2020; Martí 2020; Butler 2021). To quote American sociologist Gerardo Martí (2020, 251), "evangelicalism today might be defined more accurately not as a theological orientation but as a political one," and there has been a "marriage" between "white evangelicalism, the capitalist elite, and political control … forged out of mutual desire for power and protection" (253). For Martí, US evangelicals' strategy to reclaim a Christian America has moved on from evangelism to a strategy of gaining political control.

By contrast, evangelicals in Britain and Canada wanted me to know that they were not like evangelicals in the United States, where political partisanship seems to go hand-in-hand with evangelical faith (Gadhini 2022; Smith 2021). Research generally agrees that evangelicals outside the United States are comparatively less aligned with conservative politics and less politically engaged (Gaddini 2022a; G. Smith and Woodhead 2018; Bean 2014; Malloy 2009; Guest 2015; Hatcher 2017; Soper 1997).

Why? The list of reasons is long. British and Canadian political structures make for fewer opportunities for populist evangelical lobbying (Carwana 2021; Hatcher 2017; Soper 1994). Hatcher's (2017) comparative study of the political identities of British evangelicals found that "their religious and political identities are separate parts of their selves" (2), and thus, that there was no clear party alignment. Compared to the United States, evangelicals in both Canada and Britain tend to be more left-leaning economically, and embrace a broader spectrum of social issues, including environmentalism and support for immigration (Hatcher 2017; G. Smith 2015; Guest 2015; Hoover et al. 2002; Malloy 2011). Greg Smith (2015) notes that British evangelicals show concern for the poor and international justice, a finding that is similar to that in Canada. In addition, there is less distrust of the state and elite society in Britain and Canada (Brown and Woodhead 2016; Reimer and Sikkink 2020; Hatcher 2017). Finally, most evangelicals in Canada and Britain have long accepted their marginal status and are not keen on using political might to recreate Christendom in their countries (Malloy 2019; Hatcher 2017).

Yet, two recent events have unsettled the comparatively placid world of Canadian and British evangelical politics. The first event was the Brexit referendum of 2016 in Britain, in which a narrow majority voted to leave the European Union. Anglicans leaned toward leaving, while nonconforming evangelical denominations leaned toward remaining (Kolpinskaya and Fox 2019; Gaddini 2022a; G. Smith and Woodhead 2018). Non-Anglican evangelicals wanted to remain partly because of their support for immigration. Further, British evangelicals' political interests were piqued during Trump's presidency, since they tend to be more "international in outlook" that their US counterparts (G. Smith 2020, 18). The second event was the 2022 truckers' convoy in Canada protesting vaccination requirements. It mixed religious and political messages (K. Stiller 2022) and gained from considerable support from the American right wing (Hajiani 2022).[22] While such events reawaken concerns that the "Christian right" is coming to Canada (e.g., MacDonald 2011) or Britain (e.g., Kettell 2016), in reality, evangelical politicization is and remains comparatively weak in those countries.

In both Britain and Canada, evangelicals may tend to vote for conservatives, who are more likely to reflect their views on issues like same-sex marriage or abortion, but partisanship has not reached the levels of conservative alignment that we see in the United States (Guest 2015; Bean, Gonzalez, and Kaufman 2008; Malloy 2013; Hatcher 2017; Walton with Hatcher and Spencer 2013). Among evangelical voters, 52 per cent voted for the Conservative Party of Canada in the 2015 election, while over 80 per cent voted for the Republican Party in the 2016 US election.[23] Yet, value alignment might not be the only cause for evangelical political conservativism; they may be influenced by their churches as well.

Are evangelicals hearing political messages from the pulpit? The answer is yes, but it is more common in the United States than in Canada. If "political messages" include topics like the economy, war, abortion, and sexual identity, then about one-third of sermons in the United States include something about politics, broadly defined (Boussalis, Coan, and Holman 2021). In her study of evangelical churches in the United States and Canada, Lydia Bean (2014) found that partisan cues from American pulpits were rare, but there were subtle (and sometimes not so subtle) cues from church members that were pro-Republican. In Canadian and British churches, partisan cues were largely non-existent (Evangelical Alliance 2015; Bean 2014). I do not recall hearing any partisan cues in the churches I visited in England or Canada, either during the service or in the "parking lot" conversations before or after church.

Whatever the political alignment of evangelicals, very few of my interviewees were involved in politics. Given that active churchgoers are more (not less) likely to be involved in civil society in general, including politics (Putnam and Campbell 2010; Gerber, Gruber, and Hungerman 2016), my sample is biased toward political involvement. Yet, when asked "Are you involved in politics in any way?" nearly all respondents said no. The few who said they were involved in politics were usually non-partisan and minimally involved. By minimally involved, I mean that they voted, followed political issues, and/or occasionally signed email petitions. Much more common were responses like Cam's, a very conservative Anglican in England:

S: So, political activism – were you involved in being politically active at all?
Cam: No.
S: Do you have a position on that, one way or another, or you just haven't done it?
Cam: I just find it so fraught ... I think it's really important but I find it really frustrating because I see things just being really hyper-politicized, either in the public sphere or in the church,

and that frustrates me too. Often I seek to see the complexity of things ... so when it comes to voting, I've voted all over the place in different elections. I don't have any party affiliation.

Jackson, the Canadian Anglican youth leader we met in the previous chapter, said:

I don't think there's anything wrong with Christians being politically active and being involved in politics; however, if you're involved in pastoral ministry, leadership in the church, I do think you should keep as much as possible your political views to yourself, not because it's wrong to hold political views, but because I think it's wrong to use your influence as a pastor, as a leader in the church to try to influence others and to promote your political causes ... I think it can just become a really messy situation ... especially I think in the [United] States right now, it's become just a, a kind of glaring example of why that can be a really dangerous thing.

Jackson was not the only interviewee who thought church leaders should remain silent on political issues. Whether inside or outside of the church, the consensus was that voting was good, while promoting a political agenda was not (Hatcher 2017; Bean 2014). Politics seemed to be an uncomfortable topic, possibly because the modern zeitgeist views it as a personal decision.

VOLUNTEERING AND GIVING

In general, there is a strong correlation between church attendance and voluntarism and giving (Reimer and Wilkinson 2015; Putnam and Campbell 2010). Among the reasons for this correlation are that the kind of people who attend churches (i.e., those with higher than average education and greater social capital (see Putnam and Campbell 2010)) are more likely to volunteer; the churches' emphasis on altruism; and the opportunities provided by churches to give and volunteer. Evangelicals, partly because of their institutional religiosity, give and volunteer at higher rates than non-evangelicals, including Catholics, other Protestants, and the non-religious (C. Smith and Emerson with Snell 2008; Reimer and Wilkinson 2015). However, research shows that evangelical giving is far below the 10 per cent tithe recommended by many Christian churches (Smith and Emerson with Snell 2008; Reimer and Wilkinson 2015).

Although evangelicals volunteer and give both within and outside the church at high rates, the voluntarism and giving of my interviewees were primarily church related. Church-sponsored activities were often for community members who did not attend the church, and these activities were more likely to have a social justice than an evangelistic focus (although some social justice activities can also have an evangelistic element to them). These include immigrant/refugee support groups, soup kitchens, and more.

Reported giving was surprisingly high, and most were willing to tell me whether or not they tithe (a few even gave dollar/pound amounts). The average giving among the lay respondents was a "biblical" tithe of 10 per cent of their total family income; often they emphasized that it was 10 per cent of their gross (pre-tax) income.[24] If all those who were not clear on their percentage of giving are placed in the "less than 10 per cent" category, then roughly equal numbers of respondents were above 10 per cent and below it. Unlike devotionalism, there were no clear age differences in giving and volunteering. Several young respondents (in their thirties or younger) gave more than 10 per cent. The highest level of giving was a twenty-five-year-old from England who claimed that he gave away 25 per cent of his income. Those below 10 per cent often stated that they give regularly but not at 10 per cent, and were more likely to be without a working income. To give a sense of one of the more generous respondents, here is my conversation with Alistair, a seventy-year-old Anglican from Manchester:

S: Tell me about giving or tithing, that area of practice.
Alistair: Well, I started doing that as a child, really. I always gave something of my pocket money to – initially to the Bible class I attended as a child before I went to church. That started me in the habit of giving regularly. As soon as I earned enough to pay tax – I was twenty-five by that time – I took out a legal covenant with an organization that can recover the tax paid on the amount that I give so from time to time when I review this, I try and raise it to ... maybe more than 20 per cent of my gross income ... It usually goes to Christian charities, [but] there are organizations like Water Aid, for instance. Do you know about Water Aid?

S: Yes, I've heard of it.

Alistair: Provides sanitation water supplies in areas in the Third World where they don't have it. That's one of the charities I support through this organization.

S: ... Would the majority of your giving be to [your church]?

Alistair: No.

S: No? Just a portion of it?

Alistair: Well, I mean, goodness me, when you look at the Third World and you see the needs there, compared to the needs [here], it would be terribly selfish. I think that's one of the problems that many Christians have, or many people have. They see the needs under their nose, and they ignore the far greater needs farther away.

S: ... Do you do some volunteering that's not church related, just in the community?

Alistair: Yes.

Alistair went on to talk about several local organizations he volunteered for, including one that converts old railroad lines to walking trails. He was also a trustee of a fund that gives grants to charities in Manchester. He is typical among respondents in that his voluntarism and giving focuses on social justice issues; he is not typical in that most respondents directed at least half of their giving to their local church.

Unlike when discussing evangelism and political involvement, respondents rarely hedged or qualified their responses in areas of giving and volunteering. Since the zeitgeist of Western culture would indicate that giving and volunteering are personal decisions and a net "good," there is little social pressure to qualify responses. In addition, one should not assume that these high levels of giving stem from clear expectations communicated from the pulpit. Many pastors are hesitant to speak on giving because it's a touchy subject among parishioners and can be perceived as clergy trying to line their own pockets (Smith and Emerson with Snell 2008). As one Anglican priest near London said, "I think we really struggle to talk about giving, we struggle to talk about generosity ... [A person's attitude is] simply I need more and I'll give away a little bit if I've got some leftover."

EVANGELISM REDEFINED

Evangelicals evangelize. At least that is what they are expected to do. Their activism focuses on the Great Commandment ("Love the Lord with all your heart ... and love your neighbor as yourself," Matthew 22:37–9), and the Great Commission ("Go and make disciples of all nations," Matthew 29:19) (Reimer and Wilkinson 2015). However, as the late evangelical author Dallas Willard (2006) suggested, some wonder if the "Great Commission" has become the "Great Omission." My interviews suggest that it has.[25] Indeed, a recent study (Flourishing Congregations Institute and Alpha Canada 2021) suggests that the majority of Canadian church leaders prefer "showing" their faith through actions as opposed to "telling" people about Christ, and many did not think that one should try to convert those of another faith or no faith. It seems evangelism is unpopular in Canada, even within the church. One Canadian Anglican priest whom I interviewed said:

> When some liberal [clergy] mention to me that, "All faiths are the same. Why do you work so hard to evangelize? Even those who have no faith are still okay." But for me as an evangelical, I think if it is okay, Jesus didn't need to come, right? Jesus asked us to preach the gospel and have a Great Commission and that means nothing to you then.

What this priest is picking up on is the cultural commitment to perennialism, which, coupled with internal authority, results in a double whammy against evangelism.

Most of my respondents do not overtly evangelize – that is, they do not devote time and energy specifically to evangelism. Rather, respondents would speak of "lifestyle evangelism," noting that "actions speak louder than words." They try to talk about their faith "when the opportunity comes up," they say. This seems to mean that they try to be nice and hope someone asks them why they are kind, so they have an opportunity to witness (McAlpine et al. 2021). Not one lay respondent spoke of overt evangelism that was done privately, based on their own initiative.[26] All overt evangelism was by groups in church-sponsored (or other ministry-sponsored) events. Typical in this regard was Susan, a fifty-eight-year-old who became a Christian about twenty years ago through the Alpha program, sponsored by the independent Canadian church she still attends:

> S: Are you involved in evangelism in any way?
>
> Susan: Formally, you mean, through the church?
>
> S: Yeah.
>
> Susan: No.
>
> S: Informally?
>
> Susan: Well, informally, most of the people I deal with on a daily basis are the people I work with. So, yes, my heart is that they would understand that there's more to their lives than what they're experiencing right now.
>
> S: Do you talk to people at work much about your faith or [are there] not many opportunities?
>
> Susan: There's not a lot of opportunities. I find that if you bring up anything too specific, people are pretty quick to change the subject. You can talk to them indirectly, I find, quite easily, when just talking about your life. Without saying, "Jesus gets me through my day," you can certainly get that in there without it being quite so blatant as that and without closing their ears, which is kind of ... it's a fine line to walk. Plus, people, when they tell you about their problems, then I feel like that gives you a bit of an opportunity to talk about, "Okay, I went through that and this is what helped me."

Like most respondents, Susan said "no" when I asked if she was involved in evangelism, noting that she did not find her work context very amenable to evangelism. Her response is typical of most evangelicals, who avoid the practice entirely, unless someone shows interest. If they do talk about their faith, they normally do so in a subtle way.

Even if evangelicals rarely evangelize, most still think it's a good idea. Respondents often tried to explain their lack of evangelism while affirming that they should evangelize. Mildred, an English Baptist in her seventies, said, "I think we have to be [involved in evangelism]. It's not my top gifting. It's my bottom gifting. It's part of who we are as Christians, isn't it? Some people are gifted with evangelism and that is their priority. My priority is more pastoral." A lay Anglican academic from western Canada said, "I think most twentieth-century

Protestant evangelism has been a wasted effort ... It's something obviously we should be doing, but how we do it is a different question ... So put me down as a cautious – no, a fan of evangelism, but I haven't found a way that I could whole-heartily support."

Those who did *overtly* evangelize did so through church-supported efforts. Yet, in most cases, these efforts involved indirect evangelism: churches would sponsor events focused on hospitality, relationship building, or social justice, and participants would look for opportunities to share their faith during the event. "Seeker Sundays" were common, where church members were encouraged to invite "unsaved" friends to come to church. Some churches with charismatic leanings would offer "healing" and "prayer" ministries to people on the street. They would hang up a banner and invite people into the church for prayer or would pray for them on the street. Offering Alpha courses – where non-believers are introduced to the faith through a series of videos and discussions over shared meals, usually held in churches – was also common.

A few interviewees went to churches that engaged in more direct evangelism. For instance, a group (often young people) would go out to public spaces and seek to engage people in spiritual discussions. They might hand out flyers and invite people to the church or give out free food or drinks. Micah, a forty-year-old man from a New Frontiers church in Northern England described such events:

> Every month we have a kind of a session in [the] town centre giving something out or doing carol singing at Christmas, that sort of thing. We've done a fun day for a local community ... That went down very well. But, in terms of evangelism, I struggle to talk to new people generally (laughter) even though my job kind of forces me into speaking to new people all the time ... I find it a struggle without having a purpose from the other person's point of view for ... talking to them. So I find it very, very difficult to go out and do these kind of things ... Where I see I'm most gifted is kind of in this home group setting, where I am able to kind of develop other people and encourage other people with gifts to go out and use that gift. I think I need to gain boldness in evangelism, if anything, but I'm not a street-preacher; I'm not a guy who'll go up and down and just talk to fifty different people on the street. I find that too terrifying, as it were.

Micah was not the only one to distinguish himself from street preachers and religious people who knock on doors. Among my respondents, aggressive evangelism was roundly rejected. I did not interview anyone who felt that they had the gift of evangelism, only those who felt they did not. In general, research in Canada has suggested that evangelism is not very effective, nor is it widely practised by evangelicals (James 2011; Reimer and Wilkinson 2015). Indeed, evangelism is "frowned upon" in their societies (Wilkinson and Ambrose 2020, 17).

HOMO LITURGICUS

In his books *You Are What You Love* (2016) and *Desiring the Kingdom* (2009), philosopher James K.A. Smith attempts to recalibrate evangelical thinking about Christian devotion and discipleship. To do so, he begins with a foundational question: What is the human person? According to Smith, evangelicals embrace a faulty Cartesian view of humans ("I think, therefore I am"), believing that we are primarily "thinking things," and that our bodies are "extraneous, temporary vehicles for trucking around our ... 'minds'" (J.M.K. Smith 2016, 3). Within this view of humans, Christian discipleship is about knowledge acquisition – reading the Bible, listening to sermons, taking "world view" classes at a Christian college. Such knowledge presumably creates good Christians because they have more theologically sound information. As we all know, "right thinking leads to right living."

Not so fast, says Smith. While the life of the mind is important, such a model of humans fails to recognize that humans are not primarily "minds on a stick," but beings that *desire*. Persons love, they are emotional and passionate, and they desire the telos of human flourishing. If humans are primarily "heart" instead of "head" – beings who "can't not love" (J.M.K. Smith 2016, 10) – then, what is important is reordering our desires, or our loves. We must learn to love rightly. This is done, Smith argues, by moral habits – habits that are developed through practice. In other words, rituals, or repeated good habits, orient our loves toward the correct telos.

We all have experienced knowing what we should do – like eating healthy foods, exercising, studying, getting proper sleep – but not actually doing it. What we believe and what we do can be miles apart, because we do not actually desire the right thing. Thus, for Smith, behaviour normally comes before belief, not the other way around.

We learn to love the things we ritually practise. Of course, rituals or "liturgies" (J.M.K. Smith 2009) include practices like church attendance and prayer, but they also include surfing the internet, shopping, or hanging out with friends. All such habits shape what we love (e.g., we learn to love to shop, and the stuff we shop for, by ritually practising shopping). For Smith, we are not primarily *homo sapiens* (wise humans) but *homo liturgicus* (embodied, practising humans).

Relevant to this argument is the response of Scott, a western Canadian Anglican priest whom I quoted earlier in this chapter:

> Scott: People are used to being so entertained that, people don't really understand what church is for and so [there are] some people I think who come to church, wanting to be entertained, when really that's not what it's about, and so I think fighting against that ... I think all those media influences shape them into thinking that we want to be entertained, and to be served as well. So there's an idea that, you know, that I'm there as the priest to serve them, to give them ... spiritual goods and services, not there as their spiritual leader to help them serve their community or serve their broader context, serve God.
> S: Yeah, it's kind of a consumer thing ...
> Scott: Oh yeah, consumerism is huge, I think, as an influence.
> S: ... How can the church protect people against this?
> Scott: Well, I, I think having a liturgy ... like James K.A. Smith, I think some of his work talking about ... when we go shopping we're participating in the liturgy, and so I think we need to fight against it on the basis of a stronger liturgy, but we also need to give it time, like, so that means, Christians need to be involved daily in reinforcing the liturgy of their lives through morning prayer, evening prayer, Bible study, meditation, contemplation on the scriptures, using spiritual disciplines, I think, as a daily practice.

If James K.A. Smith and Reverend Scott are correct, practices matter. They affect not only what evangelicals do, but also what they love.

CONCLUSION

This chapter has suggested that evangelical orthopraxy is being reshaped. It is changing because of individualized, irregular schedules, which result in devotional practices and church attendance becoming more sporadic. External authorities like the church or the Bible will have less sway if church attendance and Bible reading are decreasing. Evangelicals "shop" for churches, and they stay with the one that "feels right." Few evangelize, and those who do rarely do so in overt ways. Evangelicals justify their lack of evangelism by observing that it is not their "gift" and that there are "few opportunities."

In addition, the standard for good practice has also changed. It is not based on what the church prescribes. Orthopraxy is less about living as the external authority (denomination authorities or the Bible) dictates and more about living according to one's authentic self. When the authority comes from inside, blind obedience to church requirements is inauthentic. Practices have to work for the individual. Practices that individuals feel are inconvenient, stressful, or awkward (like evangelism) are not good for the self, and thus, are done infrequently.

Evangelical beliefs are changing: they are increasingly qualified. And evangelical practices are changing as well: they are becoming increasingly sporadic. Unpopular beliefs or practices are particularly affected. Evangelicals, even the most dedicated, will distance themselves from church authority as they find their own path, and as they follow their heart.

Faith Transmission:
Will the Next Generation Commit to the Faith?

There are few things that concern evangelical parents more than the faith commitment of their children. The plethora of evangelical books on the topic indicates its importance (Anthony 2007; Frisk 2019; Garland 2012; Holmen and Siewert 2018; Keeley 2008; Kehrwald et al. 2016; Moore 2018; K. Powell and Clark 2011; Shirley 2018). When Canadian evangelical pastors were asked to rate the priorities of their churches, 80 per cent ranked "faith development of children and youth" as a "very high" priority, which was nearly 20 per cent above the next highest priority (Reimer and Wilkinson 2015). The parents among the 124 British and Canadian evangelicals interviewed for this study were no different. Many of their adult or teen children no longer attended church, and some had left the faith completely. Others had children or grandchildren who were active in their faith, but they were worried about their future. The cultural current pulling youth away from evangelical orthodoxy and orthopraxy is strong, as is evident in the words of Reverend Gideon Chow, rector of a Canadian Chinese Anglican church:

> Gideon: Our young people left the church because they feel ... that faith is personal, that faith is optional; so, if they go to university, they feel that they don't need to go to church. They can just be themselves and do their own thing. We see a great loss of our next generation coming to church ... And much of the parents of our congregation share with me how upset they are to see their children leaving church.
>
> S: Yeah, that's actually one of my questions; what needs to happen in order for the next generation to have strong Christian faith? What do you think needs to happen?

Gideon: Well, my wife and I, we have been praying for our children and we try our best to speak to them about experiencing
God in their lives, encourage them to have devotions every day,
we do devotions with them.

Reverend Gideon goes on to express his own concerns about his
teenage children, one of whom is in university. His daughter feels
pressure to avoid praying publicly before meals because "no one is
doing it," so he reminds her that her Muslim friends pray publicly, so
she can too. Gideon sees the responsibility of faith transmission as primarily resting with fathers,[1] but bemoans the fact that many churches do not teach parents well:

I think parents play a major role, particularly the father, from personal demonstration to discussing the faith. I noticed a lot of Anglican Caucasians that I talk to, even if they grew up in the church, at
home they never talk about God at all ... [My friend], he's been in
church all his life, and I would say he's around seventy-something,
and he said the church never taught him how to pray. He can hold
onto the prayer book to pray, but he cannot say a prayer by himself.
What kind of Christians are we producing?

Not only do evangelicals prioritize faith transmission, they invest in it.
Research in the United States shows that, compared to mainline Protestant churches, evangelical churches are more likely to employ a full-time
youth minister and invest in summer camps, youth mission trips, youth
groups, and children's programs.[2] James Wellman (2008) states that, in
evangelical churches, parents expect their children to enjoy church. If
not, the church needs to improve its ministries, or parents will head elsewhere. By contrast, in mainline churches, if children do not enjoy
church, the assumption is that it's the child's fault, not the church's.

THE DATA ON FAITH TRANSMISSION

In spite of efforts by churches and parents to keep their children in
the evangelical fold, many of them leave by the time they are young
adults. This should not be surprising, considering the societal trajectory toward internal authority and self-spirituality. If young adults are
to create their own path, and if the church is not perceived to be helpful in their personal quest, then they will not attend.

Despite the challenges, evangelicals are doing better at retention, on average, than mainline Protestant and Catholics. The title of a report on Canadian youth and faith transmission, *Hemorrhaging Faith*, leaves little doubt about what the authors found. Youth are leaving the church in droves. That said, Canadian evangelical churches are not "haemorrhaging" quite as badly as other denominations: 63 per cent of those raised as evangelicals maintained evangelical affiliation as young adults, whereas the retention rate was 34 per cent for mainline Protestants and 47 per cent for Catholics (Penner et al. 2012). Other data agree. A 2019 poll of over 5,000 Canadians (with 379 evangelicals) found that only 57 per cent of those raised evangelical were still evangelical as adults.[3] These data are borne out by attendance figures: only 55 per cent of those evangelicals who attended weekly as children still attend weekly as young adults (Reimer and Wilkinson 2015). It is not that youth are switching to other denominations or religions: most of those who disaffiliated between childhood and adulthood became "nones," or those with no affiliation (Penner et al. 2012). The inward turn is hard on all forms of institutional faith.

A recent book on British Catholic retention, *Mass Exodus*, reinforces these findings (Bullivant 2019). Nearly all Britons disaffiliating from the Christian religion of their youth are becoming religious nones, or what Bullivant (2017) calls "nonverts." The nones are winning the day. Evangelism is not. "For every twenty-six former Christians who now identify with No religion, there is only one former None who now identifies with a Christian label of some kind" (Bullivant 2017, 13). Linda Woodhead (2016) states that the "massive cultural shift from Christian to non-religious Britain has come about largely because of children ceasing to follow the religious commitments of their parents" (249). In the United Kingdom, 56 per cent of those raised in non-denominational or Baptist churches retain their affiliation into adulthood. In contrast to trends in the United States and Canada, this figure is below that for Catholics (63 per cent) and Anglicans (59 per cent) (Bullivant 2017). In the United States, retention rates are a bit higher than in Canada and the United Kingdom, and, as in Canada, evangelicals hold on to their youth at higher rates than Catholics and other Protestants (C. Smith and Snell 2009; Chaves 2011). According to the Pew Research Center (2015), 65 per cent of American adults raised evangelical still identify as evangelical, compared to 59 per cent of Catholics and 45 per cent of mainline Protestants.

Overall, the data from Canada, the United Kingdom, and the United States indicate that evangelical churches lose at least one-third of their childhood affiliates by young adulthood. Many more adults attend less often than they did growing up. Finally, in all three countries, youth are more likely than their elders to be (and become) nones. Seventy per cent of sixteen- to twenty-nine-year-olds in the United Kingdom claim to have no religion, compared to 49 per cent of the general population (Bullivant 2017). In Canada and the United States in 2016, about 34 per cent and 32 per cent of youth, respectively, were religious nones, proportions higher than the respective national averages (23 per cent and 22 per cent; see Thiessen and Wilkins-Laflamme 2020).

The reasons for this exodus, this haemorrhaging, are complex. As one way of uncovering those reasons, I asked clergy and parents how Western culture was influencing the faith of their youth. A thematic analysis of their responses shows that the erosion of orthodoxy and orthopraxy was their primary concern.[4] Their responses can be divided into societal *causes* and *effects*.

Regarding causes, the most common response was that youth's constant connectivity online affected their faith negatively (discussed by thirty-seven interviewees). Respondents pointed to multiple challenges associated with online activity. First, they noted that the amount of time spent online leaves little time for activities that strengthen faith. "You can't disciple on one hour a week," said one pastor, when the laity spends dozens of hours online. Second, social media and the internet reinforce messages that are incompatible with faith. They can act as "echo chambers," so that people hear only from those they already agree with. This can keep people from considering the claims of Christianity or from changing their views on a subject to align with Christian views. The internet is not a good place for reasoned dialogue or debate about things religious. Instead, it seems to feed extremism, whether religious or secular. Third, respondents noted that youth's constant need for entertainment and distraction conflicts with church attendance and devotions. Some clergy stated that exposure to media entertainment meant that laity expected to be entertained at church. These clergy recognized that their in-person and online presentations could not compete with YouTube or Netflix in entertainment value. Fourth, social media can be hard on mental health, respondents said. Shaming and cyberbullying, and comparing themselves with others, make it hard for youth to feel good about themselves. Finally, the majority of evangelical respondents viewed the internet

itself as a neutral tool, noting that the main issue was the content
(see also H.A. Campbell 2010). Some content, like sexually explicit
images, is detrimental, while other content, like religious programming, is good. The key is for parents to monitor what children and
youth are viewing.

The internet was not the only cause of eroding faith that was cited
by my respondents. They also pointed to individualism. Western society promotes individual rights, the autonomy of the self, and self-focus
on one's own well-being. This has had deleterious effects on community and church participation. The more historically informed, most
commonly Anglican clergy, also pointed to the effects of the Enlightenment, or the disestablishmentarianism and anti-institutionalism of
the 1960 and 1970s as antecedents of this individualism. Busyness was
another concern. Families were always on the go, keeping them from
church and devotional practices. Consumerism was a concern voiced
by roughly twenty respondents, particularly clergy. In their view, laity
expect churches, like grocery stores, to offer the products consumers
want at good value for the money. By conforming to consumers' taste
in worship style and stance on ethical issues, churches risk compromising their orthodoxy.

Regarding effects, the result of these societal influences that was
most commonly cited (by fifty-three interviewees) was changing
sexual ethics, particularly toward same-sex marriage and LGBTQ+
identities. Clergy, and to a lesser degree parents, were concerned
about the societal emphasis on finding one's identity, which encouraged youth to explore non-heterosexual identities. Also mentioned,
albeit less frequently, were softening attitudes toward abortion and
premarital sex/cohabitation. Another effect of Western culture's
changing sexual ethics is the tension or distance it creates between
evangelicals and most others. This tension means that evangelicals
are viewed as bigoted and narrow-minded; and it also creates a
major roadblock for outsiders who might be considering converting
to evangelical Christianity.

The second most common theme related to the effects of society on
faith was declining religiosity. Clergy noted that their congregants
now considered regular church attendance to be one to two times a
month instead of more than once a week. People come late, they don't
get involved, and yet they want a "full range of services," one clergy stated. This casual, consumeristic approach carried into their devotional
lives. Bible reading, as noted in chapter 3, is on the decline, and bibli-

cal literacy is very low, even among the committed. Low levels of other devotional practices – tithing, fasting, prayer – were also mentioned.

Another common and related theme, not surprisingly, was declining biblical authority. For my respondents, biblical authority was giving way to the authority of the self. Institutional authority was passé, and personal experience was the new authority. Respondents also used words like "relativism" and "tolerance" for diverse views to describe the eroding effects of secular culture on authority.

ALTERNATIVE AUTHORITIES

The interviews I conducted capture the alternative authorities that are promoted by Western culture and that are supplementing or replacing religious institutional authority. As I argued in chapter 1, the modern emphasis on internal authority and personal autonomy does not necessarily mean greater freedom from societal expectations and constraints. Indeed, the modern zeitgeist speaks with authority, providing clear messages that shape beliefs, values, and behavioural norms. Scholars of religion have commented on how these alternate authorities operate within evangelicalism, and their arguments are corroborated by my respondents.

Heidi Campbell (2020) argues that the internet creates an alternative authority. Digital technologies have the power to displace traditional institutional religious authority with "algorithmic authority," leveraged by those who create online content. Algorithms select which messages are received and thus shape attitudes and values. These virtual authorities often speak louder than pastors, undermining and even replacing the authority of the church. Song (2021) notes that it is not just the content youth view on the internet that can threaten faith commitments, but the medium itself (see also Brooks and Nicholas 2015). The internet is not a neutral tool (a perception that is somewhat different from that held by most of my respondents). It rewires our brains toward constant entertainment and connectivity, distracts us from spiritual disciplines, and adds to anxiety and stress.

Vaca (2019) and Grem (2017) have argued that evangelicals have also embraced the alternative authority of commercial markets. They state that evangelicals have not only occasionally borrowed secular business strategies, but that they have fully embraced such strategies along with their logics and values. Guest (2022) shows that evangelicals have embraced a "*cosmetic authority* that mirrors styles and standards popularised in entertainment media" (491, my emphasis) and that mimics secular marketing discourse and images. They have also embraced a "*strategic authority* that baptises neoliberal economic virtues of enterprise, industriousness and instrumentalism for Evangelical application" (491; my emphasis). These new authorities are not simply utilized for surface, instrumental reasons like marketing or lobbying the government; rather, the values they represent are internalized by evangelicals. Yet, these external influences do not result in complete accommodation, because "these authorities are secondary insofar as they do not ultimately supplant primary authorities like scripture or the Holy Spirit; rather, they offer templates for how Evangelical convictions may be clothed in cultural forms that are compelling to a 21st century audience" (503). My interviewees also see these alternative authorities in their churches, and they commented on the effects of secular media and commercialism on faith. Yet, external influences from Western culture are not the primary problem in faith transmission. The primary problem is internal – that is, within evangelicalism itself.

CLERGY ON FAITH TRANSMISSION

Surprisingly, clergy did not think the increasingly post-Christian culture was the greatest impediment to faith transmission. Nor did they think that the biggest problem was related to the church or its programs. Without prompting, clergy pointed to parents as the most important factor in faith transmission. The vast majority of clergy made it clear that the responsibility for faith transmission belonged primarily to parents, but that parents often passed the responsibility on to the churches. Rodney, a young Anglican priest from Manchester, stated emphatically that the key to faith transmission was "parents taking responsibility. I mean, that's it. As soon as they sub-contract discipleship to the church, we're screwed. Yeah, that's it." Patrick, an Anglican priest from Toronto agrees: "Parents often out-source discipleship and formation to the church, and you can't do formation in an hour a week. It's trying to help parents and give the parents the tools to make discipleship a part of what they're doing at home." Instead of shirking their responsibility, parents need to live out their faith at home. This involves modelling devotional practices, regularly attending church together, and talking about spiritual things with their children. Alan, pastor of a Pentecostal church in Manchester, emphasized a consistent lifestyle, so that "the Sunday morning behaviour isn't something separate from behaviour the rest of the week. The values that are spoken in church are also values that are followed and exhibited through the rest of the week so there's an authenticity and a reality and a relevance to the faith of parents." Similarly, Aidan, an Anglican rector in Manchester, says "I think encouraging families – and this is where for us, we're kind of starting from scratch in some families – is encouraging them to nurture faith outside of Sundays. It isn't the church's responsibility to raise the kids in faith. It is a parental responsibility to raise their kids, so to encourage Bible reading as a family or prayer as a family and talking about faith."

Some clergy suggested that some parents were dropping the ball. "Teaching is lacking at home," said one Anglican rector in eastern Canada. Parents allow other activities, particularly sports and vacations, to replace church attendance. Recall the clergy's concern over the "idolatry of the family," mentioned in chapter 3, where parents prioritize family activity above church. Children's sporadic attendance, weak devotionalism, and unorthodoxy reflect a lack of parental commitment, clergy surmise. Others have also noted the tendency of parents to off-load responsibility for child spiritual formation to the "professionals" at church (Frisk 2019). It may be that parents feel inadequate to the task, or feel they are too busy to do it properly (Kehrwald et al. 2016). Edwin, an Anglican priest in London, suggested that parents were afraid to impose their faith on their kids:

> Christian parents ... are terrified, or worse, apathetic about passing on the faith to their own children. And this, you know, [is] the way our society ticks, that of the best Christian faith, or any sort of religious faith, is something you should keep personal, and private, and shouldn't be imposed on anyone else. And children especially are to be nurtured in their unknowingness because you don't want to presume for them. And it's devastating.

Research consistently supports what these clergy know from experience – that parental example is the most powerful predictor in faith transmission. The following list shows, in descending order, the strongest predictors of evangelical youth faith transmission, based on research in Canada, the United States, and Britain.

1. Parental modelling: If both parents attend the same church weekly with their children, model devotional practices at home, invite conversations about spiritual things, and maintain warm, open relationships with their children, the majority (73 per cent, based on Canadian data) will be weekly attenders as young adults.[5] Research in the United States shows that parental religiosity is by far the strongest predictor of youth religiosity (Bengtson with Putney and Harris 2013; C. Smith, Ritz, and Rotolo 2020; C. Smith with Denton 2005; C. Smith, Longest, et al. 2014; Pearce and Denton 2011; K. Powell and Clark 2011). For example, Bengtson and his colleagues (2013) found that parental modelling and a warm relationship between parents and children were the most important predictors of successful faith transmission. In fact, parental influence stretches way beyond their modelling of faith. In addition, parents influence the relationships and activities their children are involved in, which, as I will show below, are also important.

2. Other reinforcing adult relationships: Active parental modelling seems to be necessary but not sufficient for successfully passing on the faith (C. Smith, Longest, et al. 2014). Youth are much more likely to stick with their faith if other adults who form relationships with them also model authentic faith (K. Powell and Clark 2011). Youth leaders, teachers, pastors, grandparents, and other adults can provide network closure – that is, relational networks where religious socialization is reinforced from multiple sources (C. Smith 2003b). Churches can offer attractive youth programming, which is important to engage youth, but, to keep young people engaged, they need to create opportunities for youth to form intergenerational relationships with non-parental adults in the church. Preferably, these relationships provide a spiritual anchor through life transitions, like the transition from high school to college or university.

3. Religious experience: A memorable conversion experience; sensing God's presence, love, and/or guidance; "supernatural experience" like divine healing – these and other experiences strengthen commitment and helps religiosity stick. Evangelical camps, mission trips, and religious youth conferences are important events at which youth and young adults experience God (Penner et al. 2012).

All three of these predictors were evident in the clergy interviews. Regarding the first, most clergy emphasized that parents need to "model" devotion, be "authentic," or be an "example." It is hard to overstate the clergy's emphasis on authenticity and modelling faith (and, as we shall see below, lay parents emphasized their importance as well). Those I interviewed seemed well aware of the centrality of authenticity to the modern zeitgeist, and they wanted the parents to emulate it and the children to see it. Scott, an Anglican rector in western Canada, stated the concern about authenticity negatively – that is, as avoiding what Frist (2019) calls the "hypocrisy gap": "I guess that I would look to James Penner, and the work that he's been doing with *Hemorrhaging Faith*, and I would say, you know, don't be a hypocrite ... Live out your faith in front of those kids, get them to participate in ways that they find meaningful." Malcolm, a Baptist pastor in northern England, found the question of faith transmission "really current," as he had children himself. Note how he chose to reword my question about how to pass on faith to the children, preferring to speak of allowing children to find their faith themselves. (This language of the self-discovery of faith was evident in many clergy interviews, and was at least as strong in lay interviews, as we shall see below.)

> I'd probably come at that question slightly differently. I think I want them to work out their faith for themselves. By that I mean that, when I was growing up, I was kind of told what to believe, and that means that your faith can go through some pretty hairy times when that's what happens if you don't own it enough. I want my children to question, I want them to know that having Jesus in their life, whatever they do, is of fundamental importance to that life, whatever that life may be. But I don't want to shy away from issues that they're already talking about. So, our eldest will talk about same-sex stuff that's been brought up in school. "What do you think about this, dad?" I'll try to be honest with him about where I'm at, but if I turn around to him and just say, "I think that's totally wrong," or "I think that's totally right," I don't know that that's helpful to him. I want him to be able to tease it out for himself; to be able to go to Scripture and say, "Well, what is it that Jesus would say in this situation? What does that mean?"

Then Malcolm used his best friend's family as a case in point:

> If I look at the relationship that my best friend has with all of his
> children, I see authenticity. I think that's incredibly important. He's
> not walked away or shied away from the tough stuff. He's had tough
> stuff in his own life, but he's been authentic and I think that's
> incredibly important for all three of his children. What happened to
> the middle one [who has walked away from faith, while the other
> two remain committed], it may well be that this is just for a time
> and he'll come back again, but I think what he has modelled to his
> family is a passion for Jesus, which is done in a way that is contextu-
> ally relevant. He's not seen as a weirdo by his children. He's seen as a
> loving father who wrestles and grapples with what it means to have
> God in his life in the bad times and the good times and how that
> can reflect in the way that he lives his life. I think authenticity is
> incredibly important. I'm really conscious as we are on this journey.

Malcolm went on to note that some pastors' children have walked
away from the faith, partly because their parents live differently on
Sunday than during the week, and that he is trying hard to avoid that
with his two children.

Ryan, the rector of an evangelical Anglican church in Sheffield,
emphasized the second key predictor of faith transmission, that of
mentoring relationships with other adults:

> So I think families [are] really key, and I think, sort of cross-genera-
> tional mentoring, you know like that one-on-one or one-on-two,
> [is] really important and ... small groups. So I think we are now
> saying to folks, "Actually, [for] a healthy Christian life, it's really
> good to be with God's people on a Sunday, it's good to be meeting
> up during the week and it's good to have at least one other person
> that either is, as it were, mentoring you or maybe you could find
> somebody to, you know, walk along side and encourage them.

Dale, a Baptist pastor in central England, emphasized the importance of experience in faith formation, the third factor identified in
the research.

> It's much more about experience than doctrine. You have to help
> them to know how to hear God for themselves and interpret what

God's saying, and that is a big challenge because that generation
tends to interpret things based on feelings and so [we are] actually
saying "No, you have to use the Bible as a yardstick," [which] is
still a bit of a challenge because they don't read either very much.
So ... it helps people to have their own experience of God. And
then authenticity is huge ... [So for] that generation if it isn't real
and you're not being honest, they don't accept it.

In addition to these three predictors, clergy felt it was important
for parents to pray for their children. Like Reverend Scott above,
clergy also emphasized an openness to talk about faith and discuss
difficult issues. Parents, they said, should not shy away from tough
questions (their examples were most commonly related to sexuality),
but share their views and allow their children to share theirs. Stanley,
the rector of a conservative Anglican church in eastern Canada, cov-
ers all these points:

We've got three kids of our own. I mean, there are three things.
The first is – these are not riveting by any sense of the word – I
think we gotta pray for them. I know we pray for them but we
really gotta pray for our kids. Secondly, we gotta model it more
than just ... these young people, they want to see the rubber on the
road. They don't care about what "the Book" says, as far as what
beliefs are laid out on paper, they want to see it, so we gotta model
it. I think the third thing is we gotta talk to them about it. Not lecture, I don't mean lecture, but we gotta listen to them and then be
willing to ask questions. We gotta be willing to be asked, we gotta
be willing to listen, and there are times – not too often – but the
right time that we need to ask them. Because if they're looking for
integrity or authenticity, then we should be looking for the same, I
think. We should be modelling that, but we should be willing to
flip that a little too. "How is your life? Where are you at?" Because
they're pretty open about this stuff. I think we gotta be real careful
about how and when, but I think it needs to be talked about.

Many clergy spoke openly about how they engage their children in
faith activities at home. They emphasized having devotions with their
children, involving them in "rhythms of prayer," as one Canadian rector put it. "We do the *examen* [a prayer reflecting of the events of the
day] with them," said another.

LAITY ON FAITH TRANSMISSION

Joseph Rourke is a white-haired eastern Canadian who regularly attends his Salvation Army corps. He has four adult children. "The four of them all put us through pretty rigorous times. They all grew up in the church, attended youth [group] but, you know, most kids they get to be teenagers and they try to say, 'okay, what's out there?' You know, so they all experimented." His oldest son no longer attends corps but continues to affirm the religious beliefs and values his dad verbalizes. His daughter still attends their corps. She is separated from her husband, who is also still attending their corps. She has recently met a young man who does not attend church, but Joseph thinks he grew up attending a Wesleyan church. His second daughter has been through some relationship difficulties but has married a "very nice young man ... both doing well. Um, she's kind of affirmative [of faith] but still ... yeah, not coming to church or whatever. She's big on philosophies and yoga and a positive outlook on life and taking responsibility for yourself. If your life is negative, then you need to do something about it yourself, not blame it on somebody else or whatever." His youngest son seemed to struggle most in life. He was a "heavy marijuana user," was married in a "toxic relationship," and now lives common law.

Mirroring Joseph's experience, the adult children of the lay parents I interviewed were more likely than not to have dropped out of church, and some had rejected their faith altogether. I asked Joseph why he thought some children end up following the faith of their parents and some do not. He said:

It's interesting, you know, you always ask yourself that question because you think, "Was I too pushy to force him to go to church? Or was I not? You know, did I not show them enough love? Or was I too soft? Should I have been more disciplinary?" You always weigh all those things out, right? And, uh, yeah, it's interesting. I'm sure that the relationship between the parent and the child has some bearing there somewhere ... Some ... men and women just seem to connect maybe better with their kids.

Considering that the laity were selected by their pastors, it is not surprising that they were all active in their churches, and that nearly all their children were either involved in a church or were raised in the church. About thirty lay interviewees had adult children, and many had grandchildren. With such a sample, it is not surprising to find general agreement between clergy parents and lay parents.

In many cases, it would be hard to distinguish between clergy and laity based on their answers to questions about faith transmission. First, they agreed that authentic parental modelling was necessary. In fact, it was the most common response. Jean, who attends a RCCG church in Canada, says:

> What can we do [to pass on our faith]? I think we need to live our faith from our home and everywhere we go. Our children have to know that this is what we believe. I believe that the word of God said to "train your children in the way of the Lord and when they grow up they will never depart from it" [Proverbs 22:6]. So basically, you do the best that you can do and the rest you leave it ... I think as a parent, if there's no contradiction between what you preach and what you live, your children will be okay ... So now, that does not guarantee that they will continue their faith, but what it does is to keep exposing them. What I believe and I always believe is that they need an encounter with God. It's not the faith of the parents, it's their own faith. But at least they have the foundation and we will keep praying for each one of them.

Many other interviewees echoed the importance of setting an example and modelling appropriate behaviour. A Canadian mother of adult children who attends the same corps as Joseph noted that some parents take their kids to sporting events instead of church. When she was young, parents made their kids go to church. She emphatically stated, "It's all about the parents. If your parents don't take you to church, you're not going to church anytime soon. So it's your parents influence, first and foremost." A British Baptist father of adult children said the key to faith transmission was to "be real." "I hope that we've [he and his wife] both always been real in the way we are. We've shared issues, they [their kids] know our past, they know the struggles we had before we were Christians, and since we've been Christians. I keep on saying but I think it's about just being real, and obviously sharing the Bible with your children, teaching them about Jesus." A father of school-aged children attending an independent church in Durham, England stated: "I think being living examples is really important. I wrestle with this one continually, I would say, it's how to express to them faith in God, not only in the words that I speak, but the actions that I take." A father of adult children from an independent church in Manchester said, "First of all, acting in accordance with your values, which is not telling them to pray if you don't pray and they don't see you pray. Not telling them to read their Bible if you don't read your Bible." Jordan, a young father from an independent church, stated:

> I think being an example, first of all. That is a massive thing already, just setting an example. I don't think you should ever force your child. I mean it just doesn't work, but I think what you must do is obviously pray for the child, setting the example, and teach the child the truth. That's the main thing. The kid just has to learn and I think when you do all those things then I think you've done the best that you could.

This emphasis among lay parents on the centrality of parental modelling seems to be at odds with the views of clergy, expressed earlier, that parents wanted to outsource religious socialization to the church. This is not what I heard from parents. Indeed, they seemed well aware of their responsibility.

Second, lay parents, like clergy, emphasized the importance of children deciding for themselves what they believe and do, of not forcing one's beliefs on a child. Many parents spoke of their adult children straying from the faith, and they seemed to let themselves off the hook to some extent, recognizing that there are no guarantees when it comes to faith transmission. As Jordan, the young father quoted above, said, "I've got friends whose parents are Christians, for example, and one is a complete atheist and one is almost an evangelist. It's the same household, same people, same parents, there's just no guarantee." Jessica, the young mother we met at the beginning of chapter 2, believes this tendency to let children discover their own faith is a generational change:

> I was brought up in a culture that was much more your parents dictate what the child believes, almost. Maybe dictate is too strong a word for that, but ... I was told what I believed growing up. "This is truth, this is how it is." And I think part of that would have been my dad's character, but part of that would have been that that was way more acceptable then, whereas I feel now none

of my friends would talk about telling their children what they believe ... They would talk about sharing what they believe and helping their children – their desire would be to help children discover truth for themselves and discover what they believe.

When I asked what needs to happen for children to become strong Christians, Zahn, a mother of three children aged fourteen to twenty attending a Chinese church in Britain, said

That's a good question. I would like to know the answer. I guess, yes, as parents, we do want to give them the best and what we think is the best; hopefully they will take them on as well. But I guess we can only try our best. If they accept it or not, if they can take it or not, I think that should have to be their choice. So, no, I don't have any good answer for that. I can just say I will try my best to teach them what I have learned and then discuss issues with them openly and tell them sometimes we don't have any absolute answer for every single question. They will have to develop their own faith themselves and hopefully, eventually, they will follow what we believe in.

In general, parents felt it was their job to model authentically their faith to their children and then leave it to them to "develop their own faith themselves." One can theorize that this approach is not new, as evangelicals have long insisted that parents cannot "save" their children, through child baptism or any other means. Each person must embrace the faith themselves to be saved. However, if this perspective is increasingly held by this generation of evangelicals, as Jessica suggests, then the modern zeitgeist, which insists that each child must find their own path, seems like a possible influence. A parent cannot dictate beliefs to their offspring if these children must discover their true selves, including their religious selves, on their own.

FAITH TRANSMISSION AND SELF-SPIRITUALITY

Many of the above findings are supported by the work of Christian Smith and his colleagues (C. Smith, Ritz, and Rotolo 2020; C. Smith and Adamczyk 2021), who interviewed hundreds of religiously affiliated American parents on faith transmission.[6] They found surprising similarities across religious groups, claiming that the parents shared an underlying "cultural model," with similar views of parenting and faith formation. Consonant with my respondents, US parents in these studies felt that they, not clergy, were primarily responsible for transmitting faith to their children, and that they took this responsibility seriously. In the main, Smith, Ritz, and Rotolo (2020) found that parents' goal was to inculcate their children with "good values," and that they wanted the church to "back them up" in this goal. In other words, good values – more than orthodoxy, devotional practices, or attendance – were what parents, even evangelical parents, wanted for their children. Inculcating such values is an instrumental goal that lines up with parents' ultimate goal of training their children up to be "good" (meaning helpful and kind) and happy adults. They were much less interested in passing on denominational or congregational loyalty. Thus, for most US parents, "religion is a matter that is essentially instrumental and therapeutic" (265). The reason parents valued religion for their children was because it provided "support, comfort, guidance, grounding and family bonding" (265–6) and help them get over obstacles in the journey of life. From the perspective of the parents they interviewed, faith was primarily about providing a strong foundation for navigating life. Their implicit cultural model held that all children have an internal, inherent, unique, "best self" that needs to be realized (105). Parents seek to maximize the likelihood of their children reaching their potential by giving them the tools to achieve their best self. Religion is one of those tools. But there are other tools to build good values. Sports, for example, can also teach children good values, and travelling to and attending sporting events are important times of family bonding.

If parents are not seeking uniquely religious or denominationally specific beliefs and practices, why would they prioritize church attendance or Sunday school over other values-building opportunities? In contrast, clergy and other religious leaders, with years of theological training, seek to pass on orthodoxy, denominational distinctiveness, and religious devotion. No wonder, then, that they think that parents are dropping the ball when it comes to faith formation. For clergy, parents' lack of commitment to orthodoxy or orthopraxy (due to their focus on values) looks like shirking their responsibility for faith formation. Lay religious parents in the US sample saw church as supplemental; good values trump correct doctrine. It seems like American adults have drunk liberally from the waters of the modern zeitgeist.

Of course, evangelical parents may be different from most American parents, so is there evidence that evangelical parents in the United States are also embracing this modern zeitgeist? After quoting a conservative Protestant mother who saw the Bible as a base from which values could be derived, Smith, Ritz, and Rotolo (2020) state: "This language difference is subtle, but we think marks a profound shift away from traditional evangelical views of the Bible in being focused on 'values' instead of truth, doctrines, or the Gospel message" (55). Religion seems to be about moral direction, functioning like rumble strips on the side of the highway, to help children avoid the ditches. The authors go on to note that, if religion is about good values and morality, then we should expect "the undermining of the importance of the *particularity* of religious traditions. Most religious parents in the United States tend toward an inclusive, ecumenical, sometimes relativistic view of religious pluralism ... That is largely because what matters about religion is not its particular theological or metaphysical claims, which are considered secondary, but rather its 'values' and moral teachings" (57). What Smith and his co-authors found in the United States is consistent with what I found in Canada and Britain, and we can conclude that there is evidence of the modern zeitgeist among evangelical parents in all three countries.[7]

If parents allow their children more freedom to find their own path, we would expect to find evidence of less restrictive parenting styles. Yet literature on parenting tends to chastise evangelical or religiously committed parents for their *authoritarian* parenting style (Baumrind 1966; Doepke and Zilibotti 2019), where parents are controlling and regulate their children as an end in itself. This is contrasted with *permissive* and, as a middle ground, *authoritative* parenting styles. However, I did not find evidence of authoritarian parenting in Canada or Britain, nor did Smith and Adamczyk (2021) in the United States. While I did not observe actual behaviour in the home, parents' words suggested that they adopted a relatively permissive style. Respondents repeatedly stated that, ultimately, their children had to make their own faith decisions and that parents had to be careful not to push them. Rebecca, a Salvation Army major in London, said: "I was forced by my parents to go to church until I was sixteen and then I could decide for myself. I let my children decide a lot earlier than that. But, I think you can't just have the faith of your parents, can you? You have to decide for yourself at some point."

Of course, evangelical parents were not attempting to give all faiths (or no faith) equal opportunity. As C. Smith, Ritz, and Rotolo (2020) state, faith formation for religiously affiliated US parents is akin to driving friends deep into the mountains while they sleep in the back seat and then, upon awakening them, asking them if they would like to go for a hike in the mountains or go to the art museum in a city several hours away. Parents want to maximize the chances of their kids embracing their faith but must be careful not to push too hard. They know that forcing religion on children often has the opposite effect, of driving them from the faith. Bengtson and his colleagues (Bengtson with Putney and Harris 2013) verify this perception. They found that religious "rebels" (young adults who reject their parent's religion) often felt forced as children or youth to adopt the faith of their over-zealous parents. Naturally, such pressure undermines a warm relationship between child and parent, one of the two key parental ingredients for successful faith transmission. The other is modelling faith commitment (Bengtson with Putney and Harris 2013). Overall, the point is that the language of evangelical parents indicates that they accept (or at least are aware) that their children cannot be forced into faith but rather, consonant with the inward turn, must find their own path.

RELIGIOUS IDENTITY FORMATION

Modern Western culture does not make it easy to pass on the faith. This is partly because the formation of a religious identity is increasingly difficult. As noted in chapter 1, often the influences to which an evangelical young person is exposed do not reinforce their faith. Since the young person is not receiving consistent messages about who they are or what they should believe, it is up to that individual to piece together their own identity. This puts a lot of pressure on them to create their own self. This need to create the self and the resulting fixation on identity formation is relatively recent (Burkitt 2011), even if its historical causes are not (Trueman 2020). Through much of history, identities were prescribed by societal constraints, providing little freedom for self-discovery. Now, however, many adolescents experience more freedom in the roles and values they assume, and, as a consequence, "the burden of creating an adult identity [is] now falling largely on the shoulders of late adolescents themselves" (Kroger 2017). The process of forming a religious identity is thus diverse and contested. It does not fit linear understandings of religion or traditional categories (Gareau, Bullivant, and Beyer 2019). In fact, some are suggesting that the language of sexual identities be applied to religious identities – particularly "bi-religious," "trans-religious," or "questioning" (e.g., Dickey Young and Shipley 2020). Identities are thought to be self-discoveries, and they are often more fluid during young adulthood than later in life.

In order to understand faith transmission, a quick overview of identity formation and the role of family and religious groups in creating group identity is important. The classic works on identity-formation theory are by Erik Erikson (1963, 1968). He emphasized the mutual interaction between the person and their social context in identity building, such that identity formation is a life-long process. Erikson identified eight stages in such development. Particularly crucial to identity forming was the fifth stage, associated with the teen years, and characterized by identity versus role confusion. In this stage, adolescents have the sometimes arduous task of self-discovery through exploration, which, ideally, results in a cohesive identity. Other possible resolutions are "negative identity," where the adolescent rejects the values and role expectations of their family and community, and "identity foreclosure," where the process of identity formation ends prematurely, without exploration or consideration of alternatives. Erikson calls the process of trying out different roles and exploring possibilities the "moratorium." If the adolescent does not successfully resolve this task, they cannot move on to subsequent stages of development, and they struggle to contribute to society.

The moratorium, a time of identity exploration and experimentation, seems to have been extended in recent generations. Jeffrey Arnett, author of *Emerging Adulthood* (2015), has argued that there is a unique stage of development that is neither adolescence nor young adulthood, typical of those eighteen to twenty-nine years old in Western countries. This unique life stage of emerging adulthood is distinguished by five features or "ages":

1. the age of identity explorations: trying out options, particularly in love and work
2. the age of instability: experiencing frequent changes in location, relationships, and work
3. the age of self-focus: having low levels of responsibilities for others, so a focus on personal choices
4. the age of feeling in-between: having a sense of being neither adult nor adolescent

5. the age of possibilities: believing that many different futures are possible

When do emerging adults become full adults? Arnett notes that emerging adults do not feel like they have reached full adulthood until they are making independent decisions, are accepting responsibility for themselves, and are financially independent. Until then, they are free from parental constraints and have social licence to explore various identities.[8] Emerging adults try out various religious, occupational, educational, relational, and sexual possibilities. They cycle through jobs and romantic relationships, relocate, and are more likely to engage in at-risk behaviours. As a result, this is the time of life when religiosity is at an all-time low (Uecker, Regnerus, and Vaalor 2007). Church attendance does not mesh well with emerging adult lifestyles – staying up late, weekend parties, shift work, college schedules, frequent moving, and sexual experimentation. As this moratorium stretches past the age of thirty for many, habits form that make a return to church less likely. And churches do not seem to be working very hard to keep emerging adults institutionally engaged. Many churches emphasize children and youth programs, but pay little attention once youth graduate from high school and leave home, after which churches lose contact (Hiemstra, Dueck, and Blackaby 2017). The church is largely absent at this crucial stage when world views, values, and habits are being formed. If the church is not shaping values and identities, who is? Are parents? Since the modern zeitgeist advocates that it is each person's responsibility to form their own identity, allowing one's parents to dictate one's religious choices is an abdication of responsibility. Each person has to find their own path. Thus, it should not be a surprise when youth reject the faith of their parents in search of their own.

Emerging adults hesitate to commit, and not just to a church. Moral commitments are often on hold, since commitments would end the moratorium (Hiemstra, Dueck, and Blackaby 2017). This does not mean that emerging adults embrace moral relativism, but simply that they have social freedom to explore values, morals, and roles in the formation of their identity. Regnerus (2020), in his research on Christian marriage across several countries, found a fear of commitment (to marriage) among young Christian men. An individual can try out "adulting," but being an adult requires commitment, and many emerging adults want to avoid getting locked into a job, relationship, or religion until they are sure that is it right for them.

None of this means that we should conclude that religious identities are created *ex nihilo* or solely by the individual. Rather, they are shaped by macrosocial forces and micro interactions with significant others. Identity formation is not just an internal process of self-determination, even if emerging adults think their identity is self-created. Consider the following illustration.[9] Imagine you are a twenty-five-year-old single adult, sitting by a campfire one evening, surrounded by your family and closest friends. They ask you to tell the story of your life, starting with your earliest memories. You close your eyes and think, and slowly some images associated with your early childhood come to mind. As you begin to verbalize these memories, more memories are triggered, and, along with them, a flood of emotions. You weave together these memories into a tale, maybe slightly embellished to keep everyone's attention. The result is a story that is more interesting and more coherent than the memory fragments that anchor them. As you speak, you begin to discern a plot, a direction in your life that you had not yet discerned. Your friends and family help. "Wow, it seems like your experiences are good preparation for ...," says one friend, suggesting a future occupation. Another states, "You have had a lot of opportunities to develop your skill in ...," pointing out a possible area of strength. Your significant others also help because they were part of your early experiences and had previously shaped your understanding of them. They help you add significance to past experiences and discern a trajectory to your life, even if the future is still hazy. They reinforce (or not) your interpretation of who you are. And the verbalizing of your story increases its coherence and allows you make sense of it.

Fast forward forty years. You once again find yourself by a campfire with close friends (and your partner) who want to hear your life story. This time, you and your closest relationships are together at your cottage, enjoying retirement. These are not the same friends that were present for your life story four decades prior, as you have lost connection with most of those and have made new connections. This time, your story is partially the same, partially different. Its sameness comes from similar memories of your early life, but it is different for several reasons. First, you tell your story in light of what has happened, and so you interpret early experiences in light of later realities. You see how experiences prepared you for your future life, and this perspective results in your translating the same early experiences differently

than you did when you were in your twenties. Second, your significant others have changed. They help you see different connections,
finding meaning and coherence where you did not see it before. They
suggest that certain experiences were moments of guidance or importance, adding significance to your life that you did not previously see.

These two scenarios illustrate that self-understanding and identity
are always in flux, shaped by significant others and new experiences.
The point is that our warm relationships help us make sense of our
lives and our selves. Identity creation is always a two-way interaction
between our inner selves and our external influences. As Erikson
(1968) notes, identities require reinforcement from others.

Identity formation is social not only because it is a symbiotic
process, but also because group identities are an important part of
personal identity. Tajfel and Turner's social identity theory (Tajfel
1978; Tajfel and Turner 1979) reminds us that people's self-identities
are also based on their belonging to social groups. If a person considers their "membership" to a group central to who they are – like
belonging to a racial or religious group – then that group identity will
shape their values and behaviours. Such group identities are maintained partially by embeddedness in the group. Typically, religious
identities require reinforcement from co-religionists, who are, historically, found in churches. If religious formation is to happen, churches and emerging adults somehow have to connect. Yet with the internal locus of authority, the next generation and institutional religion
are less likely to connect; and, even if they do, the authority of the religious leaders – an external authority – has weakened over time. Since
only a small minority of evangelical children go to evangelical
schools, most are not receiving evangelical religious socialization at
school.[10] This places the weight of religious training squarely on the
shoulders of the parents. And the data presented above show that
many parents, in spite of their best efforts, are not successful at keeping their children in the faith.

If faith transmission happens primarily at home, we need to consider how changes in the family might affect it. Eberstadt (2013)
argues that the traditional family and religion are like a double helix
and are mutually supportive.[11] The decline of the traditional family
results in declining religion, and vice versa. She argues that this lock-
step connection is ignored by secularization theory, yet it is central to
the secularization process, since societies with higher divorce and
cohabitation rates have secularized more rapidly. The traditional fam-

ily and religiosity are mutually reinforcing because, she suggests, non-married couples find dissonance between religious values and their own sexual behaviour, and because "family experience" (the "transcendent" experience of birth, selfless love for children, the death of loved ones, and so on) supports faith. Without a stable traditional family, institutional religiosity loses one of its supports.

Attachment theory (Bowlby [1969] 1982) also helps us understand the significance of this parent-faith link. This theory seeks to explain the development of affectionate bonds with others, positing that early warm relationships provide a foundation for healthy future intimate relationships. Attachment theory has also been used to understand a person's attachment to God. Those who have experienced safety and security in their bonds with primary caregivers normally can develop positive attachment to God and tend to view God as loving (Granqvist 2020; Cassibba, Granqvist, and Costantini 2013). Explanations for the link between attachment to a caregiver and attachment to God are based on the compensation hypothesis and the correspondence hypothesis. The compensation hypothesis suggests that persons compensate for a lack of early secure attachment by embracing God later in life (possibly though conversion). The correspondence hypothesis notes that those children with secure attachment to their parents are more likely to hold similar faith positions to those of their parents (Cherniak et al. 2021; Kimball et al. 2013; Greenwald et al. 2018). Thus, the correspondence hypotheses would suggest that maintaining warm relationships with children is key to faith transmission. Not surprisingly, secure attachments not only spawn positive mental health and strong relational attachments later in life, but also support positive identity formation among adolescents (Benson, Harris, and Rogers 1992; Marcia et al. 1993). So if an adolescent has cold relationships with their parents, that child is more likely to embrace internal authority and question external authority, which makes submission to divine or ecclesial authority tenuous (Eberstadt 2013).

Parental faith transmission can be undermined by the increasing encroachment of influences that are difficult for parents to control. This is potentially true of both friendships and media influences. Achieving a degree of network closure was easier for parents of children born before 1945. Often a child's friendships were formed with family friends, or at least with families that the parents knew. Parents had considerable influence over whom their children would visit, at least partly because they controlled transportation. Phone calls, television viewing, and radio listening were easier to monitor because these devices were often located in common areas in the home. Later, when the completion of high school became mandatory, friendship circles broadened, and parents lost some control of the friendship circles of their adolescent children. Still, friendship networks were spatially limited, and parents generally knew who was influencing their teen. With the ubiquity of cellphones and high-speed internet, friendship circles have broadened again, now without spatial limits. Parents have little control over whom their children converse with, or what media their children view from the privacy of their own bedroom. Common Sense Media reports that US teens are spending more than seven hours a day on their phones for entertainment reasons alone (not including school work), and children are getting smart phones at a younger age – 69 per cent of twelve-year-olds own one (Robb 2019). According to Apple, the average person unlocks their iPhone eighty times a day.[12] Obviously, there is increasing competition for a youth's attention, and parents have fewer opportunities to influence their teen. While children have long used TV and the phone to connect with peers and tune out parents, digital media have no boundaries. The teen's bedroom can become a "command centre" for monitoring emails, tweets, texts, and photos, and for streaming video (Bauerlein 2009). How can parents transmit faith when they are rarely heard above the din of digital distractions?

Not only does online saturation work against faith transmission, but it can also be hard on a young person's self-image. Social media use has been linked to anxiety, depression, and low self-esteem (Twenge et al. 2018; Keles, McCrae, and Grealish 2020). Mental health problems abound for Generation Z (those born after 1996), more than for Millennials or previous generations (Bethune 2019).[13] As Felicia Wu Song argues (2021), our "permanent connectivity" reshapes us in ways that are antithetical to the Christian world view. Add to this that religion gets very little play on social media.[14] The result: healthy self-identities, including religious identities, are difficult to form. The identities and values of youth are increasingly influenced by "likes" and "shares" from their social media posts and decreasingly by parents. While youth and emerging adults struggle to find themselves, they need secure parental attachments to anchor them through these years – years when external authorities like parents and clergy are not receiving much of an audience.

In spite of these obstacles, secure parental attachments are worth the effort. Youth with secure attachments to their parents are less likely to participate in all sorts of risky behaviours, including substance abuse, high-risk sexual behaviour, delinquency, and dropping out of school, and are less likely to struggle with depression, anxiety, or eating disorders (Moretti and Peled 2004). Although many parents spend less time with their teens, as compared to their pre-adolescent children, it is important for healthy identity development that parents maintain secure attachments into adulthood. "It is critical that the myth of adolescent detachment be dispelled," even as parents bemoan their decreasing interaction with their adolescent and emerging adult children (553).

CONCLUSION

The transcendent God of Christianity is moving inward. The generational research of Bengtson and his colleagues (Bengtson with Putney and Harris 2013) suggests that post-Depression generations (those born after 1932) see God as immanent or internal, as "a part of us," whereas previous generations view God as transcendent or external, as "out there" (28–30). The result is a growing distinction between the "spiritual" and the "religious," a distinction not made by the older respondents in their study. Bengtson and his colleagues found an increasing tendency to "internalize and de-objectify God or a Higher Power. Older generations describe an all-powerful Heavenly Father who is evidenced in nature and observed through everyday miracles. Beginning with the silent generation, respondents describe a more personal, accessible God that resides within the human spirit" (51). It is easier for parents and clergy to transmit faith in a God that is objective and external, one that is not based on personal experience. After all, they, too, are external authorities. An internal, immanent God must be discovered for one's self, and could be found only within. That is a hard thing to pass on to one's children.

In this chapter, I have shown that clergy and parents struggle to transmit their faith to the next generation. They understand that they cannot control the choices of young people, as young adults must find faith for themselves. I suggest the best explanation is that the locus of authority has moved inward, and that, along with other factors, this undermines the ability of adult authorities to shape the faith of the next generation.

Not All Evangelicals Are Trump Supporters: Exploring National Similarities and Differences

The previous chapters have emphasized commonalities between British and Canadian evangelicals, noting how globalizing cultural forces are shaping them in similar ways. In the main, interviewees identified and embodied changes in beliefs, behaviours, and attitudes that are similar on both sides of the Atlantic. Evangelical clergy and laity point to evidence of a growing internal locus of authority and self-spirituality. Yet, similar influences do not mean sameness. There is considerable diversity within evangelicalism, and national context still matters.

Since evangelicalism has no central authority that speaks for all, and since it is internally diverse and global in scope, it is difficult to identify matching groups that can be meaningfully compared across countries (Stanley 2013). In an effort to identify evangelicals and compare apples with apples in different countries, international studies of evangelicalism (e.g., Hutchinson and Wolffe 2012; B. Stiller et al. 2015) often use Bebbington's (1989) famous quadrilateral, which I discussed in the introduction. This definition is sufficiently flexible to accurately describe the diverse evangelicals I interviewed. In addition to the problem of identifying evangelicals for cross-national comparison, another danger is the possibility that such comparisons gloss over important differences within each country. In spite of these and other possible problems, I think the effort is worthwhile, as do some other scholars (Noll 1997).

Scholars of Canadian evangelicalism have argued that Canadian evangelicalism inhabits the middle ground between American and

British evangelicalism, just as Canada as a country is normally located between Britain and the United States historically and culturally (Noll 1992; Stackhouse 1994). Without a doubt, Canadian evangelicalism has been shaped by both US and British influences, and shows many similarities to both countries' brands of evangelicalism. In the past sixty years, the dominant view is that British influences on Canada (and Canadian evangelicalism) are waning, while American influences are growing stronger (Bebbington 1997; Reimer 2003; Stackhouse 1993). Yet, Canadian evangelicalism is more than just a hybrid of American and British brands (Beyer 2000; Stackhouse 1993), as it has been shaped by its own unique history and geography.

Any comparative study of British and Canadian evangelicalism benefits from excellent research by historians Bebbington, Rawlyk, and Noll (e.g., Rawlyk and Noll 1994), a Briton, a Canadian, and an American, respectively. However, comparisons between Canada and the United Kingdom have been rare in recent years,[1] partly because Canadian and British evangelicals do not make the headlines very often, and because they are a small percentage of the population in both countries. As a result, nearly all international studies compare Canadian or British evangelicalism not with each other but with evangelicals in the United States. This is not surprising, considering the size and influence of American evangelicalism. Add to this the spike in media interest in American evangelicalism since Trump's election in 2016.[2] For these reasons, a British-Canadian evangelical comparison naturally uses American evangelicalism as a foil.

Even a preliminary comparison of Canadian and UK evangelicalism shows that evangelicalism was a dominant cultural shaping force in the nineteenth century in both countries and remains influential today, and that there are substantial transatlantic influences between them, especially east to west (Bebbington 1997). As an experiment, I invite readers to go back through the proceeding chapters and read the quotations, blocking out the identifying information. Could you tell which side of the Atlantic the quote was from? The reason for such similarities is considerable international connections and subcultural flows. Evangelicals are reading the same authors (Silliman 2021) and singing the same songs (Ingalls 2018). The three countries have interconnected histories, and Canada and the United States have similar immigration patterns. Previously (2003), I argued for a pervasive interdenominational and international evangelical subculture in Canada and the United States. The strength and isomorphic tenden-

cies within the subculture lead to similarities in orthodoxy, orthopraxy, and symbolic boundaries. More than a set of beliefs and practices, evangelicals share a subculture. This chapter examines the
extent to which this globalizing evangelical subculture spans the
Atlantic as well.

EVANGELICAL INTERCONNECTEDNESS

The two church buildings could not have been more dissimilar. Holy
Trinity Anglican is an imposing gothic-style church built in the 1820s,
with pipe organ, stained glass, and vaulted ceilings. Not far away in
the same Canadian city, the Vineyard church meets in a remodelled
store in the poorer end of town. Its building is plain and simple, and
looks rather rundown from the outside. Holy Trinity's budget was
about twice that of the Vineyard church. What did these two churches
have in common? The same pastor/priest.

When I arrived at Holy Trinity, I greeted Bishop Franklin, whom I
had met previously, along with other friendly congregants. About
sixty people, mostly older, gathered for worship. The pipe organ was
not used. Instead, the worship team included keyboard, saxophone,
and guitar players, along with vocalists. There was a mix of (twenty-
to thirty-year-old) worship songs and (much older) hymns. Worship
was subdued, but several members of the congregation raised their
hands while they sang. Reverend Michael, an ordained Anglican
priest in his late fifties, wore his clerical collar and suit, adding vest-
ments for communion. After the 10:00 AM service at Holy Trinity
ended, I exited quickly to follow Michael to the 11:30 AM Vineyard
service. He replaced his suit jacket and collar with a dress shirt. The
atmosphere at the Vineyard was comparatively chaotic and noisy, with
children running around freely. Plastic stacking chairs were set up for
a similar sized group, but the congregation was younger and more
racially diverse. The band included a bass guitar, mandolin, drums,
and keyboard. All the songs were modern, with considerable repeat-
ing of the same lyrics. Some shouted "Yes, Lord!" or "Amen!" during
the songs. Many stood and raised their hands. Reverend Michael
preached basically the same sermon, although Holy Trinity received a
shorter version. At the Vineyard, a lay person interrupted Michael's
sermon to correct (perceived) inaccuracies about electricity, which
was part of an illustration. (Not surprisingly, there were no interrup-
tions at Holy Trinity when the same illustration was used.) Michael

joked and took it in stride. The casual atmosphere and the noise from the children continued throughout the service.

Despite their difference, the two churches not only share a pastor, but they have joint services on occasion. Would such pastor sharing happen in the Church of England? I was curious, so I emailed Michael's bishop, Franklin (who was formerly a priest in England and blessed Michael's dual charge). He assured me that, if he were still in England, he would bless such an arrangement there. While such local ecumenical projects were rare, they definitely existed in his diocese in England, he said. The Church of England is diverse, and has been a leader in ecumenical efforts since the 1970s. It was not the first time I had seen this ecumenical spirit. Another of my interviewees was a clergyman who was both a Pentecostal pastor and an Anglican priest, serving both a Redeemed Christian Church of God parish and Church of England parish simultaneously. Another ordained Anglican priest pastored an independent church in Manchester.

Such ecumenism across diverse traditions illustrates a broader finding in my interviews in both countries. Evangelical churches are cooperative and interconnected, as Chapman (2004) found in one Canadian city. Nearly all the clergy I interviewed were involved in local (community and/or city-wide) prayer breakfasts and interdenominational gatherings with other pastors for mutual support and cooperation. In most cases, these gatherings were open to all Christian clergy (although a few were limited to evangelicals), and some were quite large. In England, clergy were part of groups like Churches Together (formerly the Council of Churches for Britain and Ireland) and movements like Gather (an interdenominational unity movement supported by the Evangelical Alliance).[3] In both countries, local ministerial groups and participation in ecumenical efforts were common. The number of networks, affiliations, and cooperative endeavours seemed endless. Many also spoke of ecumenical outreach efforts like foodbanks, homeless shelters, services for new immigrants (often English-language classes), and disaster relief, supported by diverse local churches.

We met Pastor Brock of an independent (New Frontiers) church in England in previous chapters. Part of our conversation illustrates the connections among independent churches:

S: Are you part of a pastor breakfast or some other –
Brock: I run two of those ... That's the widest possible collection of evangelicals we can get.

S: Is it well attended?

Brock: Yeah, we do two lunches a year and we get about eighty leaders to each one.

S: That is impressive.

Brock: They range from rampant Pentecostal all the way through to utterly Reformed. We managed to pull them all together a couple of times for a couple of hours. Our aim is to build relationships with each other so we pray for all the different things that are going on, we pray for one another, all that kind of stuff. I help lead that, and then I'm also in a breakfast with four pastors. Something I'd like to replicate. We meet monthly.

S: And that's obviously much more intimate and closer relationships.

Brock: It's accountable relationships. We're genuine friends now. We've been doing this one for about eight years.

S: What are the denominational groups represented in that group of four or five?

Brock: Baptist, Methodist, Brethren.

S: Interesting. Very well-connected. Connections across the Atlantic: tell me about any connections you might have ...

Brock: Okay. We're part of the Willow Creek Association. I host the Global Leadership Summit for the northeast of England. So, Bill, Pastor Bill [Hybels], big influence in the UK.[4]

Even the most conservative churches were connected within conservative networks, but their involvements also showed broader connections. Reverend William is a minister at a British Anglican church known throughout the region for its conservativism. The church has "impaired communion" (William's words) with local bishops. William's church is active in Reform, Anglican Mission of England, Global Anglican Network, and Renew, all conservative Anglican movements. Nonetheless, they all meet three times a year with other clergy "right across the denominational spectrum" and are members of the Evangelical Alliance. Like Pastor Brock and most other clergy I interviewed, their influences also span the ocean. William spent time during one of his sabbaticals in a Baptist church in Virginia. The vicar at William's church took courses at Fuller Seminary in Pasadena, California, under John Wimber (founder of the Vineyard churches) and C. Peter Wagner. William said these "church growth people were quite influential" in his church, even though he was clear that his is not a

charismatic church. The leadership at William's church have also
attended Willow Creek's Leadership Summit.

One interviewee, Jared, a PhD student studying at a major public
university in England, came from Sydney, Australia, where his Anglican diocese was well known as staunchly conservative. I asked him
why he chose to attend the local (very) conservative Anglican church,
which was connected to William's parish. He mentioned two reasons.
First, he had friends at the church whom he knew from the past
because they had attended Moore Theological College in Sydney, a
conservative Anglican seminary. Second, he stated that the principal
at Moore College knew the pastor at his current church, and encouraged him to attend there. "I did have a feeling that if I had deliberately
decided to go somewhere else, that it might have been politically
problematic for the future," Jared said. If he were to return to Sydney
after his education, concerns about his theology after attending a
"liberal" university would be greater if he was not involved in this
conservative church.

Evangelical interconnectedness is not limited to formal and informal networks, movements, and organizations. I asked the sixty-five
clergy interviewees about who influenced them, including authors
and mentors, whether local or overseas. Regarding influential
authors, twenty-one clergy mentioned the impact of Tim Keller, an
American; twelve mentioned British Anglican N.T. Wright; eleven
pointed to the American (Reformed) theologian and pastor John
Piper; and eight mentioned former Willow Creek pastor Bill Hybels.
The late British Anglicans John Stott and C.S. Lewis also received
multiple mentions, as did Americans Richard Foster, Dallas Willard,
Francis Chan, Eugene Peterson, Joyce Meyer, Bill Johnson, Mark
Driscoll, John Maxwell, and others. Alan Hirsch was the lone Aus-
tralian mentioned more than once, and D.A. Carson the only Canadian (although he teaches in the United States). Regarding musical
influences, clergy mentioned Bethel (in the United States), Hillsong
(Australia), and the Rend Collective (Ireland). Geographic proximity
had no affect on the influences they mentioned: evangelicals in Canada were as likely as British evangelicals to mention British authors
N.T. Wright and John Stott (or American influences like Tim Keller),
just as British interviewees mentioned American evangelical leaders
as often as did Canadian interviewees.[5] Several British and Canadian
clergy mentioned travelling abroad (usually to the United States) to
attend seminary, conferences, or training schools, and occasionally to

work in American churches. These examples illustrate the interconnectedness of conservative, charismatic, and mainstream evangelicals, interconnections that are international in scope. Overall, there is plenty of evidence of transatlantic evangelical connections, and these seem to be getting denser and more deliberate as globalized flows increase.

Evangelicals learn from each other. If they see success elsewhere, they adapt their methods, contextualizing them for maximum impact in their local environments. The largest producer of evangelical cultural goods – authors, music, celebrities – is the United States, but Britons and Canadians do not import influences indiscriminately. Rather, they endeavour to take the best, from their vantage points, and leave the rest, a selectivity that spawns some national differences.

DIVERSITY WITHIN UNITY

Of course, interconnectedness does not mean that all evangelicals agree on moral and theological issues; nor does it mean that there is no friction within the subculture. In reaction to the secularizing society around them, some evangelical congregations retrench, strengthening their boundaries and distinguishing themselves from more accommodating evangelical churches. Such churches create their own networks and theologically conservative evangelistic materials. If the Alpha course is too liberal, a church can use the Christianity Explored course created by Rico Tice (minister of evangelism at London's All Souls Langham Place). One can attend churches affiliated with conservative networks like Reform or the Fellowship of Independent Evangelical Churches (FIEC). An evangelical Anglican in London can attend the conservative St Helen's Bishopsgate instead of the more charismatic Holy Trinity Brompton. In Canada, conservative Anglicans are part of the Anglican Network in Canada, which is part of the larger Anglican Churches in North America and the Global Anglican Future Conference (GAFCON). Evangelicalism is diverse, particularly in the United Kingdom. Patrick, an evangelical Anglican rector in Toronto stated:

> I think a lot of evangelicals feel a huge amount of tension now in culture. They feel unsettled, as if they're losing the place that they once had and that the world around them is rather antagonistic toward them and so in the midst of the tension, there's either, "No, we've got to put the walls up and put down our roots and

protect our convictions," or they want to resolve the tension by fig-
uring out ways to believe like the culture believes and have some
biblical basis for doing so.

In reality, the two reactions suggested by Patrick's response – of pro-
tectionists, who put up walls, and accommodationists, who align with
the culture (albeit with limits) – are part of a series of "camps" that can
be located on a conservative-liberal continuum. Evangelicals are often
not in agreement with one another over women's ordination, particular understandings of the infallibility of the Bible, or ecumenism.
However, they tend to peaceably co-exist (more so outside the United
States), and often actively cooperate. This was abundantly clear in my
interviews.

One British evangelical leader was excited about the growing unity
and cooperation he was seeing in Britain, spawned partly by the
Gather movement:

> I think what we're seeing on a national level is [church leaders]
> building relationships with each other, which usually involves
> meeting together, praying together ... As they're meeting and pray-
> ing, they are sharing their heart and passion for the community,
> their town, their city. Out of that, lots of initiatives are happening,
> which don't just carry the label of one church. So, [at the] local
> level, I think some extraordinarily encouraging stuff is happening
> ... I can't imagine that happening a few years ago. I think it was a
> tangible expression of the ground that had been taken in terms
> of unity.

Whence this growing ecumenical spirit, particularly in Britain, but
also in Canada? Not surprisingly, the same evangelical leader pointed
to the work of the Spirit to bring about an answer to Jesus' prayer
recorded in the gospel of John, chapter 17, "that they [Christians] may
be one." Sociologically, minor theological differences, which spawned
many church splits in the past, are not as salient as they were. Indeed,
in line with growing self-spirituality, many lay evangelicals are unin-
terested in denominational differences, or doctrinal precision for that
matter. Instead, evangelicals see the need to work together because of
their declining numbers and influence. Groups need to pool resources
to maximize impact and minimize costs. Nothing brings people
together like a common vision (e.g., evangelism) against a common

enemy (e.g., secularism). Furthermore, they meet each other and converse at conferences, prayer breakfasts, and other ecumenical gatherings. As sociologists have long noted, contact across cultural divides can foster mutual understanding and diminish prejudice.[6] And there are many initiatives that promote ecumenism in both countries and make it attractive. These "pull" factors include initiatives like Gather, the One People Commission, and other efforts by United Kingdom's Evangelical Alliance, which seek to bring diverse evangelicals together.[7] Canada's counterpart to the Evangelical Alliance, the Evangelical Fellowship of Canada, has a similar mission, that of "uniting Evangelicals to bless Canada in the name of Jesus."[8] Interdenominational efforts like New Wine, Fresh Expressions, other church planting networks, Inter-Varsity/Christian Union, and many conferences bring evangelicals together. The widespread use of Alpha courses, and contemporary worship music (like Hillsong, Vineyard, and Bethel music) also blunts sharp differences. One British evangelical academic stated that church services are now more focused on music and the experiential, while, in the past, they focused more on preaching or teaching. This shift likely helps mute theological differences among denominations, even as it might undermine orthodoxy. For this academic, generically evangelical Hillsong or Bethel music has replaced the theologically defining Methodist hymnbook, and teaching is shorter, less theologically precise, and more applicable to the challenges of everyday life. "Services are more like Nicky Gumbel and less like John Stott," was his memorable phrase. Similarly, the Black Majority churches in Britain, argues a Caribbean-born evangelical leader, are becoming more similar to each other over time. The African-Caribbean immigrant churches, started by the Windrush generation that arrived soon after the Second World War, are becoming less distinguishable from the later African immigrant churches. As we have seen, the de-emphasis of doctrinal differences, with the corresponding emphasis on the experiential, fits well with the modern zeitgeist.

THE AMERICAN FOIL

In eighty interviews with evangelicals in England, almost no one was able to identify substantial differences between Canadian and British versions of evangelicalism, even though I deliberately sought out interviewees who had spent time in both countries. One mentioned that Canadian evangelicals seem less comfortable than their British counterparts with imbibing alcohol or going to pubs, but my respondents could think of little else. Canadians weren't much better. Only a few Canadian Anglicans who had worked in both countries were able to identify differences with Britain, and they tended to make denominationally specific comparisons between Anglicans in Britain and Canada. In contrast, many clergy in both countries were quick to distinguish themselves from American-style evangelicalism, mentioning political differences most often. Overall, then, the interviews provided scant information on differences among contemporary Canadian and British evangelicals.

Canadian and English evangelicals more closely resemble each other than they resemble US evangelicals. This was the perception of more than a few British clergy. "You Canadians [evangelicals] are more like us, right?" said one. A few others apologized profusely (and jokingly) when they belatedly realized I am Canadian, not American. It was clear in the interviews that British and Canadian evangelicals wanted to distance themselves from their American co-religionists. They feared that outsiders were lumping them together with Americans – that is, as brash, xenophobic, right-wing, Trump supporters. In other words, evangelicals in Canada and England identified themselves by who they are not – they are not like Trump-supporting American evangelicals. This negative identity boundary, which was clear in the interviews, has also been noted by others (see M. Lee 2021; G. Smith 2020).

Note that I did not ask any questions related to attitudes toward American evangelicalism or feelings about Trump, yet this American foil came up repeatedly, particularly when I asked about political activism or when the label "evangelical" was discussed. One Canadian Anglican priest, when asked if many of his congregation were evangelical, stated, "I think those types of terms right now, particularly the 'evangelical' term, is not one that we hold onto tightly because of how it has been redefined by American politics and that bloc of evangelical voters that are said to have voted in Trump. Many have distanced themselves from that." Similarly, a pastor of a Hillsong church in England stated,

We [British evangelicals] have a love-hate relationship with America. I think we have a problem with the term "evangelical" because we tend to lump them all into a certain crowd ... They [US evangelicals like Jerry Falwell, Sr] have no care around people that are going through the stuff of life and that's what's portrayed over here, so when you say "evangelical," we think of – we don't think of what's happening in this country. We think of what's happening in America. Not Canada, because I think there's a [gentleness] ... I think probably British people would associate a lot stronger with Canadians, and maybe even vice versa as well, than with Americans.

Some had stronger reactions to Trump. A Canadian lay person, after complaining about Trump's narcissism and the repeated firings of his staff, said "I am so sick and tired of that guy," and another Canadian clergy person said, "some things [he says] are downright immoral." Hatcher (2017) found similar identity statements in her study of British evangelicals. No Canadian or British evangelical that I interviewed spoke positively of Trump. That said, not all references to American evangelicalism were negative: some Britons and Canadians had warm feelings toward certain American evangelical clergy, authors, and speakers. Still, Americans were the dominant foil, and served as an important negative part of evangelical identity.

It was ironic that English and Canadian evangelicals do to American evangelicals what they hoped others would not do to them: paint them all with the same brush. Clearly, not all American evangelicals supported Trump, and a sizable minority are not on the political right.[9] Leading American evangelicals have attempted to rescue their evangelical identity from its current political connotations (e.g., Labberton 2018; Mouw 2019; Noll, Bebbington, and Marsden 2019). British evangelicals share their concern.[10] Most were careful with what they said, but the anti-American bias was hard to miss. Even though research has shown that American and Canadian evangelicals have many more similarities than differences (Reimer 2003; Bean 2014), and it is likely that American and British evangelicals do as well (Bebbington 1994b), this is not the perception.

And, indeed, there are several ways in which Canadian and British evangelicals resemble each other more than they do their co-religionists the United States. First, Canada and Britain are distinct from the United States in that they are *further along the post-Christendom process*. The United States has often been viewed as exceptional (Torpey 2010) and as a counter-example to the secularization thesis (Greeley 1989; P. Berger, Davie, and Fokas 2008). In contrast, Voas and Chaves (2016) have shown that the trajectory of religious decline in the United

States is similar to that in Canada and Britain, albeit delayed. Canada's declining religiosity, evidenced by infrequent church attendance and a growing proportion of religious "nones," is between that in the United States and Britain, but the decline for Canada has been particularly rapid in recent decades (Thiessen and Wilkins-Laflamme 2020; Voas and Chaves 2016; Clarke and Macdonald 2017).

Interviewees feel the effects of religious decline, and distinguish their experiences from what they see in the United States. Respondents, especially Church of England clergy, noted a loss of respect and growing antagonism toward them within British society. A pastor of an independent church in Manchester, who had spent time in the United States, said,

> I felt in the States that there it was easier to be a Christian on the whole ... So generally respect for Christianity or pastoral ministry for the role of the church in a city or society was higher than here. We've moved from being seen as a bit of a joke to irrelevant to possibly dangerous and definitely intolerant. We've moved that trajectory really fast, and it's taken everyone by surprise. And I didn't feel that – outside of probably some urban centres – in America. People [in Britain] had moved very far along that [trajectory].

A few noted that visiting US evangelical speakers or church planters have more of a sense of privilege or legitimacy than they should expect in British soil. They have a more "build it and they will come" view, or they expect a more enthusiastic reception.

Second, British and Canadian evangelicals are known for their *greater eirenicism* (Bebbington 1997; Rawlyk 1993). They chafe at the aggressive "culture wars" rhetoric from US evangelicals, preferring a more reserved, deferential, or less combative tone. Historically, Canadian and British evangelicalism had a weaker fundamentalist movement in the early twentieth century (Stackhouse 1993); it was more contained and less divisive than in the United States. In general, the American version of evangelicalism has been more sectarian.[11]

Third, evangelicals make up a much *smaller proportion of the overall population* in the United Kingdom and Canada compared to the United States. British and Canadian evangelicals are a small minority, around 6 per cent of the Canadian population, and maybe 3 per cent in England. In comparison, US evangelicals represent closer to 25 per cent of the population. As a result, Canadian and British evangelicals have been quicker to accept their marginal status and are not interested in engaging the culture wars (Bean, Gonzalez, and Kaufman 2008). Hatcher (2017) found that evangelicals in Britain were not interested in reopening debates about same-sex marriage or abortion, and were more concerned about issues like the environment and poverty. My earlier work (Reimer 2003) found the same in Canada.

Fourth, Canadian and British evangelicals are *less aligned with conservative politics* (Bean 2014; Malloy 2009; Guest 2015; Hatcher 2017), as noted in chapter 3. In both countries, there may be a tendency for evangelicals to vote for conservative candidates because of their views on issues such as same-sex marriage or abortion, but this tendency has not reached the levels of conservative alignment in the United States (Guest 2015; Bean, Gonzalez, and Kaufman 2008; Malloy 2011).

Fifth, fewer *megachurches and celebrities* are associated with evangelicalism in either Canada or Britain. With the passing John Stott, British evangelicalism no longer has a central figure. Britain has famous evangelicals like N.T. Wright and Nicky Gumbel, but there are far fewer "stars" than in the United States. In that country, evangelicalism lost its central figure with the passing of Billy Graham, but Americans such as Tim Keller, Andy Stanley, Joyce Meyer, John Piper, T.D. Jakes, Tony Campolo, Rick Warren, and Joel Osteen, and many others, have international followings. One is hard-pressed to think of even one truly famous Canadian evangelical.[12]

The Hartford Institute lists thirty-five Canadian churches with weekly attendance approaching 2,000 or more, representing only 2.6 per cent of the megachurches in Canada and the United States.[13] If megachurches were as common in Canada as they are in the United States (i.e., proportionate to the population), the Canadian count would be about 140 churches, or over 10 per cent of the total (see Bird 2015). The United Kingdom has even fewer megachurches – about eighteen – many in London, and many primarily visible-minority churches.[14] For the ratio of megachurches to population to be the same as that in the United States, there would have to be about 260 in Britain. The smaller number of megachurches in Canada and the United Kingdom is partly about demographics. With lower levels of church attendance in those countries, compared to the United States, growing big churches is more difficult. Further, megachurches tend to be found in big cities, and Canada, in particular, has far fewer large urban centres than the United States.

But these numbers are not just about demographics. Interviewees suggested that there is an ethos in Britain and Canada that is sceptical about "big" religion and celebrity religious leaders. A Church of England vicar of a racially diverse parish in London complained,

> One of the things that irritates me about New Wine conferences is that loads of their speakers are from America. I always think – especially because of the context I'm in – I don't think it's transferrable. Okay, you know, great, they're doing great stuff over there, but don't tell me how to do it over here, because it's different. The gospel has to be contextualized, so I don't really feel that those generic models are necessarily helpful. Even the HTB [Holy Trinity Brompton] Alpha model – you've got to rework it to make it work here.

An independent pastor in Manchester said that, "Over here, people are more cynical, they ask more questions, they're not going to put up with 'just get in the van.' You know, ... the whole [American model of] 'I'm successful, I've got a nice suit, I'm at the front, I'm in the spotlight' – that doesn't wash with British people. Whereas in America it seems to." Another independent pastor stated that he was uncomfortable with the "celebrity treatment of [US] pastors" but recognized he might be stereotyping. An Anglican priest in Manchester stated that he interned in an Episcopalian church in South Carolina, where he learned to deal with three of his own prejudices: "against Americans," against "large church," and against "rich church." The clear indication is that American-style megachurches with celebrity pastors are not a quick sell in Britain, nor are they a strong draw in Canada.

A sixth difference is that *ecumenism* marks Canadian and British evangelicalism to a much greater extent than it does in the United States. The unity efforts discussed above provide support for this claim. Compared to the United States, Canadian Protestants have a long history of cooperation, partly because of its large land mass, small population, and regionalism, particularly as church resources were spread thin by Western expansion (Noll 1997). The United Church of Canada, which brought together Presbyterians, Methodists, and Congregationalists in a historic union in 1925, has no equivalent in the United States. In Britain, the shrinking market share of evangelicals is likely a factor in their recent ecumenical efforts. In contrast, the United States has a much higher proportion of evangelicals, and, as noted above, religious decline is more recent (Voas and Chaves 2016). These trends mean that American evangelicals often still have the critical mass to support various competing organizations, to create and sustain denomination-specific institutions, and to be more selective in their partnerships. While ecumenical efforts are alive and well in the United States, evangelicals are mostly divided, by political and socio-moral issues as well as theological differences. Clive Calver, a former general director of the Evangelical Alliance in the United Kingdom noticed this difference. "The EA [Evangelical Alliance] is not a piece of the jigsaw, it's the table on which we put the pieces of the jigsaw together," he states. "Everyone [in the United States] is trying to do something and be someone; nobody is trying to facilitate everything being together. America has no concept of working together to create unity, no concept of sacrificing their independence to do that, no concept of the vital character of being one body." In the United Kingdom, he states, there are "intelligent leaders building bridges" – not so in the United States (Mawhinney 2016). While Calver may overstate the case, his point that there is less cooperation in the United States is warranted.

EVANGELICAL DIFFERENCES

Given the above discussion, one wonders if Canadian evangelicalism is now closer culturally to British evangelicalism than it is to American evangelicalism. This is definitely true when we look at perceptions among evangelicals themselves. However, there are minor differences between British and Canadian evangelicals, even if one has to look closely to find them.

First, there are *denominational differences*. The most obvious is that roughly one-third of evangelicals attend Anglican churches in the United Kingdom (Brierley 2020). While there are evangelical Anglicans in Canada, they make up a much smaller proportion of all evangelicals. Anglican clergy who had spent time in both Britain and Canada argued that the evangelical impulse within the Church of England is larger, more established, and more respected than in Canada. Consider this exchange with a bishop, originally from England but now working in Canada:

Bishop: This was the biggest culture shock when I came here [to Canada]. The Anglican Church of Canada with its upper echelons is liberal fundamentalist.

S: What do you mean by that?

Bishop: So, if you're not a liberal, you've got rocks for brains.

S: Ah, yes, yes, okay. So, they're an intolerant kind of fundamentalist liberal?

Bishop: (nods)

He went on to tell a story of a conversation with a young Canadian who told him that he thought that all people who were against same-sex marriage were "just stupid." He perceives the same attitude among Anglican leaders in Canada, who demonstrate much less respect for conservative Anglicans than do their counterparts in Britain, even though, in both countries, Anglicans are not unified on ethics or theology (Francis, Robbins, and Astley 2006).

Furthermore, the Church in England is, not surprisingly, more established in society than the Anglican Church is in Canada (Hailes 2017). This story is from a bishop we met previously, Franklin Smith, who told me of an encounter with a front-desk clerk at a Canadian hotel:

I booked into a hotel and I went into the hotel and I said, "Room for Franklin Smith?" and eventually she said, "No." And I said, "Oh," and she said, "Well, hang on a minute. Was your first name Bishop?" I said, "Yeah, well, no." She said, "Well, we've got a room for a Bishop Franklin Smith." And I said, "Well, that's me." And she said, "Well, how can it be? You said your first name wasn't Bishop," and I said, "It's my title." She said, "Well, what sort of a title is that?" And I said, "It just means I can move diagonally on a chess board."

For the bishop, the point of the story was to illustrate the "death of Christendom" in Canada, at least among the younger generation. In Britain, the church has a more public profile, and is expected to be involved in civil ceremonies and rites of passage, the sort of vicarious religion that Davie (2015) identifies.

Due to the ubiquity and historical dominance of Anglicanism in Britain, there is a smaller proportion of traditional free churches there than in Canada. By "traditional free churches," I mean mainstream evangelical non-conformist churches, like the Baptists, Methodists, and Salvation Army, to be distinguished from newer and/or charismatic evangelical churches. In total, these free churches made up about one in four British evangelicals in 2020 (Brierley 2020). In

Canada, by comparison, non-Pentecostal and historical evangelical denominations – Baptist, Nazarenes, Salvation Army, Christian and Missionary Alliance, Mennonite, Wesleyan, and so on – represent over half of evangelicals.[15] While these mainstream evangelical denominations are not necessarily growing in Canada, it is not clear yet how much they are shrinking (Reimer and Wilkinson 2015). In Britain, Peter Brierley's data on church attendance show that Baptists have been in slow decline over thirty-five years: in 2015, their numbers were 84 per cent of those in 1980. Similarly, "smaller denominations" (the Salvation Army, Seventh-Day Adventists, and so on) were at 81 per cent of their 1980 attendance (Brierley 2017). Even more dramatically, Methodists have declined by one-half between 2000 and 2020 (Brierley 2021).

Second, evangelicalism is *more divided*, and possibly more *theologically diverse*, in Britain than in Canada. More precisely, British evangelicalism seems to be more clearly delineated into separate camps. One leading evangelical thought that evangelicalism in the United Kingdom would not hold together much longer. Bebbington (2009) notes the split between evangelicals who are conservative (represented by groups like FIEC, Reform, and so on) and those who are open and ecumenical (Fulcrum, Anglican) and charismatic (New Frontiers, Elim churches, most Black Majority churches, and so on). Yet, says Bebbington, these divisions exist not only between denominations: he sees growing divides within them "The former unity of evangelicalism had been broken," he states (2009, 105). Clive Calver (1987) spoke of twelve tribes of evangelicals in the United Kingdom, while the late John Stott pleaded for unity among evangelicals (2003). It is not surprising, then, that the Evangelical Alliance is working to create unity. While evangelical clergy in both countries are active in interdenominational gatherings, British ecumenical efforts have a higher profile.

CONCLUSION

Without a doubt, there are more differences and similarities among evangelicals in Canada and Britain than I have discussed in this chapter.[16] I focused on differences related to unity and denomination, particularly the historical dominance of Anglicanism in the United Kingdom. Yet, these differences pale in comparison to the evangelical similarities between the two countries. Even those interviewees who had been in both countries struggled to identify differences. Rather, they distinguished their brand of evangelicalism from that in the United States.

Even while plate tectonic–like change is moving Western societies toward an internal locus of authority, there is still lots of room for local and national idiosyncrasies. The gradual transition toward inwardness or subjective life does not even mean convergence between national evangelicalisms. It does, however, mean at least parallel movement, some of which can be seen on the surface. One visible area of change is ecclesiology – church structure and culture. These changes, which are intertwined with shifts in Western culture, are the subject of the next chapter.

6

Evangelical Ecclesiology:
The Changing Church

The subjective turn affects Western society on multiple levels. It is not limited to the micro-level of each person's attitudes, beliefs, and practices. It has also been a catalyst for mezzo-level organizational change. Of course, organizations are also being reshaped by a variety of other factors, including globalization, increased education, the growth of digital media, and, most recently, the COVID-19 pandemic. Businesses are being restructured around work teams as they move away from hierarchical structures (W. Powell and DiMaggio 1991). Networks of highly interconnected organizations are increasingly typical (Castells 2000). These interconnected networks of organizations mimic each other, copying successes they see elsewhere, which adds to their success and legitimacy. Some adapt well to social change, while others do not. Evangelical churches are not immune to these changes.

Yet, in some ways, churches and denominations are not like other businesses. Keeping up with social change can be detrimental for them. If a religious group is perceived to be changing in ways that undermine core religious doctrine and practice, they are likely to lose committed members. On the one hand, religious groups that are genuinely countercultural (or, in the vernacular, just plain weird) have limited growth potential (Stark and Finke 2000). On the other hand, those religious groups that conform too closely to societal norms have limited appeal as well: it's hard to attract congregants if you have nothing unique to offer. Some distinctiveness, Christian Smith argues (1998), is needed to create a sense of identity and belonging to the group, and to strengthen group boundaries. So, while thriving religious groups can adjust to cultural norms, they must avoid the erosion of the core tenets and practices of the faith.

Rodney Stark, Roger Finke, Laurence Iannacone, and other New Paradigm advocates argue that it is vital that religion maintain a degree of tension with society (see, e.g., Stark and Finke 2000). This sectarian tension makes religion "costly" for adherents, thus discouraging "free riders" (those people who warm the pew but do not contribute much), who tend to lower overall commitment. When churches are no longer in tension with society, they become comfortable and settled, and lack not only risk but also innovation. As a result, they begin to decline. According to one of my interviewees, a clergy member of an inner-city independent church, many churches go from "movement to monument to memorial to morgue."[1]

Among the most obvious institutional changes in Western society is the decline of Christian affiliation and institutional forms of religiosity. Many churches in Canada and Britain are in trouble. One Methodist academic I interviewed thought that the Methodist church in England would all but disappear in her lifetime. The denomination still has 4,000 churches in Britain but it has closed 540 churches in the last five years (Brierley 2020 and 2021). Clearly, the religious landscape is changing. Cultural change means that some religious groups will grow while others decline. Some churches will likely morph, resulting in new ecclesial forms like "emerging churches" and "network Christianity," which I briefly explore below. In this chapter, I discuss the affinity between the internal locus of authority and certain ecclesial forms, and the extent to which this affinity may explain the growth and future advantage of these forms over traditional denominations. In addition, because changing ecclesiology is highly dependent on immigration, I discuss how immigration, particularly from the global East and South, is transforming evangelicalism in Canada and Britain.

IMMIGRATION AND EVANGELICAL GROWTH

The future growth of evangelicalism in Canada and Britain is linked to several factors. Chapter 4 looked at one key ingredient, faith transmission to the next generation of evangelicals. It demonstrated that evangelical parents were struggling to keep their children in church, in spite of their best efforts and those of their churches. Indeed, they were struggling to keep them as affiliates, let alone attenders. Between one-third and one-half of evangelically raised young people became "nonverts" by adulthood (Bullivant 2017; Penner et al. 2012).

A second key ingredient is conversion, yet many pastors I interviewed admitted that there were few "seekers," or new converts, in their churches. This is not easy for an evangelical pastor to admit. These clergy made it clear that they do not want to grow through transfer growth – famously called the "circulation of the saints" by Canadian sociologists Reginald Bibby and Merlin Brinkerhoff (1973 and 1993); they want to grow primarily through evangelism that leads to new converts. In the 1970s in Calgary, Bibby found that most evangelical churches were growing from transfers (e.g., evangelicals moving into the area), and from children of evangelicals becoming members, while only about 10 per cent of congregational growth was new converts (Bibby and Brinkerhoff 1973). A study of Canadian evangelical churches in 2009 that I did with Michael Wilkinson found basically the same thing (Reimer and Wilkinson 2015). The present sample of clergy, interviewed in some sixty-five churches, reported that, on average, 13 per cent of regular attendees were people who had converted in the past five years. Since this interview sample was based partly on the reputation of the pastor or church (they were recommended by denominational leaders and academics), it is likely to be made up of relatively large and growing churches, so the average for all evangelical churches is almost certainly lower than that. Furthermore, the percentage is based on clergy responses, and evangelical clergy are probably not going to underestimate the number of conversions. That said, responses were diverse: some claimed no new converts in the past five years, while one pastor of an independent church claimed 500 converts in five years (the majority of his congregation), due to the church's aggressive outreach. But the latter church is exceptional. Even though conversionism is a historical characteristic of evangelicals (Bebbington 1989), growth through conversion is minimal, with more evangelicals switching out than joining.

A third ingredient that has the potential to contribute to future growth is fertility rates. Religious groups that include large families have greater future growth potential, even if some leave the evangelical fold. This reality is not lost on all evangelicals, particularly those involved in the "Quiverfull" movement (Joyce 2009; McGowin 2018). (This movement, whose name comes from Psalm 127:5, which likens children to an archer's quiver of arrows – "blessed is the man whose quiver is full of them" – sees having many children as a blessing from God.)[2] Thirty years ago, the fact that evangelicals had more children than average explained much of their growth at a time when mainline

Protestant denominations were declining in the United States (Hout, Greeley, and Wilde 2001). Now, however, evangelicals also follow the Western trend toward smaller families and later marriages (Regnerus 2020), and no longer have the fertility advantage. Even though evangelicals support the traditional family and transmit their faith to their children to a greater degree than do other Christian groups, the number and proportion of the population that is evangelical is declining in both Canada and Britain (Brierley 2020; Hiemstra 2020b).

Given findings that lower fertility, few conversions, and struggles with faith transmission have had a negative impact on evangelical growth, a fourth key ingredient, immigration, becomes all the more important. Many recent immigrants to Britain and Canada are from countries where non-Christian religions, such as Islam and Hinduism, dominate, or from countries that repress religion, notably China. So it is not surprising that, while the proportion of Christians in both countries is shrinking, the percentage affiliating with other world religions (or no religion) is growing. Nonetheless, sizable numbers of immigrants are evangelical, often of the Pentecostal/charismatic variety. Immigrants, on the whole, are more religious than native-born Canadians and Britons.

In the United Kingdom, about nine and a half million residents are foreign born, roughly 14 per cent of the population.[3] By 2020, most immigrants (about 70 per cent) were from outside the European Union.[4] Brierley (2020) states that roughly half of these immigrants are Christian, and it is the immigrant Christian churches and denominations in the United Kingdom that are growing. Of the fifteen fastest-growing UK denominations between 2015 and 2020, eight were "diaspora" recent immigrant churches (Brierley 2020, 5); six were Pentecostal, many of which are majority Black (African and African Caribbean) or Asian. While church attendance continues to decline among the general population (around 5 per cent of Britons attend weekly), the proportion of churchgoers who are foreign born is increasing (Goodhew and Cooper 2019; Birdsall 2021). Brierley (2020) predicts that, by 2025, non-white attenders in England will account for 30 per cent of all churchgoers.

Canada is among the world leaders in the percentage of immigrants among its population, with over eight million (21.5 per cent of the population) immigrants with permanent residency. Nearly all (90 per cent) of Canada's population growth is expected to come from immigration by the year 2050 (Simmons and Bourne 2013). Consequently, immigration is the dominant factor in the changing religious landscape in Canada (Bibby 2011 and 2012). Between 2006 and 2011, about one half (47 per cent) of immigrants to Canada were Christian, and there was a slightly higher proportion of evangelicals immigrating to Canada (about 13 per cent between 2001 and 2011) than were already in Canada in 2011 (10 per cent; Reimer and Hiemstra 2018). Significantly, evangelical immigrants attend church more often than non-immigrant evangelical Canadians (Reimer and Hiemstra 2018). As in England, the overall decline in church attendance continues in Canada, standing at about 10 per cent weekly (Clarke and Macdonald 2017; Eagle 2011), but the decline has been somewhat slowed by immigrants (Reimer 2017). However, because some Canadians raised as evangelicals are switching to become "nones" or "spiritual," evangelicals are probably not growing in numbers, and are not keeping up with population growth, in spite of being bolstered by immigration.

Evangelical immigrants bring with them new institutional forms. At the same time, some younger Canadian-born evangelicals are seeking religious groups that work better for them. Evangelical Millennials and Generation Z, not always happy with the doctrinal and behavioural rigidity of the churches in which they were raised, are looking for fresh expressions that are more "authentic" and accepting of diversity. These changes are influenced by the inward turn.

CHANGING EVANGELICAL ECCLESIOLOGY

About forty-five minutes outside of Lagos, Nigeria, is Redemption Camp, a campus that hosts the annual Holy Ghost Congress, which attracts up to four million people a year (Granberg-Michaelson 2018). The sprawling campus is really its own town, with a university, more than 5,000 homes, a power plant, banks, supermarkets, and a three-square-kilometre auditorium (Maclean 2017).[5] The Redeemed Christian Church of God (RCCG) runs Redemption Camp, led by general overseer Enoch Adeboye. Although it originated in Nigeria, the RCCG is now global, existing in nearly 200 countries. It has over 850 parishes in the United Kingdom, and nearly 200 in Canada, with thousands of parishes worldwide serving over five million adherents (Rosen 2018). Its evangelistic vision is to "plant churches within five minutes walking distance in every city and town of developing countries, and within five minutes driving distance of every city and town in developed countries" (Rosen 2018, 14). Brierley (2020) reports that the

RCCG started as a "reverse mission" – that is, missionaries coming from Africa, Asia, and so on to evangelize the secular West. It established itself in the United Kingdom in 1993 with only a few churches. Between 2003 and 2015, Pentecostal denominations in the United Kingdom added nearly 1,300 churches; roughly half of this phenomenal growth was driven by the RCCG, which has over 200 churches in London alone (Brierley 2020; see also Adedibu 2016; Aldred 2006).

Why such growth? Part of the success of the RCCG is its attraction among African and African-Caribbean immigrants, who can attend a church where they feel at home, with a familiar worship style, surrounded by other Black people. While the RCCG goal is to reach everyone in local communities, it is attracting mainly Africans (Jemirade 2017). Yet, even if it draws few whites, its growth potential is great because the number of Black people in Britain is growing rapidly, accounting for about 3 per cent of the population according to the 2011 census.[6] In addition, the RCCG pastors I interviewed in Canada and England were "tentmakers,"[7] working full-time outside the church (often as professionals), and receiving little or no pay from their parish. With low overhead, churches can start quickly and spend available funds on buildings and outreach instead of pastoral salaries. This gives them the advantage of greater efficiency over traditional denominations.

Reverend Moses is a medical doctor and co-pastor (with his wife) of a RCCG church in Canada. He confirmed that most RCCG pastors are bi-vocational, and their pastoral role is unpaid. Moses planted his church in 2009, and it had grown to an average weekly attendance of 175. I visited his church on a sunny summer Sunday in 2018, arriving around 10:00 AM, in time to catch the end of Sunday school. The place was packed, and Moses told me that the church was at least 90 per cent Black and included a few Muslim converts. The members had outgrown their present facility and were looking for a bigger building. About fifty adults (the children were downstairs) were discussing the Old Testament book of Nehemiah, led by Pastor Moses. Beside him was a woman translating from English into French. The discussion was lively, with both men and women raising their hand to respond to questions posed by Moses. He had to cut the discussion short in order to transition to the main service.

After a welcome, the worship band led the congregation in about twenty-five minutes of enthusiastic singing. Next came announcements, presentations, and some testimonials. An upcoming city-wide

"Diversity Celebration," sponsored by the church, was promoted, and congregants were encouraged to bring their friends who might be more comfortable coming to a community event than to a church. Local mayors and many others from the community would be attending. This is the kind of community activity the church promotes: they contact mayors and community leaders to see how the church can support the city, then put on events like this that raise their profile as they meet needs in the community.

Moses did not start his sermon until close to noon. As the sermon built to a crescendo, he developed his rhythm (with his translator matching it in pace and enthusiasm), and the congregation responded with loud "Amens!," standing and clapping. After the sermon, the band returned to the stage for a few songs as the service closed. We left at about 1:00 PM.

In our interview, I mentioned to Moses how quickly the RCCG was growing in the West. He stated that "one of the things that helped the growth of the church is the ability to split the church [referring to church multiplication, not schism]. In some of those cities you find that when the church grows to 100 then they'll split the church." Key to this process is training current members to lead new churches. While they do not necessarily tell members that they are training them to be pastors, "we're taking them through ministry training and we do mentorship internally, so they understand the concepts ... values ... things we are particular about at the church. We allow some of them to preach; we allow some of them to head ministries; basically, doing everything you can to prepare them." Moses has a master's degree from the RCCG Bible College in Maryland, and the RCCG encourages its pastors to get more formal training. I asked him how he has time to both run a church and work full time as a medical doctor. He replied, "That's why I said we get between 25 and 75 per cent [of] people involved. I don't do the light work. That's the benefit of empowering other people. So, all I have to do is to introduce somebody and say, 'Go to the Bank of Montreal [which is supporting the church's next event]. This is the contact; run with it.'"

The RCCG is only one of many new apostolic networks: others have started in Britain, Australia, and the United States. As discussed by William Kay (2007), these networks of interconnected congregations are led by "apostles," who, like the apostle Paul, are leaders with spiritual authority and unique giftings that allow them to be the "first builders" in an area, planting churches and establishing local elders to oversee them. The notion of apostolic leadership stems from the "five-fold ministry gifting" taught by the late C. Peter Wagner (Wagner Leadership Institute, Global Harvest Ministries) and others. Wagner promoted the restoration of the five offices mentioned in the New Testament book of Ephesians, chapter 4 – the apostle, prophet, evangelist, pastor, and teacher – for the building of the Christian church in the world. In each network, the apostolic leader is the central authority, providing general oversight. These networks include New Frontiers, Salt and Light, Pioneer, Ichthus, Jesus Fellowship, and the RCCG in Britain, and Catch the Fire Ministries in Canada. Drawing from *The Rise of Network Society* (Castells 2000), Kay notes that network organizations are dynamic, flexible, and innovative, with multiple interconnected nodes. They are efficient and responsive to changing consumer tastes and values.

According to Christerson and Flory (2017), "independent network charismatic Christianity" is the fastest-growing segment of Christianity worldwide. Traditional evangelical denominations are shrinking, while non-denominational independent congregations are growing. Unlike the RCCG or New Frontiers, however, the independent networks they focus on (including Bethel, International House of Prayer, Harvest International Ministries (HIM), Wagner Leadership Institute, and Youth with a Mission) are not primarily trying to plant churches and start new denominations; rather, they seek to influence congregations across all denominations and, ultimately, change society. They are networks of independent, but interconnected, charismatic leaders. These leaders, who include (the late) Peter Wagner and Bill Johnson (Bethel Church, Redding, California), inspire others for either "participation in hastening the return of Jesus to establish His rule on earth or actually becoming the agents of God's rule on earth," depending on the leader (42).

What makes these independent charismatic networks so successful? Christerson and Flory (2017) suggest that they have "expanded their 'market share' because of their innovative organizational structure, unique 'product' offerings, and inventive methods of marketing and financing their activities, all of which leverage the power of digital communications technologies" (13). These leaders are free to experiment with new ideas, without the limitations of bureaucracy. They are entrepreneurs, moving quickly to fill a niche in the "religious market" left by declining religious groups. They pool their resources and use their charisma to draw many to their events. They run training schools, hold conferences, and sell books and music, which greatly increase their revenue. All these are promoted virtually, increasing global impact without the costs of buildings or formal organizational structures. Importantly, their product is appealing: direct access to miraculous power and the promise of supernatural transformation. They focus on (charismatic) experience, like healings, visions, prophecies, and even exorcisms. For those who question institutional authority, networks operate outside of traditional institutions. For those seeking spiritual power, they offer direct access to the supernatural at virtual and in-person events. Another appealing feature is their flat structures, where everyone enjoys equal access to supernatural religious "products." Each person can select, from a wide range of training courses and conferences, those that best fit their felt needs. Finally, the religious consumer is not passively absorbing religious ideas or experiences, but is preparing to change the world, not only through evangelism, but also by promoting social justice (Miller and Yamamori 2007). Young people want "to go out and 'do stuff' – heal people, cast out demons, transform cities and nations – rather than sit in church and listen to a sermon and a few songs and go home" (Christerson and Flory 2017, 102). In sum, "we are seeing the beginning of a shift in the way that religious 'goods' are produced and distributed, which will change the way people experience and practice religion in the future" (Christerson and Flory 2017,17).

From the above description, it should be clear how well this new form of evangelical, charismatic Christianity meshes with the internal locus of authority. Bebbington (2008) argues that the expressivist/modernist ethos of the late twentieth century has promoted charismatic expression and an emphasis on authenticity (expressing what one feels inside). He also notes that the critique of established institutions is part of this ethos. Traditional institutional forms of religious authority are out of sync with internal spiritual quests. In other words, certain ecclesial forms are, for many reasons, more in sync with the cultural trajectory, and thus have a competitive advantage.

First, new ecclesial forms can avoid some of the negative press that evangelicalism has received in the past, and its fallout. Highly publicized scandals involving established denominational leaders have tarnished the image of all Christians, but they have been particularly hard on major traditional denominations. Such scandals, aided by a critical stance toward all kinds of external authority, have contributed to a decline of denominational loyalty, with only 8 per cent of respondents in a recent British poll saying that denomination was very important to them in choosing a church (G. Smith 2015).

Second, these new groups are run by charismatic leaders. The next generation of entrepreneurial Christian leaders are attracted to entrepreneurial apostolic leaders, and these young entrepreneurs are the best assurance of future growth. As many denominational leaders I interviewed told me, churches flourish primarily because of the leadership abilities of their pastors. Charismatic leadership, not traditional leadership, fits better within the modern zeitgeist. The authority of charismatic leaders stems from their perceived extraordinary personal qualities and the success of their own ministry, not from a position in the institutional hierarchy. As Weber made clear ([1922] 1964), charismatic authority can disrupt the status quo, a disruption that young people often embrace.

Third, in charismatic Christianity, doctrinal precision receives less emphasis than religious experience. Charismatic evangelicalism is highly experiential, with exuberant worship and emotive "ministry times." Leaders tend not to emphasize their exclusive doctrinal beliefs or moral positions, because these drive seekers away. Instead, they promote social justice, social change, personal healing, and intimacy with God. Such an approach meshes well with the experiential epistemology of self-spirituality.

Finally, these groups have a considerable online presence, which provides many options that can be individualized and consumed. The quality of these digital presentations – whether conferences, worship experiences, or sermons – is much higher than that of most local church productions. The online option also works well with the irregular schedules of younger people, who can watch and listen when it is convenient for them.

Overall, such changes to the structure of religious organizations reflect changes within Western culture, and these respective changes mutually reinforce each other.

Do these new structures have inherent weaknesses that will limit their growth and influence? Yes, say Christerson and Flory (2017). These flaws include the obvious problem of disgruntled consumers who do not experience the miraculous. This is a common problem with religious groups who rely on verifiable, and rare, religious goods (Stark and Bainbridge 1985). By definition, something that is considered miraculous is rare, and so few people have such experiences. Second, digital religiosity and dispersed networks undermine community – the kind of community that allows one to find meaning and belonging, necessary for a stable self-identity (C. Smith 1998). Third, long-term change in society requires a strong institutional base, something lacking in network Christianity. Fourth, these networks are themselves susceptible to scandal. Powerful, autonomous leaders have control over vast amounts of money, with minimal accountability. Teachings that promote "apostolic" authority, and money as a blessing from God, make them more vulnerable to scandal, as such teaching can provide religious justification for apostles to do as they please. Fifth, as one expert on diaspora churches in England that I interviewed stated, some congregants ascribe to the "cult of personality," where the charisma of the leader grows the church. The problem, of course, is succession – it is hard to find another with equal charisma or authority – and an unhealthy dependence on a single leader.

THE EMERGING CHURCH

Ecclesial change is not limited to new structures and networks, but also includes internal changes in congregational culture. Martí and Ganiel (2014) and Bielo (2011) have studied the "emerging church," an eclectic movement of younger (mostly white) evangelicals who are critical of the evangelical churches of their childhood. They are especially critical of the consumerism, bureaucracy, and right-wing politics embraced by many evangelical baby boomers. Emerging churches exist on both sides of the Atlantic, promoted by Brian McLaren, Rob Bell, Tony Jones, Peter Rollins, Nadia Bolz-Weber, and Rachel Held Evans, among others. They are marked by an anti-institutional and ecumenical ethos, consisting of informal networks more than rigid, bureaucratic denominational structures. Experimentation and creativity are encouraged. Emerging congregations seek to create a "neutral religious space" (Martí and Ganiel 2014, 29), where people are allowed to "be themselves." They form communities that are open to diverse viewpoints, so adherents can develop religious "orientations" through conversation instead of conforming to institutional doctrine.[8] These conversations are typically not to convince or convert others, but to reach mutual understanding. In fact, those in emerging churches tell "deconversion" testimonials about how they overcame their fundamentalist or evangelical past. Their former "false selves" were forced into a particular religious mould, which they must escape in order to find their true selves. They reject the megachurch approach, with its slick presentations, pastor-centredness, expensive buildings, and passive congregations. They desire non-hierarchical structures, conversational (not confrontational) "sermons," and liturgical and ancient forms of worship. The emerging church is an embodied critique of modern, conventional Christianity. Martí and Ganiel conclude that elements of the emerging church will spread within Christianity because it fits well with modern Western culture, with its flat hierarchy; emphasis on self-discovery and finding identity, even while providing community and belonging; use of technology and virtual communication; and pluralistic settings, where diversity is welcomed.

Mathew Guest's ethnographic study of an innovative evangelical congregation at St Michael's, in York, England, fits well with some characteristics of the emerging church. The young evangelicals at St Michael's hold diverse views on theology and morality, and their differences were managed by creating an ethos that was open and accepting. While many held strong views personally, they were "gentle and encouraging rather than authoritarian and prescriptive" with others (2007, 100). The authority of Scripture was liberalized, Guest suggests, by emphasizing the need for the Holy Spirit to guide interpretation, resulting in a more subjective understanding of the Bible. In order to be relevant and attractive to young people, such innovative congregations have allied with Western culture in many ways.

Even though Canada is rarely part of emerging church discussions, there is evidence of churches in Canada adjusting to the inward turn as well. Adam Stewart (2015), for example, found emerging church elements in Pentecostal churches in Canada. And, as was discussed in chapter 2, Galen Watts (2022) uncovered plenty of evidence of self-spirituality in his study of an evangelical C3 church in Toronto. I interviewed Pastor Katie from another C3 church in Canada. That church had grown to more than 500 attenders over the course of twenty years, and it continues to grow, with, she claims, some fifty to sixty baptisms of new adult believers per year. The attendees are mostly Millennials, many of whom are business entrepreneurs, with young families. Katie articulated a clear evangelical theology and conservative sexual ethics typical of evangelical churches, but emphasized "relationships," which are "always more important than the issue." I heard this "relational" emphasis from many leaders of network and some other (non-immigrant) churches. They seemed to be suggesting that relationships come before correct belief or lifestyle, and that maintaining good relationships with others is more important than "being right." For example, Pastor Katie was clear about the church's stance on traditional heterosexual relationships, but is welcoming of LGBTQ+ people, helping them in their journey without being condemning. "We believe the Holy Spirit convicts and so as, you know, if you're in the Word, in a Bible study, the Holy Spirit does the work and we are really there to support people and, uh, to help them on their healing journey. Um, whatever that [is] ... it doesn't matter; we're very much about freedom and healing."

Peter Schuurman's study of the Meeting House, a megachurch near Toronto, Ontario, with many satellite campuses, finds some features that it shares with the emerging church. Led, at the time of Schuurman's study, by Bruxy Cavey, a colourful and unconventional – and now disgraced – pastor, the Meeting House promotes itself as "a church for people not into church" (Schuurman 2019, xiv).[9] Evangelicals, Schuurman argues, find themselves in an awkward place, slapped with labels of legalism, intolerance, and traditionalism that they hope will not stick. This unconventional megachurch is attractive because it allows self-conscious evangelicals to find relief from their "spoiled identity." The main church of 5,000 attendees meets in a rented movie theatre and holds informal services that feature question-and-answer periods, along with heavy use of digital technology and marketing. Cavey has been critical of much of the evangelical subculture, as his book entitled *The End of Religion* suggests. The Meeting Place works hard to create an "irreligious" identity that provides a home for evangelicals in an increasingly secular age (Schuurman 2019).

I am not attempting to settle the question about whether or not (all or some) emerging churches are within the evangelical camp (see Martí and Ganiel 2014); rather, my point is that elements of emerging churches are making their way into evangelical churches because of the former's resonance with Western culture's inward turn. Like Watts found in the C3 church he studied, I increasingly hear the buzzwords of self-spirituality among younger and charismatic evangelicals. From the pulpit, young pastors share testimonies of their own life journeys, which typically include overcoming "adversity" to find "inner healing." They share openly about past "brokenness" – struggles with mental health, addictions, damaged relationships – so as to be "relatable" and "authentic." They encourage "experiencing" God in worship and relying on the Spirit to be one's personal "guide." They are less likely to take hard stances on divisive topics like sexual ethics or the exclusive claims of traditional Christianity (e.g., that all non-Christians are destined for hell). To be clear, such approaches do not constitute wholesale accommodation. They are changes in style, emphasis, and presentation. On a fundamental level, the leaders of these network and emerging churches I interviewed embrace orthodoxy on the central tenets of the faith and usually on moral issues.

CONCLUSION

Evangelical churches are changing, in both their culture and structure. New networks and emerging churches indicate that the inward turn can also encourage alteration at the institutional level. Other changes in churches mimic Western culture and the evolving organizational ethos. Demographic developments, especially immigration, also lead to changes in evangelicalism. What do these changes mean for evangelicalism's future? This is the question to which I now turn.

Evangelicalism's Future
in Britain and Canada

Sociologists are notoriously bad at predicting the future. We are not prophets. We can see the direction of current trends and, assuming all things continue as expected, where we are likely to be in ten or twenty years. But "assuming all things continue as expected" often assumes too much. Who would have predicted that Donald Trump would be elected US president in 2016, or that he would receive the support of the vast majority of white evangelicals? Who would have predicted a pandemic in 2020, one that would empty churches around the globe? Not me. We are much better at explaining why something happened in the past than predicting the future.

Clergy can sometimes see changes within evangelicalism better than sociologists can. They have the advantage of having an ear to the ground, since they are embedded in evangelical communities to a greater degree. The problem, of course, is that Western culture becomes taken-for-granted, like the air that surrounds us. One Anglican clergyman on the Canadian Prairies may have been able to avoid this uncritical "its just the way things are" view of culture, since he arrived in Canada from Britain only a few years prior to our interview. This was his synopsis:

> I've only been in the country five years but it feels like a huge
> wave and onslaught of secularism and liberalism [is] affecting the
> church. Basically, it's changing the culture of the church. I think
> the lovely nature of Canadians makes them susceptible to accept-
> ing things into the church that aren't of God and aren't of God's
> truth. Little step by little step, they fade away, I think, and being
> embedded farther into the culture of the world rather than the

Lord's teaching. And I think some are turning around and beginning to think, "How have we gone this far?" I think the biggest thing that's being hit by the culture is the ... confusion over what truth actually is and the desire to accept people, and accept them as they are, is causing people to almost say everybody's truth is true, which obviously can't be true. But it's what's happening. People are scared to stand up and say anything, myself included, because you're beaten down very quickly and labelled fundamentalist or homophobic or whatever it is you may be talking about. I think that's the biggest effect. It's funny, I mean the African Anglican church [is] trying to send missionaries to the Anglican Church of Canada because they perceive things have really gone downhill in that sense.

The rector is not alone. Many clergy and lay evangelicals share concerns about the infiltration of societal norms into the church. In the preceding chapters, I have suggested that these evangelicals are perceiving the visible, surface effects of a more substantial and subterranean shift from an external to an internal locus of authority. This inward turn means that institutional religiosity and attention to doctrinal differences will continue to decline. Moral views will continue to be softened and qualified. This trend, and some related trends, is so well established that it is sure to continue, and its implications for evangelicalism are important.

One obvious future change is that evangelicalism in Canada, Britain, and other Western countries is becoming increasingly non-white. Arweck and Beckford (2012) see a growth in conservative Christianity supported by waves of African and African-Caribbean immigrants in Britain. In his studies of church growth in Britain, and particularly in London, Goodhew (2012; Goodhew and Cooper 2019) has documented the prominence of immigrant churches. In Canada, the vast majority of future growth (religious or otherwise) will likely depend on immigration (Simmons and Bourne 2013; Morency, Malefant, and McIsaac 2017). With these immigrants have come new denominations and religious networks. These groups are typically charismatic/Pentecostal, and they will grow as traditional evangelical denominations decline. As Brierley (2021) and Goodhew (2012) note, these Pentecostal and charismatic groups represent a growing proportion of evangelicalism. Of the 880 Christian churches started in the United Kingdom between 2015 and 2020, 400 were Pentecostal, and 240 were independent (Brierley 2021). These figures suggest that not only will evangelicalism become increasingly populated by visible minorities, it will also become increasingly charismatic. This charismatic direction will affect worship style, but doctrine will be affected as well.

New networks, some of which originate in Western countries, point to a change that will likely influence evangelicalism, namely that, as British sociologist Linda Woodhead puts it, religion is moving simultaneously toward the "big" and the "small."[1] Younger Westerners embrace the occasional big event like a Hillsong concert or pope-led youth rally; meanwhile, others embrace the small, like mindfulness meditation, at the expense of "medium-sized" organizational level or congregational participation. This simultaneous move seems probable, aided by trends toward digital media, individualization, and self-spirituality. Early evidence indicates that COVID-19 has accelerated the trends toward private worship online and declining church attendance, as noted in chapter 3. Such changes fit well with the irregular schedules and sporadic devotionalism of younger generations. However, as I have argued elsewhere (Reimer and Wilkinson 2015), evangelicalism remains a congregational-centred faith, and congregational participation among evangelicals will decline slowly, or may even grow in certain locales (Goodhew and Cooper 2019). For the foreseeable future, evangelicals will continue to attend church (even if not every week) but will supplement this attendance with "big" conferences and concerts and "small" private practices, like prayer, listening to podcasts, watching YouTube videos, and infrequent Bible-reading.

Churches will not die quickly, because many evangelical leaders will adapt their religious style to appeal to future generations. Those that mesh well with the characteristics of self-spirituality and are efficient (with minimal bureaucracy and overhead costs) may have the competitive advantage. Evangelicalism has always had an entrepreneurial spirit and the ability to innovate. That will not change anytime soon.

As some evangelicals adapt to cultural trends, others will regroup and retrench, increasing tension between them and mainstream society. The result of these responses will be continued diversity within the fold. Will this lead to evangelical fracturing? I am not sure, although I expect to see increasing interconnectedness and cooperation among evangelicals on both sides of the Atlantic. Evangelical subcultural boundaries are amoeba-like, changing shape based on environmental stimuli, but the boundaries are strong enough to hold.

I doubt that evangelicalism in these countries will be polarized to the same degree as it is the United States. Researchers in Canada (e.g., Bean 2014) and the United Kingdom (e.g., Hatcher 2017) make it clear that political partisanship is not part of evangelical identity in these countries, and so mass mobilization in support of a political party is unlikely. In Canada and Britain, politics is unlikely to seriously divide evangelicals, even though developments like Brexit threaten unity. As in the United States, vaccination and masking requirements divided churches in Canada and Britain, but one would expect tensions to ease as restrictions are lifted.[2]

Finally, US evangelicals, and Americans more broadly (C. Smith, Ritz, and Rotolo 2020; C. Smith with Denton 2005; C. Smith and Snell 2009), are showing signs of the inward turn or the internal locus of authority. American evangelicals would be wise to look at Canada and Britain for evidence of where they are heading. While the mixing of American nationalism and evangelical faith polarizes the public sphere (e.g., Whitehead and Perry 2020), underneath operates a shift toward self-expression, self-optimization, and identity-creation based on the dictates of the heart. It is religion remixed (Burton 2020), and it is influencing evangelicals even while they resist it.

For many evangelical leaders, adjusting to inward authority and self-spirituality means changing the "packaging" (the way their product is presented) without changing the essence of the religious product (its core beliefs and practices). While the clergy I spoke to embrace evangelical orthodoxy, the presentation of the "good news" is increasingly experiential, digital, and welcoming of all, while exclusive beliefs and contentious moral positions are toned down. But can changes in presentation really leave the product unaffected? If clergy avoid uncomfortable topics like hell or sexual ethics, will not the beliefs of laity on these topics change, especially when Western culture promotes such change? Will the professionally produced worship concerts and videos of charismatic celebrity preachers leave congregants dissatisfied with the comparatively aenemic worship experience and preaching at their church? Maybe the efforts of charismatic network apostles are actually undermining the local church instead of strengthening it, as they hope. Will online services keep people from attending church? Can fellowship and mutual care take place digitally? What about the sacraments? And what about the identity-forming effects of belonging to a community? Do fewer in-person gatherings mean that community influences are weakened and that the internal locus of authority and self-spirituality will grow uninhibited? It seems inevitable that the religious product will change if the presentation changes. Evangelical clergy thus may be enabling, even accelerating, the drift toward internal authority that can undermine their own authority.[3] Evangelical leaders must think about the unintended consequences of the changes they facilitate. Some changes can enhance their efforts, while others may unintentionally undermine them. Correctly understanding the cultural change toward internal authority and self-spirituality will help them identify possible consequences of their actions. One needs to correctly identify the current before one can chart a course to best navigate through it.

Yet, there is a catch-22 here for Christian leaders. On the one hand, softening exclusivity and increasingly inclusivity – so that each person has the freedom to find their own path – will likely result in losing highly committed members who sense that the group is compromising the essence of the faith, although it may keep and attract those who feel alienated by proscriptive orthodoxy and restrictive orthopraxy. On the other hand, holding fast to the historical faith may keep the faithful in the fold and attract others who seek a community and way of life other than what they can find in the culture at large, but others will feel excluded and leave.

In both Canada and Britain, evangelical leaders are seeing changes in beliefs and practices. They see how hard it is to keep young people in the pews. They are seeing visible indicators of a massive relocation of authority. The surface looks chaotic to them, like a culture of "anything goes." But there is a coherence, a unity, to the new self-spirituality, this "religion of the heart" (Campbell 1991). People are travelling their own path toward the same telic goal, the authentic self. Beliefs that are not self-discovered and practices that are externally prescribed are often impediments in this journey toward authenticity. Yet, so many evangelical churches and denominations still operate as if Western culture has not shifted. They prescribe beliefs and practices as if external institutional authority still holds legitimacy in society. They continue to operate as if beliefs are about *assent to* a doctrinal proposition instead of about *adherence to* significant others. They are concerned about "walking the talk" and avoiding hypocrisy, but fail to see that the standard of religious authenticity has shifted. Hypocrisy is now understood, in part, as blindly adhering to institutional authority.

Evangelicals in Canada and Britain (like those in other Western countries) are not disappearing. In fact, they are a growing proportion of church-going Christians in both countries; but, at the same time, they are declining as a proportion of the broader population. Compared to other Christian groups, they are doing relatively well. However, as I have argued in this book, the more important changes are qualitative, not quantitative. They are subtle and difficult to detect by analyzing mere numbers. Over decades, Western evangelicals have been influenced by a cultural shift from an external locus of authority to internal authority. This has affected evangelicals in a myriad of ways, including the decline of institutional deference, qualified beliefs and ethics, irregular devotional and ritual practice, weakened faith transmission, and even changing institutional forms. Evangelicalism is pliable. It has always adjusted to the society around it. It is also resilient. It will not disappear anytime soon, not even in Canada and Britain.

Appendix

In 2018, I completed 124 formal interviews of evangelical clergy and active laity in England and Canada. I spent three months as Alan Richardson Fellow at the University of Durham, at which time I completed eighty formal interviews in England. I then returned to Canada to complete forty-four more formal interviews. I met face-to-face with respondents when possible, but many respondents chose online video interviews due to time and travel limitations. A few interviews were completed over the phone when video failed because of poor internet connections. In total, I interviewed sixty-seven clergy and fifty-seven active laity in sixty-seven different churches. In England, interviews were completed in Durham, Newcastle, Manchester, Sheffield, and London (and surrounding areas, to include some rural congregations). In Canada, interviews took place in Moncton, Saint John, and Fredericton, New Brunswick; the Calgary/Red Deer area, in Alberta; Winnipeg, Manitoba; and Toronto and Ottawa, Ontario.

My intention was to get a diverse sample of active evangelicals in both countries, but also to have similar samples in each country (based on denomination), where possible. Since about one-third of evangelicals in Britain attend Anglican churches, the number of Anglican interviews in Canada is disproportionately high, in order to achieve comparable samples. Independent church interviews are also disproportionately high in both countries. I focused on Anglican and independent churches to augment my previous research on the large, traditionally evangelical denominations in North America, particularly Southern Baptists, (Canadian) Convention Baptists, Pentecostal Assemblies of Canada/Assemblies of God, Nazarenes, Christian and

Missionary Alliance, Lutheran-Missouri Synod/Lutheran Church Canada, Mennonite Brethren, and Christian Reformed. I was more familiar with respondents in those traditions, and wanted more respondents within denominations that I had not yet researched.

I secured my sample in the same way in each country and location. I talked and met with local denominational leaders and academics to find out which evangelical churches I should contact. I would contact the church, identify myself as a Canadian sociologist doing a study of evangelical churches, and request an interview. I would then email the church a consent form. After interviewing the rector or lead pastor, I would ask them to put me in contact with two of their active lay members. I would ask for one older (over fifty), one younger (under thirty), a male and a female, and, where possible, a person who was a visible minority. Most clergy were willing to put me in touch with some lay members, but some failed to do so, even after several reminders.

Obviously, such a selection process is not intended to produce a sample representative of all evangelical laity or clergy in either country. Rather, it is intended to capture the beliefs, values, and attitudes of active evangelical clergy and laity from a diverse sample of churches. Due to the sampling design, I was more likely to be pointed to larger, well-known churches by evangelical leaders and academics, since referrals are partly based on reputation. However, I also scoured the internet to find churches within certain denominations and networks. The largest church in my study claimed an average weekly attendance of over 4,000, while the smallest averaged 20 weekly attendees. Table A.1 presents the denominations, number of clergy and laity, and the number of these clergy and laity who were visible minority and/or female for each country.

The majority of clergy interviewees were male, as lead clergy in evangelical churches are typically men (Reimer and Wilkinson 2015): only three Canadian and four British women clergy were in the sample. Just over half of the lay interviews were with women (31). Twenty-one lay interviews were with visible minorities, and interviews were completed in thirteen churches that were majority non-white. The roughly twenty independent churches were normally part of a network, including New Frontiers, Pioneers, FIEC (Fellowship of Independent Evangelical Churches), Victory Churches, C3 and other independent church groups. Theologically, the sample was diverse, from fundamentalist to "open" evangelical. Although all churches had

Table A.1
Interview sample

Denomination/group	England				Canada			
	Clergy	Laity	Minority	Female	Clergy	Laity	Minority	Female
Anglican / Church of England	14	12	3	7	10	14	7	7
Independent	14	14	3	7	5	3		2
Baptist	6	5	2	4	1			
Methodist	2		1	1				
Presbyterian	1				1			
Redeemed Christian Church of God	2		2		1	2	2	1
Salvation Army	2			1	2	2	1	2
Vineyard	2	3		1	1	2		2
Hillsong	1							
Elim Pentecostal	2							
Totals	**46**	**34**	**11**	**21**	**21**	**23**	**10**	**14**

the reputation of being conservative and evangelical, I interviewed three Anglican clergy whose theological and ethical positions may be considered borderline evangelical, based on the totality of their responses to theological and ethical questions. In these churches, I did not ask to interview lay members nor did I include their responses related to beliefs and ethics in chapter 2. In addition, several lay interviewees were not evangelical in belief, as traditionally understood. So, even though clergy selected the lay people I interviewed, they did not always select those that agreed with them theologically. Considerable diversity in theological positions exists among the laity in Anglican churches, especially in Canada. This not surprising, as some are operating with an internal locus of authority. I did not quote these borderline evangelical laity and clergy on theological and ethical positions, as they were not typical of the responses overall. The average length of clergy interviews was forty-six minutes, with a range from thirty-three to sixty-five minutes. Lay interviews averaged forty-one minutes, with a range from twenty-four to sixty-three minutes. All interviews were audio-recorded and were later transcribed by research assistants, resulting in over 1,000 pages of transcriptions. In addition,

I had notes from informal interviews (over lunch, over the phone, and so on) with over forty academics and evangelical leaders. Finally, I visited twenty evangelical churches, normally on Sunday morning, and took notes during these services. These visits were all in churches where I had interviewed the pastor/priest.

My goal in these interviews was to understand the "cultural models" (Smith, Ritz, and Rotolo 2020) of evangelicals – that is, the ways in which evangelicals make sense of the world around them. This requires trying to understand their unspoken assumptions and beliefs based on an analysis of their discourse. People are often not aware of the underlying schemas – their attitudes, values, dispositions, and assumptions – that they internalize over time and that guide their thinking and behaviour. The researcher must try to reconstruct these cognitive cultural models (which exist in respondents' heads), based on what they say in interviews. Evangelicals, I suggest, have shared cultural models because they draw from both the evangelical subculture (which has some clear beliefs, norms, and behavioural expectations) and broader Western culture, which also has a unity, one that I call the "modern zeitgeist." Of course, plenty of diversity can be found within and between the cultural models of individual evangelicals, but there is also a shared coherence, as I argue in this book.

INTERVIEW FORMS

All interviews were semi-formal or semi-structured, meaning that I deviated often from the questions outlined below, based on the interviewee and their responses. In each case, I started with a broad question, allowing the respondent to answer without biasing their responses. The indented questions indicate follow-up probes for clarity or more detail.

Lay Interviews

1. Tell me about your involvement in your church.
   - How long have you been attending this church?
   - Volunteer or leadership positions? How long have you been in this position?
2. Why did you choose this church, or have you been attending all your life?
   - What attracted you to it?

3. Now I have some questions about your personal religious views and practice. Remember, this is your *views personally, which may or may not match* those of your church. How would you describe your view of:
   a. The Bible
      – Would you say the Bible is divinely inspired? Authoritative? Infallible? Literal?
   b. Salvation
      – Would you say salvation is only through Jesus Christ?
   c. Conversion
      – Would you consider yourself a converted or born-again Christian?
   d. Abortion
   e. Women in leadership in the church
   f. Cohabitation/premarital sex
   g. Same-sex marriage
   h. Practices: Tell me about your devotional practices. What do you do alone for spiritual growth?
      – How often do you pray?
      – How often do you read the Bible or other Christian literature?
      – What else do you do?
   i. Church attendance
      How often do you attend your church/parish? Do you attend other church-sponsored events?
      Do you miss sometimes? How often?
   j. Are you involved in evangelism?
      In what ways?
   k. Tell me about your giving or tithing.
      To the church? Other organizations?
   l. Do you volunteer outside the church or for church-sponsored events?
   m. Are you involved in political action of any kind?
4. In your view, what is the influence of society or culture on Christian faith?
      – How is it affecting Christian beliefs?
      – How about church participation or private religious practices?
   a. What is the effect of social media/media on faith?
   b. How does faith get passed on to children? What can parents do?

   c. How have changes in the family influenced faith?

   d. How do peers (particularly of young people) shape faith?

   e. What about changing views of sex/sexuality on faith?

   f. What about the role of the church in faith development (programs, mentoring, etc.)?

5. Why do you think you have been able to keep your faith, in light of the influences of the culture?

Now some questions about your time use and other influences.

6. Media: How much time do you spend on the following activities in a typical day or week?
   - On social media (Facebook, Snapchat, Instagram, Twitter, etc.)?
   - Watching TV shows or movies?
   - How do you think the messages from media influence your faith?

7. Consumerism/shopping:
   - Do you enjoy shopping? How much time do you spend shopping or going to malls/stores or shopping on line?

8. Paid work: How many hours do you work in a typical week?

9. Parents
   - Describe the faith of your parents.
   - How do their religious beliefs/practices differ from yours, if at all?
   - How would you describe your relationship with your parents? How about as a teen or young adult?

10. Romantic relationships: Tell me about your romantic relationships and their effect on your faith.

11. Children: Do you have children, and, if so, what are their ages? Do you have concerns for your children's faith? How are they doing spirituality?

12. Faith change: Was there a time in your life when you lost or rejected your faith or were less involved in church? Why was that? Why did you return?

13. Education: What is your highest level of education? Has education affected your faith?

Clergy Interviews

1. What is your position (in this church/parish)? How long have you been at this position/church?
2. About how many people attend worship services here in an average week? Please give the total number of people, including children, for all worship services.
   – Clarify numbers if multi-site
3. Describe the attendance change over the past five years. Has it been stable, growing, declining? What accounts for the change? Has there been significant turnover or do they tend to be long-term attendees?
4. What do you/the church do to connect with newcomers/ visitors?
   – Do visitors usually stay?
5. Church demographics: What percent of your regular attendees fall into each demographic category? Your best guess is fine.
   a. per cent under the age of thirty-five
   b. per cent with bachelor's degree or higher
   c. per cent visible minority
   d. per cent unsaved seekers
   e. per cent new converts (past five years) who have been saved through the ministry of your church, not including children of church members
   f. per cent active volunteers in the church. Per cent of men who volunteer? Per cent of women? Is most work done by a few, or is it well spread out?

Theological Beliefs and Ethics

6. Compared to other churches in your denomination in this region, where would you place this church on a theologically liberal-to-conservative scale?
7. What makes this church unique compared to other Christian churches in the area?
8. Please describe your views on:
   a. The Bible
      – Would you use words like inspired, inerrant, or authoritative?

    b. Salvation
       – Through Jesus Christ alone?
    c. Conversion
    d. The importance of evangelism vs social action
       – Does your church do evangelism? Social justice work?
    e. Women's leadership in the church
    f. Abortion
    g. Same-sex marriage
    h. Political activism

Connections

9. Do you have connections – whether formal or informal ties – with any of the following types of groups or organizations?
    a. Networks
    b. Meetings with other pastors in this city or area
    c. Trans-denominational organizations like the Evangelical Alliance/EFC
10. What influences/connections do you or your church have with Christians internationally?
    – Were you or other clergy in your church trained in North America/Britain?
    – Which authors have influenced you?
    – What worship music do you use in your church?
    – Are you or your church involved in international/transatlantic Christian networks?
    – Have you spent significant time in North America/Britain?
    – Have you attended conferences or other events in or originating from Britain or North America??
11. How are social forces or Western culture influencing beliefs among Christians?
    – What about influence on practices like church attendance or devotions?
12. What do you think is most important to ensure faith transmission to our children? What is the effect of:
    – Media influences
    – Parenting influences
    – Peers
13. What can the church do to help children/youth keep the faith?

Notes

PREFACE

1 For recent scholarship on evangelicalism and race, see Martí (2020) and Butler (2021) for the United States, and Birdsall (2021) and Lindsay (2019) for Britain. On evangelicalism and gender, see Gaddini (2022b) and Fry (2021) for Britain, and du Mez (2020) for the United States.

INTRODUCTION

1 Based on my interviews, there is little doubt that evangelicals in both Britain and Canada view the society around them as increasingly hostile. A 2022 Angus Reid/Cardus poll in Canada also shows this, as over half (56 per cent) of evangelicals felt their "values and faith" are "shut out" in Canadian society, nearly twice the level of any other group (the next highest was Muslims, at 26 per cent) (Angus Reid Institute 2022). But is this perception reality? In day-to-day interactions, direct attacks or antagonism in polite society in Canada and Britain are rare (C. Smith 2000; G. Smith 2020). However, evangelicals are correct that societal support for their views is declining as Christendom declines (e.g., McIvor 2020). Indeed, evangelicals are finding their ethics and beliefs increasingly criticized by the media (Haskell 2009), and there is evidence of anti-evangelical bias, especially in higher education (C. Smith 2014; Yancey 2010; Yancey and Williamson 2015). Further, the 2022 Angus Reid/Cardus poll found that Canadians saw "Evangelical Christianity" as more damaging to Canada and Canadian society than any other religious grouping, including Islam (Angus Reid Institute 2022). Evangelicalism is clearly unpopular for many in North America and Britain.

2 "Orthodoxy" means correct belief; "orthopraxy" means correct practice or action. In this book, I use the words to refer to those beliefs and practices that are prescribed by historic evangelicalism, normally based on institutional authorities.

3 Unless otherwise specified, all quotations from the Bible are taken from the New Living Translation (NLT).

4 I struggled to find a term to best describe the broader Western culture in which British and Canadian evangelicals find themselves. "Secular culture" did not seem appropriate, because part of the argument of this book is that the "sacred" is easily found in Western culture and its institutions. Galen Watt's term "romantic liberal modernity" (2022) is a good descriptive but requires a historical explanation of romanticism and modern liberalism. Charles Taylor's "social imaginary," which he defines as "common understanding that makes possible common practices and a widely shared sense of legitimacy" (2004, 23) is close to what I have in mind but does not distinguish well between the evangelical subcultural and the wider culture that non-evangelical Westerners inhabit, which I seek to do here. Evangelicals influence and are influenced by the wider Western culture, so it is difficult to draw a line that perfectly distinguishes culture from subculture; yet, as I argue below, evangelicalism is a distinctive subculture, allowing me to talk about evangelicalism as a distinct entity. Ultimately, I settled on the term "Western culture" to refer to the broader culture external to the evangelical subculture, even though the term is far from perfect.

5 For a detailed discussion of subculture theory and evangelicalism, see Abraham (2017).

6 This is not to suggest that there is no internal diversity or disagreement within evangelicalism. There is, to the point that some evangelicals wonder if the subculture really holds together, or if it will break apart in the future. I comment at greater length about this internal diversity later in the book.

7 There are, of course, some small fundamentalist groups who separate from society and could fit within the evangelical camp (Baker 2018). These groups are rare in Canada and Britain.

8 Bramadat (2000) uses the metaphor of "bridges" (connecting to the secular culture) and "fortresses" (withdrawing to the evangelical subculture) in his study of an evangelical university group in Canada.

9 C. Smith, Ritz, and Rotolo (2020) argue that "culture" is thicker, with more shared elements than some suggest. See the discussion in chapter 4.

10 Recently, books like Kristin Kobes Du Mez's *Jesus and John Wayne*

(2020), Gerardo Martí's *American Blindspot* (2020), and Anthea Butler's *White Evangelical Racism* (2021) indicate that theological definitions of evangelicalism (like Bebbington's) may not accurately define US evangelicals. Du Mez, Butler, and Martí all indicate that US evangelicalism is more of a political movement than a theological one (see Martí 2020, 251; Butler 2021, 138), and that it is marked by racist and sexist nationalism. These arguments are specific to American evangelicalism, and we cannot define evangelicals internationally based on US politics or US nationalism. Indeed, any such attempt would be US-centric (Yeh 2018), since Americans need to consider evangelicalism globally in any attempts to redefine it (Lin 2018). Du Mez (2020, 5) herself distinguishes between an international definition and one that could apply to American evangelicalism specifically.

11 As Tim Keller (2022) states, we should see *"the primacy, but insufficiency of the theological marks* for defining evangelicalism" (emphasis in original). His point is that, when applied to global evangelicalism, the theological marks of Bebbington's quadrilateral unify the movement, but that cultural differences – including the "gender exaggeration," "nationalism," and "racism" of US white evangelicalism – are significant and cannot be ignored. Further, evangelicalism in Canada and Britain is more distinct from the broader (secular) culture than in the United States because Canada and Britain are more secular than the United States (Reimer 2000), and because the US evangelical influence on American culture is more powerful at present than evangelicalism's influence on Britain or Canada.

12 In defence of using Bebbington's definition, I note, first, that the flagship evangelical organizations in the United States (the National Association of Evangelicals), Canada (the Evangelical Fellowship of Canada), and the United Kingdom (the Evangelical Alliance) all define evangelicalism based on Bebbington's quadrilateral (with minor variation), which they all cite on their websites. We should define evangelicals in ways that they accept themselves. Second, I am not aware of any scholars who define evangelicalism as a political or nationalist movement in Canada and Britain. Instead, international treatments of evangelicalism use Bebbington's quadrilateral as the foundation of their definitional strategies (see, e.g., Stackhouse 2022; Birdsall 2021; Stiller et al. 2015; Hutchinson and Wolffe 2012), as I do. Third, Bebbington recently defended his classic definition (Noll, Bebbington, and Marsden 2019), insisting that evangelicals must be defined based on theological, not cultural, criteria. See also Noll (n.d.).

13 In his definition, Stackhouse (2022) recommends six characteristics of evangelicals: Trinitarian, Biblicist, Conversionist, Missional, Populist, and Pragmatic. Stackhouse's list overlaps with that of Bebbington but includes a historical emphasis on all three Persons of the Godhead (Trinitarian), and an impulse toward evangelism, social action, and service (Missional, which overlaps with Bebbington's activism). It also includes a populist impulse (based on the priesthood of all believers) and pragmatism (going with what works).

14 That said, biblical literacy is likely declining, according to the Canadian Bible Engagement Study from 2013. For highlights, see the Canadian Bible Engagement Study page on the Evangelical Fellowship of Canada website, at https://www.evangelicalfellowship.ca/Topics/Church-Faith-Trends/Canadian-Bible-Engagement-Study-(CBES).

15 I use "Britain" and "British" instead of "England" and "English" in this book, even though my research was limited to England, because it is confusing to use "English" to refer to a geographic area. I recognize, of course, some differences in pockets of evangelicalism – in Scotland, particularly – that would not fit my overall description. See Guest, Olson, and Wolffe (2012). I refer to the "United Kingdom" when the research I cite includes all of the United Kingdom.

16 I intentionally created an interview sample that was disproportionately Anglican/Independent and British. I focused on Anglican and independent churches because I had previously done extensive research on the large, traditionally evangelical denominations. I completed fewer interviews in Canada because I previously had already done hundreds of interviews with evangelicals there (Reimer 2003; Reimer and Wilkinson 2015). I have also completed over one hundred interviews of evangelicals in the United States (Reimer 2003; 2011b). I do not draw directly from these previous studies in this book, but simply note them here as they provided background knowledge for the present study. See the appendix for more details on the sample.

17 Gauvreau (1991) called Canada's nineteenth century "the evangelical century." Noll (1992) sees evangelical dominance in both the United States and Canada through much of the nineteenth century. Bebbington (1989) states that evangelicalism had considerable influence in Britain and reached the height of its influence around 1850. Callum Brown (2009) argues that an evangelical Christian metanarrative dominated Britain from around 1800 to 1950, at which point it quickly broke down.

CHAPTER ONE

1 For those interested in a more complete historical development of this inward turn, which has early roots in the Enlightenment and Romanticism, but blossomed in the 1960s, see Watts (2022) and Taylor (2007).

2 For a thorough discussion on authority, see Koyzis (2014). For him, authority is not a bad thing, something that represses personal freedom. Rather, it is necessary for human flourishing.

3 While it may not be widely known that the inward turn is evident within evangelicalism, this is not a new discovery. James Davison Hunter wrote about the "subjectivization" of evangelicalism back in the 1980s (Hunter 1982).

4 Experts in all areas, including science and medicine, have lost much of their authority. This became obvious during the COVID-19 pandemic and throughout the Trump presidency, which have been associated with a variety of conspiracy theories (see Houtman, Aupers, and Laermans 2021). Thanks to Galen Watts for this insight. However, I would still contend that not all institutional authority has weakened at an equal pace. Religion has been particularly hard hit in terms of institutional authority.

5 When we speak of internal authority, this authority is perceived to come from the self, from the individual's own inner sense or intuition. My point is that one's intuition is socially shaped. For example, one's experiences become authoritative, but these experiences are bounded by social norms and are interpreted based on "schemas" available in society. One's moral inner sense is authoritative, but the reason an ethical position "seems right" to a person is because it is associated with positive feelings, which stem, at least partially, from reinforcement by people with whom the individual has close relationships and by "likes" on social media. Thus, the triumvirate of authorities – personal experience, algorithmic reinforcement, and the influence of warm relationships – are all social factors that shape internal authority, which is replacing institutional religious authority. Many Westerners view internal authority as free, while external authority is viewed as oppressive.

6 My perusal of the academic and popular uses of "individualism" shows at least five different but related definitions of the term, which sometimes refers to a macro societal reality and sometimes a micro personal reality: 1) a society is individualistic when individuals are paramount

and individual rights trump group rights; 2) a society is individualistic when people are separated from community and lack integration in society; 3) persons are individualistic if they show little concern for what others think, are self-reliant, or are rugged individualists; 4) persons are individualistic if they are self-focused; and 5) persons who are idiosyncratic/peculiar are sometimes referred to as individualistic.

7 One can debate how new this modern multi-vocality really is. Durkheim noted the growing diversity in society with the increased division of labour and institutional differentiation around the beginning of the twentieth century. My point here is not that it is new, but that Western society's multi-vocality increased quickly after the 1960s.

8 A reviewer wondered if I was critical of internal authority, and, if so, suggested that I should make that clear. The point I want to make is that, in many ways, internal authority undermines evangelicalism. It is hard to embrace the "lordship" of Jesus Christ (an external authority) if your authority comes from yourself. As I will show, orthodoxy and orthopraxy (as prescribed by church authorities) are also hard to maintain when one has an internal locus of authority. Outside of evangelicalism, I am more ambivalent about the notion. On the one hand, societies are more diverse, and so, to avoid oppressing minorities, our modern zeitgeist's emphasis on personal freedoms and self-determination is a sensible adaption. On the other hand, I share the concerns of others that Western cultures undermine the kind of community integration required for the healthy development of the self, and the kind of moral regulation that combats the "utilitarian individualism" and consumerism that dominates the economic sphere (see Watts 2022, 222). For a more general critique of modern spirituality, see Bregman 2014.

9 This section is heavily indebted to the work of Galen Watts (2020, 2022), whose masterful condensing of the literature on spirituality (which he calls "religion of the heart") results in ten "interrelated tenets" (2022, 48): 1) experiential epistemology; 2) immanence of god or the super-empirical; 3) benevolent god/universe; 4) redemptive self as theodicy; 5) self-realization as teleology; 6) self-ethic (voice from within); 7) natural virtue; 8) sacralization of individual liberty; 9) mind-body-spirit connection; and 10) methodological individualism.

10 In his book, *The Easternization of the West* (2007), Campbell summarizes this new ethos:

> We are now finally in a position to see precisely what is meant by the claim that the West is undergoing a process of Easternization. It

means that the worldview characteristic of the East is in the process of replacing the formerly dominate Western view – in other words, that metaphysical monism is replacing materialistic dualism. More precisely, it means that belief in a transcendental, personal god is giving way to belief in an immanent and impersonal one; that all dualisms are being rejected, whether that of god and mankind, mankind and nature, mind and body, or body and soul, in favor of generally holistic assumptions. That the idea of there being a single overriding principle guiding human history (whether religious or secular in form) is rejected in favor of either a cyclical notion of time or a belief in reincarnation and cosmic or spiritual evolution. That belief in sin is replaced by the idea of ignorance and error, and the striving of salvation is succeeded by a search for self-knowledge and enlightenment. At the same time, faith in reason is replace by an emphasis on intuition and insight and a stress on analysis, mea-surement, and calculation by contemplation and meditation, with direct experience of "the real" valued more highly than literal truth. Finally, church religion, and a concern with the division between believer and unbeliever, is being replaced by a pluralistic and diffuse spirituality in which the idea of seekership prevails. (66–7)

11 At least forty-six of my fifty-seven lay interviewees showed evidence of internal authority, while roughly ten did not, and a few were unclear in their responses. I was surprised that this tendency was so widespread, because the lay interviewees were clearly among the most institutional-ly committed, many serving in leadership positions within the church. I considered the person to be showing internal authority if 1) they per-sonally disagreed with an official position of their church, and often stated that they knew they were doing so; 2) if they made it clear that their position was a personal choice that they needed to discover by themselves, apart from an external authority; or 3) if they had different standards for themselves and others, often indicating that what others do or believe is "up to them."

12 The RCCG originated in Nigeria in 1952 and is led by Enoch Adeboye. It has now spread to 180 countries globally and is one of the fastest-growing Christian networks. According to its websites, it claims over 170 parishes in Canada (https://rccgcanada.org/), over 600 in the United States (https://rccgna.org/regions/parishes/usa-parishes/), and 850 in the United Kingdom (https://www.rccguk.church/our-history/).

13 Molly Worthen (2014, 258) argues that "the problem with evangelical intellectual life is not that its participants obey authority ... The prob-

lem is that evangelicals attempt to obey multiple authorities at the same time. They demand that presuppositions trump evidence while counting the right kind of evidence as universal fact. They insist that modern reason must buttress faith, that scripture and spiritual feeling align with scientific reality." Authority has long been contested within evangelicalism, and it is not unified on its understanding of *sola scriptura*, the authority of the Bible. I am suggesting that authority within evangelicalism will continue to be contested, driven increasingly by the embrace of subjective authority versus the external authority of the Bible and church hierarchy.

14 Table 1.2 uses data from the 2019 Maru Blue/EFC Church and Faith Trends survey, which was conducted in English and French with 5,011 Canadians over the age of eighteen on 12–16 August 2019, on the Maru/Blue online research panel. The Maru/Blue panel is highly respected and representative of the Canadian population. The estimated margin of error for this survey is +/- 1 per cent, nineteen times out of twenty. For more information about the reliability and validity of Maru/Blue panel surveys, see https://www.marublue.com/blog. I want to thank Rick Hiemstra and the Evangelical Fellowship of Canada for allowing me use of this survey data.

15 According to their website, C3 Churches Global (formally Christian City Church International) was started by Phil and Chris Pringle in 1980 in Sydney, Australia. There are over 500 churches in 38 countries, including 25 churches in Canada (https://c3churchglobal.com /regions/c3-canada).

CHAPTER TWO

1 Throughout this book, the names of persons and churches are pseudonyms to protect the confidentiality of the respondents.

2 The "Fall" refers to the time when the first humans, Adam and Eve, ate the fruit from the tree in the garden of Eden that God had commanded them not to eat from, and thus "fell" into sin.

3 For the nineteenth-century definition, see Merriam-Webster 1828, at http://webstersdictionary1828.com/Dictionary/belief. Now, Merriam-Webster defines belief as "a state or habit of mind in which trust or confidence is placed in some person or thing." None of the definitions include religion, although some of the examples of the usage of the word do. https://www.merriam-webster.com/dictionary/belief.

4 Evangelicals believe that God is unchanging, a belief based on multiple

Bible passages (e.g., Hebrews 13:8; Malachi 3:6). The words of God, as re-corded in the Bible, are also unchanging (e.g., Isaiah 40:8; Matthew 24:35).

5 Here Day nods to Durkheim (1915), who argued that religious beliefs come into being through the performance of rituals. I am not convinced by Durkheim's explanation that religion originated through collective ritual, although I am convinced that beliefs are reinforced through ritual.

6 In my view, religious belief's meaning-making function and belonging function are mutually reinforcing. Religion does both. I agree with Berger (1967) that religion provides meaning and order in the face of the chaos of the world, and provides us with moral orientation. These beliefs are reinforced by belonging to a group of co-religionists, who support our waning belief in times of crisis. I also do not think that beliefs are simply "performative" in the Durkheimian sense. Beliefs are also cognitive, and stem not just from social interaction but also from the need to make sense of the world through narratives that provide meaning (see C. Smith 2003a).

7 This tendency toward softening unpopular beliefs has been demonstrated among Pentecostals in Canada (Stewart 2015; Wilkinson and Ambrose 2020).

8 In the United States, Smith called "moralistic therapeutic deism" the dominant religious view of young Americans (C. Smith with Denton 2005, 162). In Canada, Hiemstra, Dueck, and Blackaby (2018, 107) refer to the "Universal Gnostic Religious Ethic" as dominant among Canadian youth. In the United Kingdom, Guest (2019, 51) found that Christian university students had a "tendency toward syncretism." Each of these concepts has considerable overlap with perennialism.

9 "Average Daily Time Spent on Social Media," Broadband Search, https://www.broadbandsearch.net/blog/average-daily-time-on-social-media.

10 The pastor is referring to anthropomorphisms, those passages that metaphorically speak of God as having a human body or body part, like God's "outstretched arm" (e.g., Exodus 6:6).

11 Similarly, Perrin's (2016) research on the hermeneutics of young evangelicals in England found a focus on questions of historical context as key to interpretation. For views of the Bible among British youth, also see Ford, Mann, and Phillips 2019.

12 "Saying the sinner's prayer" refers to the moment of conversion, where the repentant person confesses their sin and receives salvation through Jesus. The "Damascus road" conversion refers to St Paul's sudden and

dramatic conversion on the road to Damascus recorded in the book of
Acts, chapter 9.

13 However, evangelicals are not as unanimous as some think on issues
such as abortion. For example, while 42 per cent of British evangelicals
in 2010 agreed that "abortion can never be justified," 41 per cent disagreed (G. Smith 2020).

14 For Evangelical Fellowship of Canada (EFC), "Sanctity of Life,"
https://www.evangelicalfellowship.ca/Themes/Sanctity-of-Life; for UK's
Evangelical Alliance (EA), "Both Lives Matter,"
https://www.eauk.org/about-us/nations/northern-ireland/both-lives-mat-
ter; for the US National Association of Evangelicals (NAE),
https://www.nae.net/abortion-2/. On the traditional definition of marriage, EFC, "When Two Become One,"
https://files.evangelicalfellowship.ca/si/Marriage%20and%20Family/Mar
riage%20booklet%202006.pdf; EA "Biblical and Pastoral Responses to
Homosexuality," https://www.eauk.org/resources/what-we-offer/reports
/biblical-and-pastoral-responses-to-homosexuality; NAE, "God Defined
Marriage," https://www.nae.net/god-defined-marriage/.

15 Bruce (2020), who interviewed 217 Americans on their attitudes toward
abortion, also found that responses were more complicated, nuanced,
and fluid than the "pro-life" and "pro-choice" labels suggest. However,
she found that, in the United States, "abortion is frequently attributed
to personal selfishness or moral failing, against God's will" (2020, 35),
whereas Canadian and British evangelicals were more likely to attribute
it to societal problems.

16 "Sacrificing to Molech" refers to Old Testament passages where the
penalty for child sacrifice to Molech, the "detestable god of the
Ammonites," was death (e.g., Leviticus 20:2).

17 Charismatic and Pentecostal evangelicals believe that the Holy Spirit
imparts information to persons that they could not otherwise know.
Such divinely imparted knowledge can be a "word of knowledge" (normally dealing with the present) or a "prophetic word" (normally dealing
with future events).

18 Of course, I recognize that some are hurt by the non-affirming message
of evangelical churches, in spite of attempts to be "gentle." My point
here is that most evangelicals in both Canada and England present their
conservative ethical positions gently, attempting not to offend. However,
the inclusivity of these churches has limits. For example, official membership or leadership positions in the church may exclude those in non-
traditional relationships.

CHAPTER THREE

1 Based on data from the Pew Research Centre: see Martínez and Smith (2016) and Lipka and Smith (2020).

2 60 *Minutes* interviewed Daniels, and the story was covered by many newspapers (Luckhurst 2018).

3 The actual divorce rates of evangelicals in comparison to non-evangelicals in the United States are debated. What seems to be clear is that church attendance and religious homogeneity (both spouses have the same religious affiliation and views) work against marriage dissolution, whereas inactive evangelicals (especially those who marry young) have higher rates of divorce (Vaaler, Ellison, and Powers 2009; W.B. Wilcox and Williamson 2007; W.B. Wilcox and Wolfinger 2016; Wright 2010). See also the argument by Park, Tom, and Andercheck (n.d.) for higher divorce rates among American evangelicals compared to their compatriots who claim no religion, and the response to that claim by Zylstra (2014).

4 Research seems to suggest that religiosity, including church attendance, decreases intimate partner violence (IPV) (see W.B. Wilcox 2004; W.B. Wilcox and Wolfinger 2016), although less religious evangelicals (i.e., those with sporadic attendance) may have the highest rates of IPV in the population (Westenberg 2017). Some argue that male headship and complementarianism are used to justify abuse, to keep women in violent relationships, or to cover up IPV (Giles 2020).

5 A few cautions are warranted when it comes to comparing rates of divorce among evangelicals and non-evangelicals. First, evangelicals are more likely to marry, and obviously higher rates of marriage will be related to higher rates of divorce. A better measure, therefore, would be the percentage of marriages that end in divorce. Second, evangelical churches may attract previously divorced people, if they offer a sense of community and support. Alternatively, divorce may increase disaffiliation. Both of these possibilities can also influence divorce rates (Bowen 2004).

6 In Canada, if evangelicalism is measured based on denomination (those who affiliate with evangelical denominations, like Baptists, Alliance, Wesleyans, Pentecostals, and so on), there is no statistically significant difference in the divorce ratio (percentage divorced divided by percentage married) or in the percentage who have ever been divorced for evangelicals (23.5 per cent) compared to non-evangelicals (21.5 per cent). A statistically significant difference can be found in the divorce ratio between evangelicals ("evangelically aligned," 16.3 per cent) and non-evangelicals (22.2 per cent), when evangelicalism is measured based

on those who hold to evangelical beliefs (the CES scale, based on questions that tap Bebbington's quadrilateral), where evangelicals are slightly less likely to be divorced. These data come from the 2019 Maru Blue/EFC Church and Faith Trends Poll.

7 Of course, authenticity is not the same as fully autonomous self-expression, as all social situations contain some norms and expectations that shape behaviour and limit choices. Thus, the culture (or evangelical subculture) and our individual self-expression are "co-determiners" of our beliefs, actions, and identities (Abraham 2017, 43).

8 Carey Nieuwhof, "5 Things Millennials Are Looking for in a Church," undated blog post, https://careynieuwhof.com/5-things-millennials-are-looking-for-in-a-church/.

9 For the United States, see Roach (2020); for Australia, see Lake (2018). In Britain, a meta-analysis sees decline in all forms of bible engagement (Field 2014).

10 Evangelical Alliance, "21st Century Evangelicals: Time for Discipleship?" (2014), https://www.eauk.org/church/resources/snapshot/upload/Time-for-Discipleship-PDF.pdf

11 Based on the 2019 MaruBlue/EFC Church and Faith Trends Survey.

12 Evangelical research organizations provide insight into what Americans pray for. See "Americans Pray for Friends and Family, but Rarely for Celebrities or Sport Teams," 1 October 2014, Lifeway Research, https://lifewayresearch.com/2014/10/01/americansprayforfriendsandfamily-2/, and "Silent and Solo: How Americans Pray," 15 August 2017, Barna, https://www.barna.com/research/silent-solo-americans-pray/.

13 While it may be that desirability bias would encourage evangelicals to over-report their spiritual practices, it is also possible that some would under-report because of biblical teaching against public displays of piety, including alms-giving, prayer, and fasting (see Jesus' teaching in Matthew, chapter 6).

14 Edith is referring to the monastic practice of "unceasing prayer," where the Christian tries to remain constantly in prayer through their day. She refers to classic works on this practice, including Brother Lawrence's seventeenth-century work *Practicing the Presence of God*, and *The Way of the Pilgrim*, a nineteenth-century Russian work where the pilgrim recites the "Jesus Prayer," "Lord Jesus Christ, son of God, have mercy on me, a sinner."

15 Note that Edith's reading includes American evangelical authors Foster and Yancey, and Briton Wright. This indicates the international nature of evangelical subcultural influences, something I will say more about in chapter 5.

16 Evangelical Alliance, "21st Century Evangelicals."

17 See also Sophia Bernazzani, "What Millennials Want from Work: Flexibility, Not Salary," undated blog post, The Predictive Index, https://www.predictiveindex.com/blog/why-flexibility-is-a-better-perk-than-salary/, and many other articles citing research in this area. There are similar findings in the United Kingdom (Burnford 2019).

18 Meagan Drillinger, "The Tired Generation: 4 Reasons Millennials Are Always Exhausted," Healthline, updated 29 March 2020, https://www.healthline.com/health/millennials-exhausted-all-the-time.

19 In addition, a Lifeway research study in January 2022 reported that 83 per cent of American Protestant pastors said that new people were attending their churches (Earls 2022).

20 Research in Canada by the Angus Reid Institute (2021) shows that evangelicals are split down the middle on whether or not governmental restrictions were "unfairly harsh on places of worship compared to other public venues," with 47 per cent feeling they were and 46 per cent thinking they were not.

21 *Premier Christianity*, a Christian magazine out of the United Kingdom, reports that about one-third of younger cohorts who attended at least monthly will not return to church after COVID (Faro 2022). Research in Canada found that, in February 2022, when 85 per cent of churches were meeting in person, Christian church leaders reported that church attendance was at about 60 per cent of what it had been before the pandemic. See "The Future of Christian Churches and Ministries," National Survey Results, Spring 2022, WayBase, https://www.waybase.com/research/reports.

22 There is also evidence of American political influence in politically conservative Alberta (Banack 2016; Reimer 2021).

23 Data from EFC/Angus Reid Forum provided to me by EFC include results from Angus Reid's public opinion polls from 2004 to 2015. The data show that 51.9 per cent of evangelicals in Canada (identified based on questions developed to tap the four characteristics of Bebbington's quadrilateral) voted for conservative parties in 2015, and that, between 2004 and 2011, no more than 61 per cent of evangelicals voted for conservative parties. However, evangelicals were consistently more likely than the general Canadian population to vote for conservatives.

24 It is possible that some respondents were overreporting their giving here, but many answered with the sort of precision (e.g., "10 per cent of my pre-tax income") that suggests accurate reporting.

25 Similarly, Hatcher (2017) notes that evangelism is not a "defining attribute" of evangelicals (9).

26 One respondent, who had started a ministry to the homeless in his city, spoke of going out (by himself) with a thermos of coffee and "sharing Christ" with people on the street. This was at least partially connected to a larger ministry and was the only example of a solo evangelizing effort from the lay interviews.

CHAPTER FOUR

1 Some research (e.g., Bengtson with Putney and Harris 2013) also indicates that a father's faith modelling is more important than a mother's. Of course, Gideon may not be aware of this research but may simply be stating a personal view.

2 "Mark Chaves: Evangelicals Lose Fewer Youth than Liberals," Faith and Leadership, 8 July 2019, https://faithandleadership.com/mark-chaves-evangelicals-lose-fewer-youth-liberals. See also Chaves 2011.

3 Thanks to Rick Hiemstra of the Evangelical Fellowship of Canada for use of their 2019 Maru/EFC poll.

4 For a description of thematic analysis, see Ryan and Bernard (2003).

5 Based on secondary analysis of the data in *Hemorrhaging Faith* (Penner et al. 2012).

6 Note that their sample of US parents was not representative of the national population, as C. Smith, Ritz, and Rotolo (2020) make clear. Instead, they interviewed 235 adults who were involved in congregations and therefore were assumed to be more religious than the average.

7 One difference between Smith, Ritz, and Rotolo's sample and mine is that the individuals in mine were probably even more institutionally active and committed, so concern for doctrinal orthodoxy was slightly more common. At least a few parents in my sample voiced concerns about the orthodoxy of their children, which was rare in the American sample. For example, a mother in a Canadian independent church with children in their twenties said, "I'm concerned about their understanding of biblical truth, because I consider it to be biblical truth and fact, whereas I'm not sure … I think they believe in Jesus, I think they're saved, I think they love God, but I'm not sure they think that it's the only way." This concern for doctrinal truth was also evident in a minority of interviews in C. Smith, Ritz, and Rotolo (2020) and was greater among evangelical parents.

8 Some have critiqued Arnett's suggestion that emerging adults are free to explore lifestyle choices, unrestrained by macroeconomic and demo-

graphic factors. Instead, say his critics, macrosocial factors like class and race constrain choice and contribute to delayed adulthood (see, e.g., Coté and Allahar 2006).

9 The idea to connect identity to telling your story comes from Vermeer (2009).

10 In the United States, about 8 per cent of evangelical children go to private Christian schools (Reimer and Sikkink 2020). We don't know the percentage in Canada or in Britain. There are many state-funded religious schools in Britain, but the number of "new Christian schools" is small (roughly 100, according to the website New Christian Schools, https://newchristian schools.org/history/). Canada has about 500 non-Catholic "Christian" schools, with some 80,500 students (Allison, Hasan, and Van Pelt 2016), possibly attracting 10 per cent of children from evangelical families.

11 Similarly, Jenkins (2020) and Inglehart (2021) have also connected secularization to the family, specifically to declining fertility and fertility norms.

12 Conor Heneghan, "The Number of Times the Average iPhone User Unlocks Their Phone Every Day Has Been Revealed," Joe, n.d., https://www.joe.ie/tech/the-number-of-times-the-average-iphone-user-unlocks-their-phone-every-day-has-been-revealed-540973.

13 These mental health concerns are often linked to technology and social media in research (see, e.g., McMaster 2020).

14 A recent poll shows that Canadians are hesitant to talk about religion, politics, sex, and money on social media or in polite company in general. "Money, Religion, Politics and Sex: Canadians Share Their Taboo Topics," Cision, 25 February 2020, https://www.newswire.ca/news-releases/money-religion-politics-and-sex-canadians-share-their-taboo-topics-860346993.html.

CHAPTER FIVE

1 An exception is Stackhouse (2018).

2 Press coverage of evangelical nationalism may have peaked with the storming of the US Capitol in January 2021, during which Confederate flags, white supremacist symbols, and "Jesus saves" banners waved together. This and similar events were subsequent to my 2018 interviews.

3 See the Churches Together website, at https://cte.org.uk/.

4 Subsequent to my 2018 interviews, Bill Hybels retired with a tarnished reputation, so we can assume his influence has diminished since then.

5 A pastor of a network church thought that the reason the American

Presbyterian and prolific author Tim Keller was so popular in England
was because he was a theologically sophisticated evangelical who filled
the void left by the late John Stott.

6 I refer here to contact theory, which argues that, under certain condi-
tions, intergroup contact reduces prejudice (Allport 1958).

7 See the One People Commission page on the Evangelical Alliance website,
at https://www.eauk.org/what-we-do/networks/one-people-commission
and the Gather Movement website, at http://www.gather.global/about/.

8 See The Evangelical Fellowship of Canada's website, https://www
.evangelicalfellowship.ca/.

9 I have in mind here US evangelical groups like Sojourners and Evangelicals for Social Action (see Swartz 2014). In April 2018, about fifty evangelical leaders met at Wheaton College, Illinois, partly to address their
concern that evangelicalism was being too closely aligned with Trump's
political rhetoric, although Trump was not the main focus of the meeting. The event was reported in the Washington Post (E. Miller 2018),
Christianity Today magazine ("About That Evangelical Summit in
Wheaton This Week," 19 April 2018, https://www.christianitytoday.com
/ct/2018/april-web-only/Evangelical-summit-conference-wheaton.html);
and other venues ("World Evangelical Leaders Confer at Wheaton,"
Wheaton Record, 19 April 2018, http://www.wheatonrecord.com/news
/world-Evangelical-leaders-confer-wheaton/).

10 A British evangelical leader in London told me that the debate as to
whether or not their (evangelical) organization should be identified
with the word "evangelical" is a "conversation we're regularly having.
What's happening in the States doesn't help us." So far, they have decided to retain the label in their organization's title. Canadians seem to be
responding in similar fashion (Stiller 2021).

11 Historically, evangelicals in Britain and Canada would also be known
for their more decorous, less exuberant worship (Bebbington 1997;
Reimer 2003). However, my experience in churches influenced by the
Toronto Blessing in both Canada and the United Kingdom, and the
exuberance of many new independent and charismatic churches in
both countries, including the growing number of immigrant churches,
lead me to wonder if this is still true. Bebbington (2007) also finds
more informality and expressive worship in churches in the United
Kingdom over time.

12 Recently disgraced megachurch pastor Bruxy Cavey and pop icon Justin
Bieber (reportedly converted at Hillsong, New York) may be the best-
known Canadian evangelicals, but others include scholars James K.A.

Smith and D.A. Carson, TV/radio personality Lorna Dueck, theologians
Clark Pinnock and Gordon Fee, novelist Jeanette Oke, World Vision's
David Toycen, pastors Charles Price and Leon Fontaine, EFC's Bruce
Clemenger, spiritual writer Mark Buchanan, evangelical global leader
Brian Stiller, singer-songwriters Steve Bell and Carolyn Arends, and ethi-
cist/historian John Stackhouse Jr, among others.

13 See the "Database of Megachurches in the US" page on the website of
the Hartford Institute for Religious Research, at http://hirr.hartsem.edu
/megachurch/database.html (scroll down to the "Listing of Canadian
Megachurches" hyperlink for Warren Bird's list).

14 A list of world megachurches is maintained by Warren Bird of the Leadership Network, which lists eighteen in the United Kingdom. Leadership
Network, "World Megachurches," https://leadnet.org/world/?%2Fworld.

15 Based on denominational statistics collected by Bruce Guenther and
made available to the author.

16 I considered two other differences between Britain and Canada, but
could not find enough comparative data to make a strong argument.
The first is that evangelicalism is less visible on university campuses in
Canada than in Britain. In the United Kingdom, research suggests that
about one-quarter of Christian students participate in a Student Union
(Guest et al., 2013; see also Guest 2019; Perfect, Ryan, and Aune n.d.). In
the United States, groups like Inter-Varsity, Cru, Navigators, and many
evangelical denominational ministries engage some 270,000 students on
college/university campuses (Schmalzbauer and Mahoney 2018). In
Canada, groups like Inter-Varsity, Power to Change, and Navigators
work actively with roughly 6,000 university students with another
2,000–3,000 who are broadly connected (based on personal conversations with Inter-varsity). A second possible difference is that evangelicals
in Canada have a greater focus on multiculturalism and Indigenous
peoples than those in Britain. Awareness of and reconciliatory efforts
with Indigenous peoples (treaty acknowledgements, blanket exercises,
and so on) seem much more common among Canadian evangelicals.

CHAPTER SIX

1 Another independent pastor argued that it is more efficient to create
small multi-site churches that rent public buildings instead of investing
in "Lazarus projects" (referring to Jesus resurrecting the dead Lazarus in
John 11), in which millions are spent trying to renovate and re-energize
a large, old church. He said he embraced the old Methodist, itinerant

preacher model from the nineteenth century, noting that it is more efficient to employ young leaders with less education who are raised up
from within and released with his support, than to employ academically
trained, traditionally ordained clergy. He does not think that congregants care whether or not their pastor has certain degrees, as long as
that individual cares for them and helps them grow spiritually. Respect
is earned by action, not by degrees, he avows. This pastor's network of
churches was growing quickly.

2 The Quiverfull movement is more common in the US Midwest and
South, but represents a small proportion of evangelical families. They
tend to embrace male headship and home schooling, and reject birth
control. The television series *19 Kids and Counting*, featuring Michelle
and Jim Bob Duggar, increased interest in the movement, even though
the Duggars stated that they were not part of the movement.

3 Migration Statistics, UK Parliament, House of Common Library, 27
April 2021, https://commonslibrary.parliament.uk/research-briefings
/sn06077/.

4 Net Migration Statistics, Migration Watch UK, https://www.migration
watchuk.org/statistics-net-migration-statistics.

5 There is a fair bit of variation in reports of the size of the Lagos auditorium (e.g., one mile long, two miles long and a mile wide), but it is likely the biggest in the world.

6 Ethnic Group by Measures, 2011 (table), Nomis, https://www.nomis
web.co.uk/census/2011/KS201EW/view/2092957699?cols=measures.

7 "Tentmakers" refers to those (such as the Apostle Paul, who made tents
for a living) who serve as pastors but do not receive money from their
congregation(s).

8 Martí and Ganiel (2014) prefer the term "religious orientations" as
opposed to "religious identities," because of the fluid nature of the emerging church (and the identities of those in it), which is always in flux.

9 In 2022, Cavey resigned as pastor due to allegations of sexual impropriety and was later convicted.

CONCLUSION

1 Private correspondence with Professor Woodhead.

2 In 2020–21, churches in both countries were not allowed to meet in
person. They later required masking and/or social distancing, along
with proof of vaccination. On tensions within evangelicalism caused by
vaccination passports and requirements, see Coren (2022) on Canada,

Sherwood (2021) on the United Kingdom, and Alberta (2022) in the United States.

3 For example, Wilkinson and Ambrose (2020) suggest that the leaders of the Pentecostal Assemblies of Canada borrowed from secular business models in their creation of religious programming in such a way as to appeal to, and even promote, individualistic understandings of religious belief and practice.

References

Abraham, Ibrahim. 2017. *Evangelical Youth Culture: Alternative Music and Extreme Sports*. New York: Bloomsbury.

Adedibu, Babatunde. 2016. "Missional History and the Growth of the Redeemed Christian Church of God in the United Kingdom (1988–2015)." *Journal of the European Pentecostal Theological Association* 36 (1): 80–93.

Alberta, Tim. 2022. "How Politics Poisoned the Evangelical Church." *Atlantic*, 10 May. https://www.theatlantic.com/magazine/archive/2022/06/evangelical-church-pastors-political-radicalization/629631/.

Aldred, Joe. 2006. *Respect: Understanding Caribbean British Christianity*. Peterborough, UK: Epworth Press.

Alexander, Jeffrey C. 2003. *The Meanings of Social Life: A Cultural Sociology*. Oxford: Oxford University Press.

Allison, Derek J., Sazid Hasan, and Deani Van Pelt. 2016. "A Diverse Landscape: Independent Schools in Canada." Fraser Institute. https://www.fraserinstitute.org/studies/a-diverse-landscape-independent-schools-in-canada.

Allport, Gordon. 1958. *The Nature of Prejudice*. New York: Anchor.

Ammerman, Nancy T. 2014. *Sacred Stories, Spiritual Tribes: Finding Religion in Everyday Life*. Oxford: Oxford University Press.

Angus Reid Institute. 2021. "Religious Canadians Praying for Return to In-Person Worship, but Won't Forsake Online Services in Future," 1 April. https://angusreid.org/wp-content/uploads/2021/03/2021.04.01_Religion_Easter_COVID.pdf.

– 2022. "Canada across the Religious Spectrum: A Portrait of the Nation's Inter-Faith Perspectives during Holy Week." https://angusreid.org/canada-religion-interfaith-holy-week/.

Anthony, Michael, ed. 2007. *Perspectives on Children's Spiritual Formation:*

Scottie May, Gregory C. Carlson, Trisha Graves, and Tim Ellis. Nashville: B&H Academic.

Armstrong, Chris. 2016. "Sound, Style, Substance: New Directions in Evangelical Spirituality." In *The Future of Evangelicalism in America*, edited by Candy Gunther Brown and Mark Silk, 54–91. New York: Columbia University Press.

Arnett, Jeffrey. 2015. *Emerging Adulthood: The Winding Road from the Late Teens through the Twenties*. 2nd ed. Oxford: Oxford University Press.

Arnett, Jeffery, and Lene Arnett Jensen. 2002. "A Congregation of One: Individualized Religious Beliefs among Emerging Adults." *Journal of Adolescent Research* 17 (5): 451–67.

Arweck, Elisabeth, and James A. Beckford. 2012. "Social Perspectives." In *Religion and Change in Modern Britain*, edited by Linda Woodhead and Rebecca Catto, 352–72. London: Routledge.

Asad, Talal. 1993. *Genealogies of Religion: Discipline and Reasons of Power in Christianity and Islam*. Baltimore: Johns Hopkins University Press.

Aune, Kristin. 2004. "Postfeminist Evangelicals: The Construction of Gender in the New Frontiers International Churches." PhD diss., University of London.

– 2006. "Marriage in a British Evangelical Congregation: Practising Postfeminist Partnership?" *Sociological Review* 54 (4): 638–57.

– 2008. "Evangelical Christianity and Women's Changing Lives." *European Journal of Women's Studies* 15 (3): 277–94.

Bailey, Sarah Pulliam. 2018. "In the Age of Trump and Stormy Daniels, Evangelical Leaders Face Sex Scandals of Their Own." *Washington Post*, 20 March. https://www.washingtonpost.com/news/acts-of-faith/wp/2018/03/30/in-an-age-of-trump-and-stormy-daniels-evangelical-leaders-face-sex-scandals-of-their-own/.

Baker, Joseph. 2018. "Christian Sectarianism, Fundamentalism, and Extremism." In *Routledge Handbook on Deviance*, edited by Stephen Brown and Ophir Sefiha, 187–98. London: Routledge.

Banack, Clark. 2016. *God's Province: Evangelical Christianity, Political Thought, and Conservatism in Alberta*. Montreal and Kingston: McGill-Queen's University Press.

Bartkowski, John P. 1996. "Beyond Biblical Literalism and Inerrancy: Conservative Protestants and the Hermeneutic Interpretation of Scripture." *Sociology of Religion* 57 (3): 259–72.

Bauerlein, Paul. 2009. *The Dumbest Generation: How the Digital Age Stupefies Young Americans and Jeopardizes our Future*. New York: Penguin Books.

Baumrind, Diana. 1966. "Effects of Authoritative Parental Control on Child Behavior." *Child Development* 37 (4): 887–907.

Beaman, Lori G., and Peter Beyer. 2013. "Betwixt and Between: A Canadian Perspective on the Challenges of Researching the Spiritual but Not Religious." In *Social Identities between the Sacred and the Secular*, edited by Abby Day, Giselle Vincett, and Christopher R. Cotter, 127–42. Farnham, UK: Ashgate.

Bean, Lydia. 2014. *The Politics of Evangelical Identity: Local Churches and Partisan Divides in the United States and Canada*. Princeton, NJ: Princeton University Press.

Bean, Lydia, Marco J. Gonzalez, and Jason Kaufman. 2008. "Why Doesn't Canada Have an American-Style Christian Right? A Comparative Framework for Analyzing the Political Effects of Evangelical Subcultural Identity." *Canadian Journal of Sociology* 33 (4): 899–943.

Bean, Lydia, and Brandon Martinez. 2014. "Evangelical Ambivalence toward Gays and Lesbians." *Sociology of Religion* 75 (3): 395–417.

Bebbington, David. 1989. *Evangelicalism in Modern Britain*. New York: Routledge.

– 1994a. "Evangelicalism in Its Settings: The British and American Movements since 1940." In *Evangelicalism: Comparative Studies of Popular Protestantism in North America, the British Isles, and Beyond, 1700–1990*, edited by David Bebbington, Mark A. Noll, and George A. Rawlyk, 365–88. New York: Oxford University Press.

– 1994b. "Evangelicals in Modern Britain and America: A Comparison." In *Amazing Grace: Evangelicalism in Australia, Britain, Canada, and the United States*, edited by George A. Rawlyk and Mark Noll, 183–212. Montreal and Kingston: McGill-Queen's University Press.

– 1997. "Canadian Evangelicalism: A View from Britain." In *Aspects of the Canadian Evangelical Experience*, edited by George A. Rawlyk, 38–54. Montreal and Kingston: McGill-Queen's University Press.

– 2007. "Evangelicals and Public Worship, 1965–2005." *Evangelical Quarterly* 79 (1): 3–22.

– 2008. "Gospel and Culture in British Evangelicalism." Unpublished paper.

– 2009. "Evangelical Trends, 1959–2009." *Anvil* 26: 93–106.

Bebbington, David, and David Ceri Jones, eds. 2013. *Evangelicalism and Fundamentalism in the United Kingdom during the Twentieth Century*. Oxford: Oxford University Press.

Beck, Ulrich. 2010. *A God of One's Own*. Cambridge: Polity Press.

Becker, Penny E. 1999. *Congregations in Conflict*. New York: Cambridge University Press.

Bellah, Robert N., Richard Madsen, William M. Sullivan, Ann Swidler, and Steven M. Tipton. 1985. *Habits of the Heart: Individualism and Commitment in American Life*. Berkeley and Los Angeles: University of California Press.

Bengtson, Vern L., with Norella M. Putney and Susan Harris. 2013. *Families and Faith: How Religion Is Passed Down across Generations*. Oxford: Oxford University Press.

Benson, Mark J., Paula B. Harris, and Cosby S. Rogers. 1992. "Identity Consequences of Attachment to Mothers and Fathers among Late Adolescents." *Journal of Research on Adolescence* 2 (3): 187–204.

Berger, Peter. 1967. *The Sacred Canopy: Elements of a Sociological Theory of Religion*. New York: Anchor Books.

– 1979. *The Heretical Imperative: Contemporary Possibilities of Religious Affirmation*. New York: Doubleday.

Berger, Peter, Brigitte Berger, and Hansfried Kellner. 1974. *The Homeless Mind: Modernization and Consciousness*. New York: Vintage.

Berger, Peter, Grace Davie, and Effie Fokas. 2008. *Religious America, Secular Europe? A Theme and Variations*. London: Routledge.

Berger, Peter, and Thomas Luckmann. 1965. *The Social Construction of Reality: A Treatise in the Sociology of Knowledge*. New York: Anchor Books.

Bethune, Sophie. 2019. "Gen Z More Likely to Report Mental Health Concerns." *American Psychological Association* 50 (1) January. https://www.apa.org/monitor/2019/01/gen-z.

Beyer, Peter. 2000. "Modern Forms of the Religious Life: Denomination, Church, and Invisible Religion in Canada, the United States and Europe." In *Rethinking Church, State and Modernity: Canada between Europe and America*, edited by David Lyon and Marguerite Van Die, 189–210. Toronto: University of Toronto Press.

Beyer, Peter, Scott Craig, and Alyshea Cummins. 2019. "Religious Identity Construction among Young Adults in Canada: The Religious, the Spiritual, and the Non-Religious." In *Youth, Religion and Identity in Globalizing Context: International Perspectives*, edited by Paul Gareau, Spencer Culham Bullivant, and Peter Beyer, 35–52. Leiden: Brill.

Bibby, Reginald. 1987. *Fragmented Gods: The Poverty and Potential of Religion in Canada*. Toronto: Irwin.

– 2006. *The Boomer Factor: What Canada's Most Famous Generation Is Leaving Behind*. Toronto: Bastian Books.

– 2011. *Beyond the Gods and Back: Religion's Demise and Rise and Why It Matters*. Lethbridge, AB: Project Canada Books.

– 2012. *A New Day: The Resilience and Restructuring of Religion in Canada*. Lethbridge, AB: Project Canada Books.

– 2017. *Resilient Gods: Being Pro-Religious, Low Religious, or No Religious in Canada*. Vancouver: UBC Press.

Bibby, Reginald, and Merlin B. Brinkerhoff. 1973. "The Circulation of the

Saints: A Study of People Who Join Conservative Churches." *Journal for the Scientific Study of Religion* 12: 273–83.

– 1993. "Circulation of the Saints, 1966–1990: New Data, New Reflections." *Journal for the Scientific Study of Religion* 33: 273–80.

Bibby, Reginald, Joel Thiessen, and Monetta Bailey. 2019. *The Millennial Mosaic: How Pluralism and Choice Are Shaping Canadian Youth and the Future of Canada*. Toronto: Dundurn Press.

Bielo, James. 2011. *Emerging Evangelicals: Faith, Modernity, and the Desire for Authenticity*. New York: New York University Press.

Bird, Warren. 2015. "Large Canadian Churches Draw an Estimated 300,000 Worshippers Each Week: Findings from a National Study." Leadership Network. https://ureachcanada.ca/wp-content/uploads/2018/06/Large-Canadian-Churches-Warren-Bird.pdf.

Birdsall, Jessimin. 2021. "Racial Diversity in British Evangelicalism: Frames, Barriers and Practices." PhD diss., Princeton University.

Boch, Anna. 2020. "Increasing American Political Tolerance: A Framework Excluding Hate Speech." *Socius: Sociological Research in a Dynamic World* 6: 1–12.

Bouma, Gary. 2008. "The Challenge of Religious Revitalization to Multicultural and Multifaith Australia." *International Journal of Diversity in Organizations, Communities and Nations* 8 (1): 1–4.

Boussalis, Constantine, Travis G. Coan, and Miyra R. Holman. 2021. "Political Speech in Religious Sermons." *Politics and Religion* 14: 241–68.

Bowen, Kurt. 2004. *Christians in a Secular World: The Canadian Experience*. Montreal and Kingston: McGill-Queen's University Press.

Bowlby, John. [1969] 1982. *Attachment and Loss*. Vol. 1. *Attachment*. 2nd ed. New York: Basic Books.

Bowler, Kate. 2013. *Blessed: A History of the American Prosperity Gospel*. Oxford: Oxford University Press.

Bramadat, Paul. 2000. *The Church on the World's Turf: An Evangelical Christian Group at a Secular University*. New York: Oxford University Press.

Bregman, Lucy. 2014. *The Ecology of Spirituality: Meanings, Virtues, and Practices in a Post-Religious Age*. Waco, TX: Baylor University Press.

Brenner, Phillip. 2011. "Exceptional Behavior or Exceptional Identity? Overreporting of Church Attendance in the US." *Public Opinion Quarterly* 75 (1): 19–41.

Brierley, Peter. 2017. *UK Church Statistics No. 3: 2018 Edition*. Tonbridge, UK: ADBC Publishers.

– 2020. *UK Church Statistics No. 4: 2021 Edition*. Tonbridge, UK: ADBC Publishers.

– 2021. "Numbers and Trends: 21st Century Church Statistics." *Preach Magazine* 27: 27–31.

Brooks, Ed, and Pete Nicholas. 2015. *Virtually Human: Flourishing in a Digital World.* Nottingham, UK: Intervarsity Press.

Brophy, Sorcha. 2016. "Orthodoxy as Project: Temporality and Action in an American Protestant Denomination." *Sociology of Religion* 72 (2): 123–43.

Brown, Andrew, and Linda Woodhead. 2016. *That Was the Church That Was: How the Church of England Lost the English People.* London: Bloomsbury.

Brown, Callum. 2009. *The Death of Christian Britain: Understanding Secularisation, 1800–2000.* 2nd ed. London: Routledge.

Brubaker, Rogers, Mara Loveman, and Peter Stamatov. 2004. "Ethnicity as Cognition." *Theory and Society* 33 (1): 31–64.

Bruce, Steve. 2011. *Secularization: In Defense of an Unfashionable Theory.* Oxford: Oxford University Press.

Bruce, Tricia C. 2020. "How Americans Understand Abortion: A Comprehensive Interview Study of Abortion Attitudes in the US." McGrath Institute for Church Life, University of Notre Dame. https://f.hubspotuser content40.net/hubfs/2077093/Content%20Offers/AAS%20Research %20Report/Research%20Report_How%20Americans%20Understand %20Abortion.pdf?__hstc=246422427.9d88dcaee400664d67e1d6e2504 ac547.1657044097873.1657044097873.1657044097873.1&__hssc=246422 427.1.1657044097874&__hsfp=3568165056&hsCtaTracking=42c4a036-ecac-4883-abac-1f44f79b47c2%7C0f7049fb-43e3-41af-8e1a-94f97d25d45c.

Bullivant, Stephen. 2017. "The 'No Religion' Population in Britain." *Catholic Research Forum Reports* 3. St Mary's University, Twickenham, London. https://www.google.com/url?sa=t&rct=j&q=&esrc=s&source=web&cd=1 &ved=2ahUKEwjr7fLu4PoAhUHU98KHfwwDzgQFjAAegQIBhAB &url=https%3A%2F%2Fwww.stmarys.ac.uk%2Fresearch%2Fcentres %2Fbenedict-xvi%2Fdocs%2F2017-may-no-religion-report.pdf&usg =AOvVaw3w2nHIkQDJsnJ78JY2mWJR.

– 2019. *Mass Exodus: The Catholic Disaffiliation in Britain and America since Vatican II.* Oxford: Oxford University Press.

Burkitt, Ian. 2011. "Identity Construction in Sociohistorical Context." In *Handbook of Identity Theory and Research: Structures and Processes.* Vol. 1, edited by Seth J. Schwartz, Koen Luyckx, and Vivian L. Vignoles, 267–83. New York: Springer.

Burnford, Joy. 2019. "Flexible Working: The Way of the Future." *Forbes,* 28 May. https://www.forbes.com/sites/joyburnford/2019/05/28/flexible-working-the-way-of-the-future/#4422cfab4874.

Burton, Tara Isabella. 2020. *Strange Rites: New Religions for a Godless World.* New York: PublicAffairs.

Busch, Beverly G. 1998. "Faith, Truth, and Tolerance: Religion and Political Tolerance in the United States." PhD diss., University of Nebraska.

Butler, Anthea. 2021. *White Evangelical Racism: The Politics of Morality in America*. Chapel Hill: University of North Carolina Press.

Callaway, Lindsay, Rick Hiemstra, and Joel Murphy. 2020. "Canadian Evangelical Family Faith Formation Study Literature Review." Unpublished paper.

Calver, Clive. 1987. *Where Truth and Justice Meet*. London: Hodder and Stoughton.

Campbell, Colin. 2004. "I Shop Therefore I Know that I Am: The Metaphysical Basis of Modern Consumerism." In *Elusive Consumption*, edited by Karin Ekstrom and Helen Brembeck, 27–44. Oxford: Berg.

– 2007. *The Easternization of the West: A Thematic Account of Cultural Change in the Modern Era*. Boulder, CO: Paradigm Publishers.

Campbell, Heidi A. 2010. *When Religion Meets New Media*. London: Routledge.

– 2020. *Digital Creatives and the Rethinking of Religious Authority*. London: Routledge.

Campbell, Ted A. 1991. *The Religion of the Heart: A Study of European Religious Life in the Seventeenth and Eighteenth Centuries*. Eugene, OR: Wipf and Stock.

Carte, Katherine. 2021. *Religion and the American Revolution: An Imperial History*. Williamsburg, VA: Omohundro Institute of Early American History and Culture; Chapel Hill: University of North Carolina Press.

Carwana, Brian. 2021. "Evangelicals, the Liberal State, and Canada's Family Values Debates: The Struggle to Shape Selves." PhD diss., University of Toronto.

Cassibba, Rosalinda, Pehr Granqvist, and Alessandro Costantini. 2013. "Mothers' Attachment Security Predicts Their Children's Sense of God's Closeness." *Attachment and Human Development* 5: 51–64.

Castells, Manuel. 2000. *The Rise of the Network Society*. Oxford: Wiley-Blackwell.

Castle, Jeremiah. 2019. *Rock of Ages: Subcultural Religious Identity and Public Opinion among Young Evangelicals*. Philadelphia: Temple University Press.

Chandler, Siobhan. 2008. "The Social Ethic of Religiously Unaffiliated Spirituality." *Religion Compass* 2 (2): 240–56.

Chapman, Mark. 2004. "No Longer Crying in the Wilderness: Canadian Evangelical Organizations and Their Networks." PhD diss., University of Toronto.

Chaves, Mark. 1994. "Secularization as Declining Religious Authority." *Social Forces* 72 (3): 749–74.

– 2011. *American Religion: Contemporary Trends*. Princeton, NJ: Princeton University Press.

Cherniak, Aaron D., Mario Mikulincer, Phillip R. Shaver, and Pehr Granqvist. 2021. "Attachment Theory and Religion." *Current Opinion in Psychology* 40: 126–30.

Christerson, Brad, and Richard Flory. 2017. *The Rise of Network Christianity: How Independent Leaders Are Changing the Religious Landscape*. Oxford: Oxford University Press.

Clarke, Brian, and Stuart Macdonald. 2017. *Leaving Christianity: Changing Allegiances in Canada since 1945*. Montreal and Kingston: McGill-Queen's University Press.

Clydesdale, Tim. 2007. *The First Year Out: Understanding American Teens after High School*. Chicago: University of Chicago Press.

Coleman, Simon. 2000. *The Globalisation of Charismatic Christianity: Spreading the Gospel of Prosperity*. Cambridge: Cambridge University Press.

Coren, Michael. 2022. "At the Trucker Protest, the Political Hard Right Is Co-opting Christianity." *Globe and Mail*, 7 February 2022. https://www.theglobeandmail.com/opinion/article-at-the-trucker-protests-the-political-hard-right-is-co-opting/.

Cornelissen, Louis. 2021. Religiosity in Canada and Its Evolution from 1985 to 2019." Insights on Canadian Society, Statistics Canada. Catalogue no. 75-006-X. https://www150.statcan.gc.ca/n1/en/pub/75-006-x/2021001 /article/00010-eng.pdf?st=2Ung-66T.

Coté, James E., and Anton L. Allahar. 2006. *Critical Youth Studies: A Canadian Focus*. Toronto: Pearson.

Crapanzano, Vincent. 2000. *Serving the Word: Literalism in America from the Pulpit to the Bench*. New York: New Press.

Cusack, Carole. 2011. "Some Recent Trends in the Study of Religion and Youth." *Journal of Religious History* 35 (3): 409–18.

D'Antonio, William, Michelle Dillon, and Mary Gautier. 2013. *American Catholics in Transition*. Lanham, MD: Rowman & Littlefield.

Davie, Grace. 2015. *Religion in Britain: A Persistent Paradox*. 2nd ed. West Sussex: Blackwell Publishers.

Davis, Joshua T., and Samuel L. Perry. 2021. "White Nationalism and Relative Political Tolerance for Racists." *Social Problems* 68 (3): 513–34.

Day, Abby. 2011. *Believing in Belonging: Belief and Social Identity in the Modern World*. Oxford: Oxford University Press.

– 2013. "Varieties of Belief over Time: Reflections from a Longitudinal Study of Youth and Belief." *Journal of Contemporary Religion* 28 (2): 277–93.

Day, Abby, and Gordon Lynch. 2013. "Introduction: Belief as Cultural Performance." *Journal of Contemporary Religion* 28: 199–206.

Dayton, Donald W., and Robert K. Johnston, eds. 1991. *The Variety of American Evangelicalism.* Knoxville: University of Tennessee Press.

Demerath, N.J. III, Peter Dobkin Hall, Terry Schmitt, and Rhys H. Williams, eds. 1998. *Sacred Companies: Organizational Aspects of Religion and Religious Aspects of Organizations.* Oxford: Oxford University Press.

Dickerson, John. 2013. *The Great Evangelical Recession: 6 Factors that Will Crash the American Church ... and How to Prepare.* Grand Rapids, MI: Baker.

Dickey Young, Pamela, and Heather Shipley. 2020. *Identities under Construction: Religion, Gender and Sexuality among Youth in Canada.* Montreal and Kingston: McGill-Queen's University Press.

Dimock, Michael. 2019. "Defining Generations: Where Millennials End and Generation Z Begins." Pew Research, 17 January. https://www.pewresearch.org/fact-tank/2019/01/17/where-millennials-end-and-generation-z-begins/.

Doepke, Matthias, and Fabrizio Zilibotti. 2019. *Love, Money, and Parenting: How Economics Explains the Way We Raise Our Kids.* Princeton, NJ: Princeton University Press.

Du Mez, Kristin Kobes. 2020. *Jesus and John Wayne: How White Evangelicals Corrupted a Faith and Fractured a Nation.* New York: Liveright.

Durkheim, Emile. 1915. *The Elementary Forms of the Religious Life.* London: George Allen and Unwin.

Eagle, David. 2011. "Changing Patterns of Attendance at Religious Services in Canada, 1986–2008." *Journal for the Scientific Study of Religion* 50 (1): 187–200.

Earls, Aaron. 2022. "Churches Still Recovering from Pandemic Losses." Lifeway Research, 1 March. https://research.lifeway.com/2022/03/01/churches-still-recovering-from-pandemic-losses/.

Eberstadt, Mary. 2013. *How the West Really Lost God: A New Theory of Secularization.* West Conshohocken, PA: Templeton Press. Kindle.

Eisenstein, Marie A. 2006. "Rethinking the Relationship between Religion and Political Tolerance in the USA." *Political Behavior* 28: 327–48.

– 2008. *Religion and the Politics of Tolerance: How Christianity Builds Democracy.* Waco, TX: Baylor University Press.

Eliasoph, Nina, and Paul Lichterman. 2003. "Culture in Interaction." *American Journal of Sociology* 108 (4): 735–94.

Erikson, Erik H. 1963. *Childhood and Society.* 2nd ed. New York: W.W. Norton.

– 1968. *Identity, Youth and Crisis.* New York: W.W. Norton.

Evangelical Alliance. 2015. "21st Century Evangelicals: Faith in Politics?"

https://www.eauk.org/assets/files/downloads/21st-Century-Evangelicals-
Faith-in-politcs-2015.pdf.

Faro, Anna. 2022. "Will Covid Empty the Pews?" *Premier Christianity*, 27 January. https://www.premierchristianity.com/news-analysis/will-covid-
empty-the-pews/6001.article.

Farrell, Justin. 2011. "The Young and the Restless? The Liberalization of
Young Evangelicals." *Journal for the Scientific Study of Religion* 50 (3):
517–32.

Field, Clive D. 2014. "Is the Bible Becoming a Closed Book? British Opinion
Poll Evidence." *Journal of Contemporary Religion* 29 (3): 503–28.

Fitzgerald, Frances. 2017. *The Evangelicals: The Struggle to Shape America*.
New York: Simon and Schuster.

Flory, Richard, and Donald E. Miller. 2008. *Finding Faith: The Spiritual Quest
of the Post-Boomer Generation*. New Brunswick, NJ: Rutgers University Press.

Flourishing Congregations Institute and Alpha Canada. 2021. "The Priority
and Practice of Evangelism: Canadian Church Leader Perspectives in
2021." https://5c6ae412-7eda-4fd5-aa92-49c06363da01.filesusr.com/ugd
/68e091_25df2ee227b64fcda1509ee01b0b757c.pdf.

Ford, David G., Joshua L. Mann, and Peter M. Phillips. 2019. *The Bible and
Digital Millennials*. London: Routledge.

Francis, Leslie J., Mandy Robbins, and Jeff Astley. 2006. *Fragmented Faith?
Exposing the Fault-lines in the Church of England*. Glasgow: Paternoster.

Freitas, Donna. 2017. *The Happiness Effect: How Social Media Is Driving a
Generation to Appear Perfect at Any Cost*. Oxford: University of Oxford Press.

Frisk, Natalie. 2019. *Raising Disciples: How to Make Faith Matter for Our Kids*.
Harrisonburg, VA: Herald Press.

Fry, Alex. 2021. "Postfeminist, Engaged and Resistant: Evangelical Male Clergy Attitudes toward Gender and Women's Ordination in the Church of
England." *Critical Research on Religion* 9 (1): 65–83.

Gaddini, Katie. 2022a. "Identities in Flux: Evangelical Identity in the Time
of Brexit and Trump." *Journal of Contemporary Religion* 37 (1): 125–44.

– 2022b. *The Struggle to Stay: Why Single Evangelical Women Are Leaving the
Church*. New York: Columbia University Press.

Gallagher, Sally K. 2003. *Evangelical Identity and Gendered Family Life*. New
Brunswick, NJ: Rutgers University Press.

Gareau, Paul L., Spencer Culham Bullivant, and Peter Beyer, eds. 2019.
*Youth, Religion, and Identity in a Globalizing Context: International Perspec-
tives*. Leiden: Brill.

Garland, Diana R. 2012. *Family Ministry: A Comprehensive Guide*. 2nd ed.
Downer's Grove, IL: IVP Academic.

Gauvreau, Michael. 1991. *The Evangelical Century: College and Creed in English Canada from the Great Revival to the Great Depression*. Montreal and Kingston: McGill-Queen's University Press.

Gerber, Alan, Jonathan Gruber, and Daniel M. Hungerman. 2016. "Does Church Attendance Cause People to Vote? Using Blue Laws' Repeal to Estimate the Effect of Religiosity on Voter Turnout." *British Journal of Political Science* 46 (3): 481–500.

Giles, Kevin. 2020. *The Headship of Men and the Abuse of Women: Are They Related in Any Way?* Eugene, OR: Cascade Books.

Goodhew, David, ed. 2012. *Church Growth in Britain: 1980 to the Present*. Farnham, UK: Ashgate.

Goodhew, David, and Anthony-Paul Cooper, eds. 2019. *The Desecularisation of the City: London's Churches, 1980 to the Present*. Abingdon, UK: Routledge.

Granberg-Michaelson, Wesley. 2018. *Future Faith: Ten Challenges Reshaping Christianity in the 21st Century*. Minneapolis: Fortress Press.

Granqvist, Pehr. 2020. *Attachment in Religion and Spirituality: A Wider View*. New York: Guilford Press.

Greeley, Andrew. 1989. *Religious Change in America*. Cambridge, MA: Harvard University Press.

Greenwald, Yaakov, Mario Mikulincer, Pehr Granqvist, and Phillip R. Shaver. 2018. "Apostasy and Conversion: Attachment Orientations and Individual Differences in the Process of Religious Change." *Psychology of Religion and Spirituality* 13 (4): 425–36. https://doi.org/10.1037/rel0000239.

Grem, Darren E. 2017. *The Blessings of Business: How Corporations Shaped Conservative Christianity*. Oxford: Oxford University Press.

Grenville, Andrew. 1997. "Development of the Christian Evangelicalism Scale." Unpublished paper.

Guest, Mathew. 2007. *Evangelical Identity and Contemporary Culture: A Congregational Study of Innovation*. Milton Keynes, UK: Paternoster.

– 2015. "Evangelicalism and Politics." In *21st Century Evangelicals: Reflections on Research by the Evangelical Alliance*, edited by Greg Smith, 82–99. Herts, UK: Instant Apostle.

– 2017. "The Emerging Church in Transatlantic Perspective." *Journal for the Scientific Study of Religion* 56 (1): 41–51.

– 2019. "The Hidden Christians of the UK University Campus." In *Young People and the Diversity of (Non)Religious Identities in International Perspective*, edited by Elizabeth Arweck and Heather Shipley, 51–67. London: Springer.

– 2022. "From Protestant Ethic to Neoliberal Logic: Evangelicals at the

Interface of Culture and Politics." *Research in the Social Scientific Study of Religion* 32: 482–507. https://doi.org/10.1163/9789004505315_025.

Guest, Mathew, Kristin Aune, Sonya Sharma, and Rob Warner. 2013. *Christianity and the University Experience.* London: Bloomsbury Academic.

Guest, Mathew, Elizabeth Olson, and John Wolffe. 2012. "Christianity: Loss of Monopoly." In *Religion and Change in Modern Britain*, edited by Linda Woodhead and Rebecca Catto, 57–78. London: Routledge.

Hackett, Conrad, and Michael D. Lindsay. 2008. "Measuring Evangelicalism: Consequences of Different Operationalization Strategies." *Journal for the Scientific Study of Religion* 47 (3): 499–514.

Hailes, Sam. 2017. "How Evangelicals Took Over the Church of England." *Premier Christianity*, 25 October. https://www.premierchristianity.com/features/how-evangelicals-took-over-the-church-of-england/3081.article.

Hajiani, Riyana Karim. 2022. "The American Influence on the Canadian Trucker Convoy: Culture under Siege?" *McGill Journal of Political Studies*, 25 February 2022. https://mjps.ssmu.ca/2022/02/25/the-american-influence-on-the-canadian-trucker-convoy-culture-under-siege/.

Halafoff, Anna, and Laura Gobey. 2019. "'Whatever?' Religion, Youth and Identity in 21st Century Australia." In *Youth, Religion and Identity in Globalizing Context: International Perspectives*, edited by Paul Gareau, Spencer Culham Bullvant, and Peter Beyer, 255–77. Leiden: Brill.

Hargreaves, Julian, Edward Kessler, David Izamoje, and Alissa Symon. 2020. "How We Get Along: The Diversity Study of England and Wales 2020." Executive Study, Woolf Institute. https://www.woolf.cam.ac.uk/assets/file-downloads/How-We-Get-Along-Executive-Summary.pdf.

Haskell, David M. 2009. *Through a Lens Darkly: How the News Media Perceive and Portray Evangelicals.* Toronto: Clements Academic.

Hatcher, Andrea C. 2017. *Political and Religious Identities of British Evangelicals.* Cham, CH: Palgrave Macmillan.

Heelas, Paul. 1996. *The New Age Movement: The Celebration of the Self and the Sacralization of Modernity.* Oxford: Blackwell.

– 2008. *Spiritualities of Life: New Age Romanticism and Consumptive Capitalism.* Oxford: Blackwell.

Heelas, Paul, and Linda Woodhead. 2005. *The Spiritual Revolution: Why Religion Is Giving Way to Spirituality.* Malden, UK: Blackwell.

Hexham, Irving, and Karla Poewe. 1997. *New Religions as Global Cultures: Making the Human Sacred.* Boulder, CO: Westview Press.

Hiemstra, Rick. 2017. "YATR Young Adult Interviews Report: A Preliminary Report to Project Partners." Unpublished paper.

– 2020a. "Bible Engagement Trends in Canada, 1993 to 2019." Unpublished paper.

– 2020b. "Not Christian Anymore." *Faith Today*, January/February. https://www .faithtoday.ca/Magazines/2020-Jan-Feb/Not-Christian-anymore.

Hiemstra, Rick, Lorianne Dueck, and Matthew Blackaby. 2017. "YATR Literature Review: A Preliminary Report to Project Partners." Unpublished paper.

– 2018. *Renegotiating Faith: The Delay in Young Adult Identity Formation and What It Means for the Church in Canada*. Toronto: Faith Today. https://p2c .com/wp-content/themes/avada-corp/files/Renegotiating-Faith-Report.pdf.

Hoffman, John, and John P. Bartkowski. 2008. "Gender, Religious Tradition and Biblical Literalism." *Social Forces* 86 (3): 1245–72.

Holmen, Mark, and Brian Siewert. 2018. *Faith@Home Revealed: An Inside Look at Churchgoing Parents*. Crosslake, MN: Faith@Home Press.

Hoover, Dennis, Michael Martinez, Sam Reimer, and Ken Wald. 2002. "Evangelical Protestantism Meets the Continental Divide: Moral and Economic Conservatism in the United States and Canada." *Political Research Quarterly* 55 (2): 351–74.

Hout, Michael, Andrew M. Greeley, and Melissa J. Wilde. 2001. "The Demographic Imperative of Religious Change." *American Journal of Sociology* 107: 458–500.

Houtman, Dick, and Stef Aupers. 2010. "Religions of Modernity: Relocating the Sacred to the Self and the Digital." In *Religions of Modernity: Relocating the Sacred to the Self and the Digital*, edited by Stef Aupers and Dick Houtman, 1–29. Leiden: Brill.

Houtman, Dick, Stef Aupers, and Rudi Laermans, eds. 2021. *Science under Siege: Contesting the Secular Religion of Scientism*. London: Palgrave Macmillan.

Hunter, James Davison. 1982. "Subjectivization and the New Evangelical Theodicy." *Journal for the Scientific Study of Religion* 20 (1): 3 9–47.

– 1987. *Evangelicalism: The Coming Generation*. Chicago: University of Chicago Press.

Hutchinson, Mark, and John Wolffe. 2012. *A Short History of Global Evangelicalism*. Cambridge: Cambridge University Press.

Ingalls, Monique M. 2018. *Singing the Congregation: How Contemporary Worship Music Forms Evangelical Community*. Oxford: Oxford University Press.

Inglehart, Ronald F. 2021. *Religion's Sudden Decline: What's Causing It, and What Comes Next?* Oxford: Oxford University Press.

James, William Closson. 2011. *God's Plenty: Religious Diversity in Kingston*. Montreal and Kingston: McGill-Queen's University Press.

Jemirade, Dele. 2017. "Reverse Mission and the Establishment of Redeemed Christian Church of God (RCCG) in Canada." *Missionalia* 45 (3): 263–84.

Jenkins, Philip. 2011. *The Next Christendom: The Coming of Global Christianity*. 3rd ed. Oxford: Oxford University Press.

. – 2020. *Fertility and Faith: The Demographic Revolution and the Transformation of World Religions*. Waco, TX: Baylor University Press.

Joyce, Kathryn. 2009. *Quiverfull: Inside the Christian Patriarchy Movement*. Boston: Beacon Press.

Kane, Gerald C. 2013. "Psychosocial Stages of Symbolic Action in Social Media." Semantic Scholar. https://pdfs.semanticscholar.org/7afd/4e6a10850f1d012e783db73791d1bcbccd06.pdf.

Kay, William K. 2007. *Apostolic Networks in Britain: New Ways of Being Church*. Eugene, OR: Wipf and Stock.

Keeley, Robert J. 2008. *Helping Our Children Grow in Faith: How the Church Can Nurture the Spiritual Development of Kids*. Grand Rapids, MI: Baker Books.

Kehrwald, Leif, John Roberto, Gene Roehlkepartain, and Jolene Roehlkepartain. 2016. *Families at the Center of Faith Formation*. Cheshire, CT: Lifelong Faith Associates.

Keles Betul, Niall McCrae, and Annmarie Grealish. 2020. "A Systematic Review: The Influence of Social Media on Depression, Anxiety and Psychological Distress in Adolescents." *International Journal of Adolescence and Youth* 25 (1): 79–93.

Keller, Timothy. 2022. "The Decline and Renewal of the American Church: Part 2 – The Decline of Evangelicalism." *Life in the Gospel*, Winter 2022. https://quarterly.gospelinlife.com/the-decline-of-evangelicalism/.

Kelley, Melissa Morgan. 2022. "Christians Are Going Back to Church – But Maybe Not the Same One." *Christianity Today*, 18 January. https://www.christianitytoday.com/news/2022/january/church-switch-turnover-leave-covid-pandemic.html.

Kettell, Steven. 2016. "Always Read the Label: The Identity and Strategy of Britain's 'Christian Right.'" *Politics, Religion and Ideology* 17 (1): 1–17.

Kimball Cynthia N., Chris J. Boyatzis, Kaye V. Cook, Kathleen C. Leonard, and Kelly S. Flanagan. 2013. "Attachment to God: A Qualitative Exploration of Emerging Adults' Spiritual Relationship with God." *Journal of Psychological Theology* 41: 175–88.

Kolpinskaya, Ekaterina, and Stuart Fox. 2019. "Praying on Brexit? Unpicking the Effect of Religion on Support for European Union Integration and Membership." *Journal of Common Market Studies* 57 (6): 1–19.

Kroger, Jane. 2017. "Identity Development in Adolescence and Adulthood," 27 February. https://oxfordre.com/psychology/view/10.1093/acrefore/9780190236557.001.0001/acrefore-9780190236557-e-54?print.

Koyzis, David T. 2014. *We Answer to Another: Authority, Office, and the Image of God*. Eugene, OR: Pickwick Publications.

Labberton, Mark, ed. 2018. *Still Evangelical? Insiders Reconsider Political, Social and Theological Meaning*. Downer's Grove, IL: IVP Books.

Lake, Meredith. 2018. "Why Our Declining Biblical Literacy Matters." *The Conversation*, 15 April. https://theconversation.com/why-our-declining-biblical-literacy-matters-94724.

Lasch, Christopher. 1979. *The Culture of Narcissism: American Life in an Age of Diminishing Expectations*. New York: W.W. Norton.

– 1984. *The Minimal Self: Psychic Survival in Troubled Times*. New York: W.W. Norton.

Lee, Francis L.F. 2013. "'Tolerated One Way but Not the Other': Levels and Determinants of Social and Political Tolerance in Hong Kong." *Social Indicators Research* 118: 711–27.

Lee, Morgan. 2021. "How American Politics Complicates Evangelicalism in the UK." *Christianity Today*, 2 February. https://www.christianitytoday.com/ct/2021/february-web-only/evangelical-alliance-uk-trump-british-church-brexit-covid.html.

Lin, Tom. 2018. "Hope for the Next Generation." In *Still Evangelical? Insiders Reconsider Political, Social and Theological Meaning*, edited by Mark Labberton, 184–200. Downer's Grove, IL: IVP Books.

Lindsay, Ben. 2019. *We Need to Talk about Race: Understanding the Black Experience in White Majority Churches*. London: SPCK.

Lipka, Michael, and Gregory A. Smith. 2020. "White Evangelical Approval for Trump Slips, but Eight-in-Ten Say They Would Vote for Him." Pew Research Center, 1 July. https://www.pewresearch.org/fact-tank/2020/07/01/white-evangelical-approval-of-trump-slips-but-eight-in-ten-say-they-would-vote-for-him/.

Lipset, Seymour M. 1990. *Continental Divide: The Values and Institutions of the United States and Canada*. New York: Routledge.

Luckhurst, Toby. 2018. "Why the Stormy Daniels–Donald Trump Story Matters." BBC News, 2 May. https://www.bbc.com/news/world-us-canada-43334326.

Luhrmann, Tanya M. 2012. *When God Talks Back: Understanding the American Evangelical Relationship with God*. New York: Knopf.

MacDonald, Marci. 2011. *The Armageddon Factor: The Rise of Christian Nationalism in Canada*. Toronto: Vintage.

Maclean, Ruth. 2017. "Eat, Pray, Live: The Lagos Megachurches Building Their Very Own Cities." *Guardian*, 11 September. https://www.the guardian.com/cities/2017/sep/11/eat-pray-live-lagos-nigeria-megachurches-redemption-camp.

Malley, Brian. 2004. *How the Bible Works: An Anthropological Study of Evangelical Biblicism*. Walnut Creek, CA: AltaMira Press.

Malloy, Jonathan. 2009. "Bush/Harper? Canadian and American Evangelical Politics Compared." *American Review of Canadian Studies* 39: 352–63.

– 2011. "Between America and Europe: Religion, Politics and Evangelicals in Canada." *Politics, Religion and Ideology* 12 (3): 315–31.

– 2013. "The Relationship between Canadian Evangelicals and the Conservative Party of Canada." In *Conservatism in Canada*, edited by James Farney and David Rayside, 184–206. Toronto: University of Toronto Press.

– 2019. "Canada's Marginal 'Christian Right.'" *The Conversation*, 11 August. https://theconversation.com/canadas-marginal-christian-right-121024.

Marcia, James E., Alan S. Waterman, David R. Matteson, Sally L. Archer, and Jacob L. Orlofsky. 1993. *Ego Identity: A Handbook for Psychosocial Research*. New York: Springer.

Marler, Penny Long. 2008. "Religious Change in the West: Watch the Women." In *Women and Religion in the West: Challenging Secularization*, edited by Kristin Aune, Sonya Sharma, and Giselle Vincett, 23–56. London: Routledge.

Martí, Gerardo. 2017. "Forum on the Emerging Church Movement: New Concepts for New Dynamics – Generating Theory for the Study of Religious Innovation and Social Change." *Journal for the Scientific Study of Religion* 56 (1): 16–18.

– 2020. *American Blindspot: Race, Class, Religion and the Trump Presidency*. Lanham, MD: Rowman & Littlefield.

Martí, Gerardo, and Gladys Ganiel. 2014. *The Deconstructed Church: Understanding Emerging Christianity*. Oxford: Oxford University Press.

Martin, David. 2002. *Pentecostalism: The World Their Parish*. Oxford: Blackwell.

Martínez, Jessica, and Gregory A. Smith. 2016. "How the Faithful Voted: A Preliminary 2016 Analysis." Pew Research Center. https://www.pewresearch.org/fact-tank/2016/11/09/how-the-faithful-voted-a-preliminary-2016-analysis/.

Mawhinney, Ruth. 2016. "Does Evangelicalism Have A Future? Yes, Says Clive Calver – But Only If It Puts Jesus First." *Christian Today*, 1 October. https://www.christiantoday.com/article/does-Evangelicalism-have-a-future-yes-says-clive-calver-but-only-if-it-puts-jesus-first/95628.htm.

McAlpine, Bill, Joel Thiessen, Keith Walker, and Arch Chee Keen Wong. 2021. *Signs of Life: Catholic, Mainline, and Conservative Protestant Churches in Canada*. Toronto: Tyndale Academic Press.

McDonnell, Jean. 2017. "What Does Authenticity Really Mean to Millennials?" https://www.linkedin.com/pulse/what-does-authenticity-really-mean-millennials-jean-mcdonnell.

McGowin, Emily Hunter. 2018. *Quivering Families: The Quiverfull Movement and Evangelical Theology of the Family*. Minneapolis: Fortress Press.

McIvor, Méadhbh. 2020. *Representing God: Christian Legal Activism in Contemporary England*. Princeton, NJ: Princeton University Press.

Mcmaster, Geoff. 2020. "Millennials and Gen Z Are More Anxious Than Previous Generations: Here's Why." University of Alberta Folio, 28 January. https://www.ualberta.ca/folio/2020/01/millennials-and-gen-z-are-more-anxious-than-previous-generations-heres-why.html/.

Miller, Claire Cain and Sanam Yar. 2019. "Young People Are Going to Save Us All from Office Life." *New York Times*, 17 September. https://www.nytimes.com/2019/09/17/style/generation-z-millennials-work-life-balance.html.

Miller, Donald E., and Tetsunao Yamamori. 2007. *Global Pentecostalism: The New Face of Christian Social Engagement.* Berkeley and Los Angeles: University of California Press.

Miller, Emily McFarlan. 2018. "There's a 'Red Evangelicalism and a Blue Evangelicalism': Faith Leaders Gather to Discuss Their Common Future." *Washington Post*, 18 April. https://www.washingtonpost.com/news/acts-of-faith/wp/2018/04/18/theres-a-red-Evangelicalism-and-a-blue-Evangelicalism-faith-leaders-gather-to-discuss-Evangelical-future/?utm_term=.2496c0a856ef.

Moore, Russell D. 2018. *The Storm-Tossed Family: How the Cross Reshapes the Home.* Nashville, TN: B&H Books.

Morency, Jean-Dominique, Éric Caron Malefant, and Samuel MacIsaac. 2017. "Immigration and Diversity: Population Projections for Canada and its Regions, 2011–2036." Statistics Canada. https://www150.statcan.gc.ca/n1/pub/91-551-x/91-551-x2017001-eng.htm.

Moretti, Marlene M., and Maya Peled. 2004. "Adolescent-Parent Attachment: Bonds That Support Healthy Development." *Paediatrics and Child Health* 9 (8): 551–5.

Mouw, Richard. J. 2019. *Restless Faith: Holding Evangelical Beliefs in a World of Contested Labels.* Grand Rapids, MI: Brazos Press.

Nason-Clark, Nancy, Barbara Fisher-Townsend, Steve McMullin, and Catherine Holtmann. 2013. "Family Violence in Canada." In *Family Violence from a Global Perspective: Strengths-Based Research and Case Studies*, edited by Sylvia M. Asay, John DeFrain, Marcee Metzger, and Bob Moyer, 182–99. Thousand Oaks, CA: Sage Publications.

Nichols, Tom. 2017. *The Death of Expertise: The Campaign against Established Knowledge and Why It Matters.* Oxford: Oxford University Press.

Noll, Mark A. n.d. "Evangelicalism in the Early Twenty-First Century." IVP. https://www.ivpress.com/pages/content/evangelicalism-early-twenty-first-century.

– 1992. *A History of Christianity in the United States and Canada.* Grand Rapids, MI: Eerdmans.

– 1997. "Canadian Evangelicalism: A View from the United States." In *Aspects of the Canadian Evangelical Experience*, edited by George Rawlyk. Montreal and Kingston: McGill-Queen's University Press.

Noll, Mark A., David W. Bebbington, and George M. Marsden, eds. 2019. *Evangelicals: Who They Have Been, Are Now and Could Be*. Grand Rapids, MI: Eerdmans.

Nunn, Clyde Z., Harry J. Crockett, Jr, and J. Allan Williams, Jr. 1978. *Tolerance for Nonconformity*. San Francisco: Jossey-Bass.

Ogland, Curtis P., and John P. Bartkowski. 2014. "Biblical Literalism and Sexual Morality in Comparative Perspective: Testing the Transposability of a Conservative Protestant Religious Schema." *Sociology of Religion* 75 (1): 3–24.

Park, Jerry Z., Joshua Tom, and Brita Andercheck. n.d. "CCF Civil Rights Symposium: Fifty Years of Religious Change, 1964–2014." Council on Contemporary Families. https://contemporaryfamilies.org/50-years-of-religious-change/.

Pearce, Lisa D., and Melinda Denton. 2011. *A Faith of Their Own: Stability and Change in the Religiosity of America's Adolescents*. Oxford: Oxford University Press.

Penner, James, Rachael Harder, Erika Anderson, Bruno Désorcy, and Rick Hiemstra. 2012. *Hemorrhaging Faith: Why and When Canadian Young Adults Are Leaving, Staying and Returning to the Church*. Toronto: EFC Youth and Young Adult Ministry Roundtable..

Penning, James M., and Corwin Smidt. 2002. *Evangelicalism: The Next Generation*. Grand Rapids, MI: Baker Book House.

Perfect, Simon, Ben Ryan, and Kristin Aune. n.d. "Faith and Belief on Campus: Division and Cohesion." Theos. https://www.theosthinktank.co.uk/cmsfiles/Reportfiles/Theos—Faith-and-Belief-on-Campus—Executive-Summary.pdf.

Perrin, Ruth. 2016. *The Bible Reading of Young Evangelicals: An Exploration of the Ordinary Hermeneutics and Faith of Generation Y*. Eugene, OR: Pickwick Publications.

Pew Research Center. 2014. Religious Landscape Study. https://www.pewforum.org/religious-landscape-study/.

Placher, William C. 1996. *The Domestication of Transcendence: How Modern Thinking about God Went Wrong*. Louisville, KY: Westminster John Knox.

Powell, Kara, and Chap Clark. 2011. *Sticky Faith: Everyday Ideas to Build Lasting Faith in Your Kids*. Grand Rapids, MI: Zondervan.

Powell, Ruth. 2013. "Trends in Protestant Church Vitality over Twenty Years (1991–2011)." NCLS Occasional Paper 23. https://shop.ncls.org.au/products/ncls-occasional-paper-23.

Powell, Walter W., and Paul J. DiMaggio. 1991. *The New Institutionalism in Organizational Analysis*. Chicago: University of Chicago Press.

Putnam, Robert D., and David E. Campbell. 2010. *American Grace: How Religion Divides and Unites Us*. New York: Simon and Schuster.

Quebedeaux, Richard. 1978. *The Worldly Evangelicals*. San Francisco: Harper and Row.

Rah, Soong-Chan. 2009. *The Next Evangelicalism: Releasing the Church from Western Cultural Captivity*. Downer's Grove, IL: IVP books.

Rawlyk, George A. 1993. *Is Jesus Your Personal Saviour? A Search for Canadian Evangelicalism in the 1990s*. Montreal and Kingston: McGill-Queen's University Press.

Rawlyk, George A., and Mark Noll, eds. 1994. *Amazing Grace: Evangelicalism in Australia, Britain, Canada and the United States*. Montreal and Kingston: McGill Queen's University Press.

Regnerus, Mark. 2020. *The Future of Christian Marriage*. Oxford: Oxford University Press.

Reimer, Sam. 1996. "North American Evangelicalism: A Look at Regional and National Variation in Religiosity." PhD diss., University of Notre Dame.

– 2000. "A More Irenic Canadian Evangelicalism? Comparing Evangelicals in Canada and the US." In *Revival, Baptists and George Rawlyk*, edited by Daniel C. Goodwin, 153–80. Wolfville, NS: Gaspereau Press.

– 2003. *Evangelicals and the Continental Divide*. Montreal and Kingston: McGill-Queen's University Press.

– 2011a. "'Civility without Compromise': Evangelical Attitudes toward Same-Sex Issues in Comparative Context." In *Faith, Politics, and Sexual Diversity in Canada and the United States*, edited by David Rayside and Clyde Wilcox, 71–86. Vancouver: UBC Press.

– 2011b. "Orthodoxy Niches: Diversity in Congregational Orthodoxy among Three Protestant Denominations in the US." *Journal for the Scientific Study of Religion* 50 (4): 763–79.

– 2017. "Conservative Protestants and Religious Polarization in Canada." *Studies in Religion* 46 (2): 187–208.

– 2021. "Political Tolerance in Canada: Are Religious Canadians and Americans More Intolerant?" *Canadian Journal of Sociology* 58 (4): 531–48.

Reimer, Sam, and Rick Hiemstra. 2018. "The Gains/Losses of Canadian Religious Groups from Immigration: Immigration Flows, Attendance and Switching." *Studies in Religion* 47 (3): 327–44.

Reimer, Sam, and David Sikkink. 2020. "Comparing the Social Attitudes of Young Adult Evangelicals in Canada and the United States: Differences in Subcultural Boundaries among Evangelical School Graduates." *Canadian Review of Sociology* 57 (1): 80–104.

Reimer, Sam, and Michael Wilkinson. 2015. *A Culture of Faith: Evangelical Congregations in Canada.* Montreal and Kingston: McGill-Queen's University Press.

Repstad, Pål. 2008. "From Sin to a Gift from God: Constructions of Change in Conservative Christian Organizations." *Journal of Contemporary Religion* 23 (1): 17–31.

Roach, David. 2020. "Bible Reading Drops during Social Distancing." *Christianity Today*, 22 July. https://www.christianitytoday.com/news/2020/july/state-of-bible-reading-coronavirus-barna-abs.html.

Robb, Michael. 2019. "Tweens, Teens, and Phones: What Our 2019 Research Reveals." Common Sense, 29 October/ https://www.commonsensemedia.org/blog/tweens-teens-and-phones-what-our-2019-research-reveals.

Roof, Wade Clark. 1999. *Spiritual Marketplace: Baby Boomers and the Remaking of American Religion.* Princeton, NJ: Princeton University Press.

Rosen, Armin. 2018. "Redemption Camp." *First Things* (January). https://www.firstthings.com/article/2018/01/redemption-camp.

Ryan, Gery W., and Russell H. Bernard. 2003. "Techniques to Identify Themes." *Field Methods* 15 (1): 85–109.

Schmalzbauer, John, and Kathleen A. Mahoney. 2018. *The Resilience of Religion in American Higher Education.* Waco, TX: Baylor University Press.

Schneider, Daniel, and Kristen Harknett. 2019. "Consequences of Routine Work-Schedule Instability for Worker Health and Well-being." *American Sociological Review* 84 (1): 82–114.

Schuurman, Peter. 2019. *The Subversive Evangelical: The Ironic Charisma of an Irreligious Megachurch.* Montreal and Kingston: McGill-Queen's University Press.

Schwadel, Philip, and Christopher R.H. Garneau. 2019. "Sectarian Religion and Political Tolerance in the United States." *Sociology of Religion* 80 (2): 168–93.

Sewell, William H., Jr. 1999. "The Concept(s) of Culture." In *Beyond the Cultural Turn: New Directions in the Study of Society and Culture*, edited by Victoria E. Bonnell and Linda Hunt, 35–61. Berkeley and Los Angeles: University of California Press.

Shellnutt, Kate. 2018. "Do Christians Focus Too Much on the Family?" *Christianity Today*, 21 November. https://www.christianitytoday.com/news/2018/november/christians-family-faith-pew-research-meaning.html.

Sherwood, Harriet. 2021. "UK Church Leaders Warn against 'Dangerous' Vaccine Passport Plans." *Guardian*, 17 April. https://www.theguardian.com/world/2021/apr/17/uk-church-leaders-warn-against-dangerous-vaccine-passport-plans.

Shibley, Mark A. 1998. "Contemporary Evangelicals: Born-Again and World Affirming." *Annals of the American Academy of Political and Social Science* 558: 67–87.

Shipley, Heather. 2019. "Apathy or Misunderstanding? Youth's Reflections on Their Religious Identity in Canada." In *Youth, Religion and Identity in Globalizing Context: International Perspectives*, edited by Paul Gareau, Spencer Culham, and Peter Beyer, 191–201. Leiden: Brill.

Shirley, Chris. 2018. *Family Ministry and the Church: A Leader's Guide for Ministry through Families*. Nashville: Randall House Publications.

Silliman, Daniel. 2021. *Reading Evangelicals: How Christian Fiction Shaped a Culture and a Faith*. Grand Rapids, MI: Eerdmans.

Simmons, Jim, and Larry S. Bourne. 2013. *The Canadian Urban System in 2011: Looking Back and Projecting Forward*. Toronto: Cities Centre, University of Toronto.

Smith, Christian. 1998. *American Evangelicalism: Embattled and Thriving*. Chicago: University of Chicago Press.

– 2000. *Christian America? What Evangelicals Really Want*. Berkeley and Los Angeles: University of California Press.

– 2003a. *Moral Believing Animals: Human Personhood and Culture*. Oxford: Oxford University Press.

– 2003b. "Religious Participation and Network Closure among American Adolescents." *Journal for the Scientific Study of Religion* 42 (2): 259–67.

– 2014. *The Sacred Project of American Sociology*. Oxford: Oxford University Press.

– 2017. *Religion: What It Is, How It Works, and Why It Matters*. Princeton, NJ: Princeton University Press.

Smith, Christian, and Amy Adamczyk. 2021. *Handing Down the Faith: How Parents Pass Their Religion on to the Next Generation*. Oxford: Oxford University Press.

Smith, Christian, with Kari Christoffersen, Hilary Davidson, and Patricia Snell Herzog. 2011. *Lost in Transition: The Dark Side of Emerging Adulthood*. Oxford: Oxford University Press.

Smith, Christian, with Melinda Lundquist Denton. 2005. *Soul Searching: The Religious and Spiritual Lives of American Teenagers*. Oxford: Oxford University Press.

Smith, Christian, Michael O. Emerson, with Patricia Snell. 2008. *Passing the Plate: Why American Christians Don't Give Away More Money*. Oxford: Oxford University Press.

Smith, Christian, Kyle Longest, Jonathan Hill, and Kari Christoffersen. 2014. *Young Catholic America: Emerging Adults In, Out of, and Gone from the Church*. Oxford: Oxford University Press.

Smith, Christian, Bridget Ritz, and Michael Rotolo. 2020. *Religious Parenting: Transmitting Faith and Values in Contemporary America*. Princeton, NJ: Princeton University Press.

Smith, Christian, and Patricia Snell. 2009. *Souls in Transition: The Religious and Spiritual Lives of Emerging Adults*. Oxford: Oxford University Press.

Smith, Greg, ed. 2015. *21st Century Evangelicals: Reflections on Research by the Evangelical Alliance*. Herts, UK: Instant Apostle.

– 2020. "Trans-Atlantic Evangelicalism: Toxic, Fragmented or Redeemable?" William Temple Foundation. https://williamtemplefoundation.org.uk /temple-tracts/.

Smith, Greg, and Linda Woodhead. 2018. "Religion and Brexit: Populism and the Church of England." *Religion, State and Society* 46 (3): 206–23.

Smith, James K.A. 2009. *Desiring the Kingdom: Worship, Worldview and Culture Formation*. Grand Rapids, MI: Baker Academic.

– 2016. *You Are What You Love*. Grand Rapids, MI: Brazos Press.

Snyder, Cynthia, and Anne-Marie Chang. 2019. "Mobile Technology, Sleep, and Circadian Disruption." In *Sleep and Health*, edited by Michael Grandner, 159–70. San Diego: Elsevier Academic Press.

Song, Felicia Wu. 2021. *Restless Devices: Recovering Personhood, Presence and Place in the Digital Age*. Downer's Grove, IL: IVP Academic.

Soper, Christopher J. 1994. *Evangelical Christianity in the United States and Great Britain: Religious Beliefs, Political Choices*. New York: New York University Press.

– 1997. "Divided by a Common Religion: The Christian Right in England and the United States." In *Sojourners in the Wilderness: The Christian Right in Comparative Perspective*, edited by Corwin E. Smidt and James M. Penning, 171–92. Lanham, MD: Rowman and Littlefield.

Stackhouse, John G., Jr. 1993. *Canadian Evangelicalism in the Twentieth Century: An Introduction to Its Character*. Toronto: University of Toronto Press.

– 1994. "More than a Hyphen: Twentieth-Century Canadian Evangelicalism in Trans-Atlantic Context." In *Amazing Grace: Evangelicalism in Australia, Britain, Canada, and the United States*, edited by George A. Rawlyk and Mark A. Noll, 375–400. Kingston and Montreal: McGill-Queen's University Press.

– 2018. "What Has Happened to Post-Christian Canada?" *Church History* 87: 1152–70.

– 2022. "Evangelicalism Defined." In *Evangelicalism: A Very Short Introduction*. Oxford: Oxford University Press.

Stanley, Brian. 2013. *The Global Diffusion of Evangelicalism: The Age of Billy Graham and John Stott*. Downer's Grove, IL: IVP Academic.

Stark, Rodney, and William Sims Bainbridge. 1985. *The Future of Religion: Secularization, Revival and Cult Formation*. Berkeley and Los Angeles: University of California Press.

Stark, Rodney, and Roger Finke. 2000. *Acts of Faith: Explaining the Human Side of Religion*. Berkeley and Los Angeles: University of California Press.

Stasson, Anneke. 2014. "The Politicization of Family Life: How Headship Became Essential to Evangelical Identity in the Late Twentieth Century." *Religion and American Culture: A Journal of Interpretation* 24 (1): 100–38.

Steensland, Brian, and Philip Goff. 2014. *The New Evangelical Social Engagement*. Oxford: Oxford University Press.

Stewart, Adam. 2015. *The New Canadian Pentecostals*. Waterloo, ON: Wilfrid Laurier University Press.

Stiller, Brian. 2021. "Now That Trump Has Gone: What Does Evangelical Mean in Our Society Today?" *Faith Today*, May/June, 35–7.

Stiller, Brian C., Todd M. Johnson, Karen Stiller, and Mark Hutchison. 2015. *Evangelicals around the World: A Global Handbook for the 21st Century*. Nashville: Thomas Nelson.

Stiller, Karen. 2022. "Christians at the Convoy." *Faith Today*, May/June, 49–51.

Stott, John. 2003. *Evangelical Truth: A Personal Plea for Unity, Integrity and Faithfulness*. London: Intervarsity Press.

Stouffer, Samuel. 1955. *Communism, Conformity, and Civil Liberties*. Garden City, NJ: Transaction Publishers.

Strhan, Anna. 2013a. "The Metropolis and Evangelical Life: Coherence and Fragmentation in the 'Lost City of London.'" *Religion* 43 (3): 331–52.

– 2013b. "Practising the Space Between: Embodying Belief as an Evangelical Anglican Student." *Journal of Contemporary Religion* 28 (2): 225–39.

Stringer, Dan. 2021. *Struggling with Evangelicalism: Why I Want to Leave and What It Takes to Stay*. Downer's Grove, IL: IVP Press.

Sullivan, John L., James Piereson, and George E. Marcus. 1982. *Political Tolerance and American Democracy*. Chicago: University of Chicago Press.

Swartz, David R. 2014. *Moral Minority: The Evangelical Left in an Age of Conservatism*. Philadelphia: University of Pennsylvania Press.

Tajfel, Henri. 1978. "The Achievement of Inter-Group Differentiation." In *Differentiation between Social Groups*, edited by Henri Tajfel, 77–100. London: Academic Press.

Tajfel, Henri, and John C. Turner. 1979. "An Integrative Theory of Inter-Group Conflict." In *The Social Psychology of Inter-Group Relations*, edited by William G. Austin and Stephen Worchel, 33–47. Monterey, CA: Brooks/Cole.

Taylor, Charles. 1989. *Sources of the Self: The Making of Modern Identity*. Cambridge, MA: Harvard University Press.

– 1991. *The Ethics of Authenticity*. Cambridge, MA: Harvard University Press.

– 2004. *Modern Social Imaginaries*. Durham, NC: Duke University Press.

– 2007. *The Secular Age*. Cambridge, MA: Harvard University Press.

Thiessen, Joel. 2015. *The Meaning of Sunday: The Practice of Belief in a Secular Age*. Montreal and Kingston: McGill-Queen's University Press.

Thiessen, Joel, and Sarah Wilkins-Laflamme. 2020. *None of the Above: Nonreligious Identity in the US and Canada*. New York: New York University Press.

Torpey, John. 2010. "American Exceptionalism?" In *The New Blackwell Companion to the Sociology of Religion*, edited by Bryan S. Turner, 141–59. Oxford: Wiley-Blackwell.

Trueman, Carl R. 2011. *The Real Scandal for the Evangelical Mind*. Chicago: Moody Press.

– 2020. *The Rise and Triumph of the Modern Self: Cultural Amnesia, Expressive Individualism, and the Road to Sexual Revolution*. Wheaton, IL: Crossway.

Twenge, Jean M., Thomas E. Joiner, Megan L. Rogers, and Gabrielle N. Martin. 2018. "Increases in Depressive Symptoms, Suicide-Related Outcomes, and Suicide Rates among US Adolescents after 2010 and Links to Increased New Media Screen Time." *Clinical Psychological Science* 6 (1): 3–17.

Uecker, Jeremy, Mark D. Regnerus, and Margaret Vaaler. 2007. "Losing My Religion: The Social Sources of Religious Decline in Early Adulthood." *Social Forces* 85: 1667–92.

Vaaler, Margaret L., Christopher G. Ellison, and Daniel A. Powers. 2009. "Religious Influences on the Risk of Marital Dissolution." *Journal of Marriage and Family* 71: 917–34.

Vaca, Daniel. 2019. *Evangelicals Incorporated: Books and Business of Religion in America*. Cambridge, MA: Harvard University Press.

Vermeer, Paul. 2009. "Denominational Schools and the (Religious) Socialization of Youths: A Changing Relationship." *British Journal of Religious Education* 31 (3): 201–11.

Voas, David, and Mark Chaves. 2016. "Is the United States a Counterexample of the Secularization Thesis?" *American Journal of Sociology* 121 (5): 1517–56.

Voas, David, and Stefanie Doebler. 2011. "Secularization in Europe: Religious Change between and within Birth Cohorts." *Religion and Society in Central and Eastern Europe* 4: 39–62.

Wang, Mei-Chuan, Sharon G. Horne, Heidi M. Levitt, and Lisa M. Klesges.

2009. "Christian Women in IPV Relationships: An Exploratory Study of Religious Factors." *Journal of Psychology and Christianity* 28 (3): 224–35.

Walton, Andy, with Andrea Hatcher and Nick Spencer. 2013. "Is There a 'Religious Right' Emerging in Britain?" London: Theos. https://www.the osthinktank.co.uk/cmsfiles/archive/files/Reports/IS%20THERE%20A %20RELIGIOUS%20RIGHT%20(NEW).pdf.

Waters, Malcolm. 1995. *Globalization*. London: Routledge.

Watts, Galen. 2018. "On the Politics of Self-Spirituality: A Canadian Case Study." *Studies in Religion* 47 (3): 345–72.

– 2019. "Religion, Science, and Disenchantment in Late Modernity." *Zygon* 54 (4): 1022–35.

– 2020. "Religion of the Heart." PhD diss., University of Toronto.

– 2022. *The Spiritual Turn: The Religion of the Heart and the Making of Romantic Liberal Modernity*. Oxford: Oxford University Press.

Weber, Max. [1922] 1964. *Economy and Society*. Berkeley and Los Angeles: University of California Press.

Wellman, James K. 2008. *Evangelical vs Liberal: The Clash of Christian Cultures in the Pacific Northwest*. Oxford: Oxford University Press.

Westenberg, Leonie. 2017. "'When She Calls for Help': Domestic Violence in Christian Families." *Social Sciences* 6 (3): 71. https://www.mdpi.com /2076-0760/6/3/71/htm.

Whitehead, Andrew, and Samuel Perry. 2020. *Taking America Back for God: Christian Nationalism in the United States*. Oxford: Oxford University Press.

Wilcox, Clyde, and Ted Jelen. 1990. "Evangelicals and Political Tolerance." *American Politics Quarterly* 18: 25–46.

Wilcox, W. Bradford. 2004. *Soft Patriarchs, New Men: How Christianity Shapes Fathers and Husbands*. Chicago: University of Chicago Press.

Wilcox, W. Bradford, and Elizabeth Williamson. 2007. "The Cultural Contradictions of Mainline Family Ideology and Practice." In *American Religions and the Family*, edited by Don S. Browning and David A. Clairmont, 37–55. New York: Columbia University Press.

Wilcox, W. Bradford, and Nicholas H. Wolfinger. 2016. *Soul Mates: Religion, Sex, Love and Marriage among African Americans and Latinos*. Oxford: Oxford University Press.

Wilkinson, Michael, and Linda Ambrose. 2020. *After the Revival: Pentecostalism and the Making of a Canadian Church*. Montreal and Kingston: McGill-Queen's University Press.

Willard, Dallas. 2006. *The Great Omission: Reclaiming the Essential Teachings on Discipleship*. New York: HarperOne.

Wolfe, Alan. 2003. *The Transformation of American Religion: How We Actually Live Our Faith*. New York: Free Press.

Woodhead, Linda. 2016. "The Rise of 'No Religion' in Britain: The Emergence of a New Cultural Majority." *Journal of the British Academy* 4: 245–61.

– 2017. "The Rise of No Religion: Toward an Explanation." *Sociology of Religion* 78 (3): 247–62.

Worthen, Molly. 2014. *Apostles of Reason: The Crisis of Authority in American Evangelicalism*. New York: Oxford University Press.

Wright, Bradley R.E. 2010. *Christians Are Hate-Filled Hypocrites ... and Other Lies You've Been Told*. Minneapolis: Bethany House.

Wuthnow. Robert. 1998. *After Heaven: Spirituality in America since the 1950s*. Berkeley and Los Angeles: University of California Press.

Yancey, George. 2010. *Compromising Scholarship: Religious and Political Bias in American Higher Education*. Waco, TX: Baylor University Press.

Yancey, George, Sam Reimer, and Jake O'Connell. 2015. "How Academics View Conservative Protestants." *Sociology of Religion* 76 (3): 1–22.

Yancey, George, and David A. Williamson. 2015. *So Many Christians, So Few Lions: Is There Christianophobia in the United States?* Lanham, MD: Rowman and Littlefield.

Yeh, Allen. 2018. "Theology and Orthopraxis in Global Evangelicalism." In *Still Evangelical? Insiders Reconsider Political, Social and Theological Meaning*, edited by Mark Labberton, 97–119. Downer's Grove, IL: IVP Books.

Zylstra, Sarah. 2014. "Are Evangelicals Bad for Marriage?" *Christianity Today*, 14 February. https://www.christianitytoday.com/ct/2014/february-web-only/are-evangelicals-bad-for-marriage.html.

Index